All About Growing Fruits & Berries

Edited by
Will Kirkman

Designed by
Craig Bergquist

Photography by
William Aplin
Clyde Childress
Michael Landis
William Reasons

Illustrations by
Leavitt Dudley
Ron Hildebrand

Contents

2   **What this book is all about**
Fruit in the landscape *4*, Containers with fruit *8*, Dwarf and semidwarf *12*, Fruit climates *16*

20   **Tree fruits**
Apples *22*, Pears *32*, Peaches and nectarines *34*, Plums *38*, Apricots *42*, Cherries *44*, Crabapples *46*

48   **Home garden specialties**
A selection of fruit especially for home gardens in the eastern and central states.
A picture gallery *56*

58   **The small fruits**
Strawberries *59*, Raspberries *62*, Blackberries *64*, Blueberries *66*, Grapes *68*, Currants and gooseberries *72*

74   **Pests and diseases**

78   **Space-saver training**
How to create hedges, espaliers, and wall plantings with your fruit plants

86   **Pollination, Pruning, and Grafting**
Pollination *87*, Common-sense pruning *88*, Grafting is easy *98*

104   **Care from the ground up**

111   **List of catalog sources**

113   **Index**

What this book is all about

Let your garden do more for you. Plant fruit in the living-space portion using ideas and answers from the pages that follow to help you blend it into your landscape.

That old equation, Fruit Tree=Orchard hangs on, even in the minds of the most up-to-date gardeners, but it's just not valid.

Fruiting plants these days come in such a range of sizes and kinds that you can use them anywhere, from containers on the terrace to hedges, ground cover, or shade trees. Let us help you plan a fruit garden with the ideas included here. We discuss landscape uses of fruit, container care, dwarf trees, and varieties to suit your climate. Then we list kinds of fruit, following page 20, and finally we discuss care and training, following page 74.

As a quick example of how fruit can and should be used in a landscaped garden, here's a little story.

While planning this book, we went to talk to one of the most experienced and imaginative gardeners we know. After talking a while he paused, thinking of the subject in terms of his own garden. Then he said, "I guess I don't have much fruit here."

The fact is, he does have fruit—everywhere on his suburban lot. But it fits in so well that he'd forgotten it. We took him on a mental tour of his own place.

"You have the persimmon, the pomegranate, and the fig beside the driveway. And your two dwarf apple espaliers behind the zinnias."

"Oh, yes," he said, "I do have some trees in front."

"Then you have the quince in the sideyard, a dwarf mandarin, and the espaliered lemon and Rangpur lime outside the bedroom."

"That's right," he said. "I've got quite a bit of fruit."

"You've got some in back, too," we went on. "The kumquat, and the Japanese plum—in fact, this garden is really an orchard."

Forgetting 11 fruit trees on a 50-foot lot may seem like an extreme case of absent-mindedness, but this man's trees fit right into the landscape, and take no more care than his shrubs and a lot less than his annuals or his lawn. He enjoys the spring flowers, picks ripe fruit in most seasons, does a bit of spraying and pruning along with his other garden chores, and never thinks of his town orchard as special.

◊

Top: This elegant row of espaliered apple trees in full leaf makes a striking hedge.
Far left: 'Bonanza,' genetic dwarf peach, provides a big harvest.
Left: A trained dwarf apple tree planted in a box is a perfect addition to a deck or terrace.

Fruit plants are different now

Even years ago a gardener might put an apple tree in the center of his lawn, or grow grapes over the summerhouse, but until fairly recently a single fruit tree took up a great deal of space and created so much shade that low-growing fruit plants beneath it couldn't get enough sun for a crop. All that has changed. Modern techniques of dwarfing and simplified methods of training let you grow a dozen apple varieties in the same garden and still have plenty of sunny garden space for peaches, strawberries, and a row of petunias.

We show you pictures on the following pages of a garden that is only 15 feet by 50 feet and still holds 17 fruit trees, several grape varieties, cane berries, and vegetables. And in the photographs opposite this page you can see three distinct ways of planting fruit in small spaces, all of which add to the beauty of the landscape: You can train plants as hedges and espaliers (we discuss techniques following page 78); you can buy genetic dwarf plants like the little peach opposite; or you can combine dwarf plants, training, and container gardening for an orchard right on the terrace.

Using this book to plan your garden

The focus throughout this book is small-space gardening. We draw from the work of plant scientists on dwarfing rootstocks and genetic or natural dwarfs; from old and new techniques of pruning and training that confine plants; and from the experience of home gardeners willing to try something new in landscape mixtures or container planting.

Start with the idea that anything is possible. Perhaps you have a large deck with a few pots of annuals and succulents on it, but you want fruit. Look at the container discussion following page 8 for ideas on planting and care of container trees. Read on into the discussion of dwarf trees immediately following. Then choose your fruit from the variety lists: perhaps a couple of apples, a peach, a nectarine, some strawberries, and a grape vine.

You'll want the apples small, so choose a nursery, either near you or from our catalog list, that can supply full dwarf trees on Malling 9 or Malling 26 roots (or the new Malling 27 when it's available). See the chart on page 13. Among peaches and nectarines, the new genetic dwarfs have abundant double flowers and attractive leaves and are just right in a container. Your strawberries can go into a special jar or barrel, your grapes into a trellis container. Look at the final section of the book for discussions of planting, container soil, pruning, and training, then set out your plants and enjoy them.

What this book is all about 3

Fruit in the landscape

When you landscape with fruit plants, you combine beauty with down-to-earth practicality. On these pages we show a charming garden entirely devoted to fruit plants, more than 20 kinds, all growing in a space just 15 feet by 50. We'll discuss this garden in detail, but first we'd like to outline some of the many possibilities for working fruit plants into a more usual landscape. We'll break our suggestions down by the standard landscape categories.

Trees for shade or for ornament

For shade over an outdoor sitting area, use standard-sized apples or large crabapples, pruning them to branch high, or try a spreading cherry such as 'Napoleon' ('Royal Ann').

For a medium-sized lawn tree for shade and ornament, use an apple on semidwarf roots (MM 106), or an apricot if climate permits.

Good ornamental trees for the middle distance include showy-flowered peaches, semidwarf cherries, figs, the larger crabapples, and citrus.

For an especially striking effect in mild climates use a persimmon for its fall color and winter fruit, or a pomegranate for its big orange flowers and globes of red fruit.

Shrubs and hedge plants

Genetic dwarf peaches make splendid flowering hedges with abundant spring bloom and ornamental fruit among the leaves. Train showy-flowered semidwarf or standard peaches the same way.

Apples and pears on Malling 9, 26, or 7 roots can be trained to an informal hedge against trellis or fence, and as formal espaliers. See page 78.

For shrub borders try the smallest crabapples, blueberries, or currants. The last are especially rewarding, with ornamental flowers and clusters of scarlet fruit. Or try edible ornamentals such as chokecherry, cornelian-cherry (*Cornus mas*), Oregon grape, pyracantha, *Viburnum trilobum* (high-bush cranberry), or elderberry.

Ground covers

For small areas of ground cover, use fruiting strawberry, but plan to replace it every three years with new plants if you want a heavy crop. For larger areas use cranberry, low-bush blueberry, or some of the low and spreading pyracanthas and mahonias.

Especially striking flowers or fruit

Among temperate region fruit trees, the most striking in bloom are apples, crabapples, showy-flowered peaches, cherries, and quince.

Among tender crops, citrus offers the best perfume, and there are beautiful flowers on pineapple guava and passionvine.

For showy fruit, crabapple is the hardiest and most striking. In mild climates, persimmons and pomegranates are good, and citrus is showy over a long season.

Among edible ornamentals the best effect of all comes from mountain-ash *(Sorbus),* bearing huge clusters of scarlet berries on a small tree.

Big fruit garden, 15 by 50

The garden shown in our photographs belongs to David Whiting of St. Helena, California. You may not want a

Top, Whiting garden looking north at entrance. Bottom, looking south, where one variety of nectarine, and multiple varieties of raspberries, currants, grapes, berries, and pears are planted.

The 15' x 50' garden

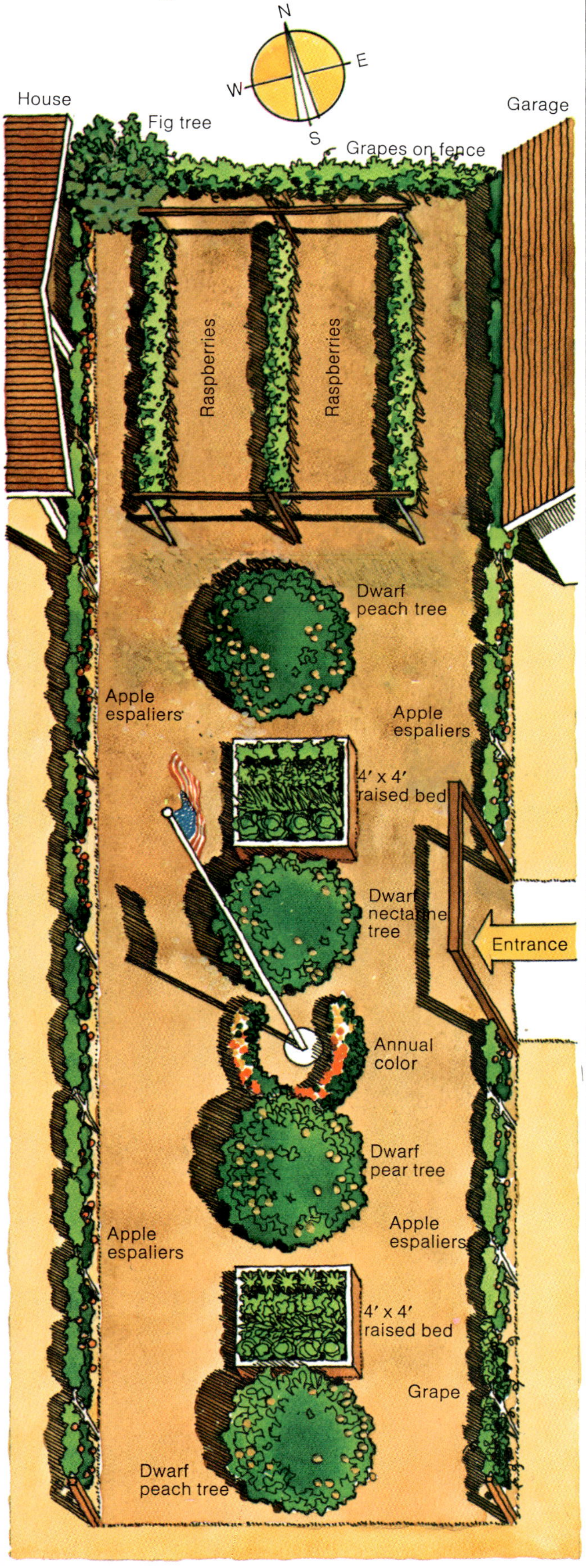

garden of only fruiting plants, but you can borrow Mr. Whiting's techniques, even if fruit will form only part of your landscape.

The important basics

Look over the plan on page 5 and notice first the orientation of the garden. The sun, in passing from east to west, lights both sides of all the plants. Fruit needs sun to set a crop. You should always plan to have fruit plants exposed to the south or west sun if you can't manage the all-day exposure of this garden.

Examine, too, the training of these plants. Dwarf apples and pears on open trellises form an attractive hedge, and the training exposes the branches to a maximum of light for heavy crops. Cane berries are also trellised and oriented approximately north and south. They take little space and bear heavily. In the center of the garden a pruned dwarf pear and genetic dwarf peaches and nectarines act as decorative shrubs, offering bloom and fruit. Grapes are mainly planted on the north side of the garden with full southern exposure to develop good sugar in the fruit. Raised beds produce vegetables in this garden, but could also be planted with small fruits or annuals for cut flowers and color.

If you choose to combine fruiting plants with more standard ornamentals, one of many possible variations on this garden might be to plant an apple or pear hedge as shown on the entrance side, backed by a lawn. A paved sitting area where Mr. Whiting grows berries could hold a few genetic dwarf peaches or nectarines in containers, and perhaps a few strawberry barrels.

At the rear, among ornamental shrubs, you could use a fruiting crabapple for its spring bloom and decorative edible fruit.

Efficient training cuts your work

Fruit plants need maintenance if you hope for crops, but you don't want to spend your life as an apple babysitter. Mr. Whiting's training takes an initial effort, but once plants are established this way they get good light, perfect air circulation and plenty of rootspace, so they need the least possible babying with sprays, fertilizers, and shears. On page 84 we tell you how to do formal espaliers like those on the Whiting trellises, but we also suggest a method that takes less time at the start. You bend young trees at an angle, then trim all new growth to stubs with four leaves each. In a couple of seasons you have a handsome fruit hedge.

Trained dwarf plants make maintenance a lot easier since you can reach every part of them. The necessary sprays for pests or diseases go on in minutes when the distance from root to branch tip is only four or five feet. Pruning is quicker too, for a couple of reasons. First, you practice summer pruning. An occasional nip with the shears during the warm months means that winter pruning is almost entirely finished before winter; whatever branches you missed on your ordinary garden inspections are down where you can reach them. No ladders or pole pruners are necessary.

Even feeding and watering are easier with trained dwarf plants. The roots are shallow, so you don't need deep watering basins and hours of soaking. And since you want controlled growth, you apply less fertilizer and save money.

◁
Top: Looking north, the Whiting garden as it looked in spring. Spray emitters in raised beds maintain even moisture.
Bottom: In mid-summer, crops in raised beds have grown to provide vegetables along with the ripening fruit.

David Whiting harvests fruit from one of three different peach trees in his garden.

Above two photos: Training one of his 19 grafted apple trees.
Below: Espaliered apples form a fence on side of garden.

Containers with fruit

At Versailles in the 1600's, Louis XIV's gardeners grew orange trees in pots. In summer they lined the walks of the palace gardens, then wheeled the trees indoors to the orangerie, a special greenhouse, when snow fell. Some of the trees are said to have lasted 75 years.

The general techniques of caring for a container orchard really haven't changed much in the last few hundred years, but modern dwarfing techniques cut the work of caring for container trees considerably, since dwarf trees are far less likely to get rootbound and cause problems with watering and feeding.

Following page 12 we discuss dwarf trees in detail, both grafted and natural, but first we'll outline the step-by-step techniques of planting and care that will keep your portable orchard healthy and productive for years.

Climate and container trees

The historical anecdote above gives you one good reason for planting in containers. Even tender plants far from their natural climate zone will grow well, since you can move them to shelter when cold weather comes (or wheel them to a shady spot if desert heat is your problem).

With containers, there's no reason not to try 'Meyer' lemons in Michigan or peaches in North Dakota. Your winter holding site should have plenty of light, but not too much heat, and you'll have to be careful not to overwater while the plants are inactive. Citrus is decorative enough to come into the house and fill a south window, but deciduous material can probably survive a season in the garage if you get it into the sun on fine spring days.

One warning: just because a plant can survive winter in the ground where you live doesn't mean it can manage cold weather in a container. If your garden soil freezes, then container soil will also freeze, killing your plants. Gardeners in the coldest northern zones should plan to protect even hardy deciduous plants in the coldest months.

What plants to choose

Our variety lists and the pages on dwarf trees will give you more extensive information on plants that suit containers. Here are just a few ideas to guide you: apples on Malling 9, 26, or 7 rootstocks; pears on quince roots; genetic dwarf peaches, nectarines, apricot, or cherry; any fig; the smaller crabapples; citrus on trifoliate orange roots where available; strawberries; spur-pruned grape varieties. When the new Malling 27 rootstock becomes widely available for apples, it should be ideal for container planting.

Size of container

Begin your container orchard with containers that are just 2 or 3 inches wider than the roots of your plants. If you start with a bareroot apple or pear, or one of the genetic dwarf fruits, your first container will be about the size of a 5-gallon lard can. In fact, since it will only be in use for one growing season, you might use a lard can and cover it with a basket or box. Let the young tree grow for a season and fill the container with roots, then repot it the following spring.

Evergreen fruit plants such as citrus should start their lives in a container that's not too much bigger than their rootball. If your soil mix is well drained you can go to a box 3 or 4 inches wider than the roots all around. For large nursery plants, the first container may be the permanent container.

Grapes in containers (Muscat above, 'Kings Ruby' below) take frequent attention to water and feeding, but look good. Supply a trellis for training.

Espaliered 'Gravenstein' apple is pretty and sets a good crop.

Breakfast comes fresh from your own 'Sequoia' strawberry "tree."

The maximum for permanent containers should be about bushel-basket size. Anything bigger will be too bulky to handle or move. (But consider a platform on wheels for any large container.) Half barrels are about the right size, or any box or pot that holds about that volume of soil. The minimum permanent size should be about 18 inches on a side and 18 inches deep. The smaller the container, the more work is involved in feeding, watering, and root pruning.

Any container is more practical if it can be taken apart. One side can be attached with screws, or better yet, all four sides can be screwed together for easy removal. The reason: container trees must be removed from their pots every two or three years for root pruning as described in the sketches on pages 10 and 11. Otherwise all the feeder roots bunch at the walls of the container and the plant languishes.

Move plants from the first, 5-gallon size container to the bushel size over two or three seasons. The right size of container lets the plant find water and nutrients easily, keeps soil from going sour around and beneath the roots, and slows top growth.

Container soil mix

We discuss synthetic soils on page 107. Some gardeners like to add a little rich loam to the mix of sand and organic material. It holds water better and helps keep nutrients available. Add up to one-third loam if you like, but be careful not to include clay soil. It holds water too well for a container mix, and you may drown your plants. For a purely synthetic mix, you'll have to be careful about feeding. The nutrients you add leach away when you water. Keep to a regular schedule as outlined below.

Feeding container fruit

Use the growth of the plant and its general appearance as your main guides to feeding. It should leaf out and grow vigorously in the spring and early summer, and leaves should be a healthy medium green. Yellowed leaves suggest a lack of nitrogen, while very dark leaves may mean you're feeding too much.

One method is to give each plant about half the recommended quantity of complete fertilizer (containing nitrogen, phosphoric acid, and potassium or potash) about every two to three weeks. A liquid fertilizer is easy to handle and less likely to burn roots. If the container says 1 tablespoon per gallon of water, use 1½ teaspoons instead.

Another good method is to use one of the pelleted slow-release fertilizers. These dissolve slowly over a period of time so you won't wash them away in the first week or so.

Feed through the growing season if the plant is to receive winter protection. Stop about mid-July if it is to stay outdoors. That will give it a chance to harden up new growth.

A note of caution: Fertilizer can build up in a pot when the drainage is poor and begin to burn the plant. You'll probably see brown, dry-looking leaf edges first. If you do, water heavily as described in the section below on watering. This heavy watering, or leaching, will clean the soil.

Citrus requires about the same amount of feeding as deciduous fruit, but it may also require a few extra nutrients. Special citrus foods containing iron, zinc, and sometimes other minerals are available at nurseries. Use them regularly, or switch to them if you see leaves with yellowed portions between bright green veins. If the leaf is uniformly yellow, veins and all, the plant lacks nitrogen. Citrus food won't hurt deciduous plants if you want to use it—but it may cost more.

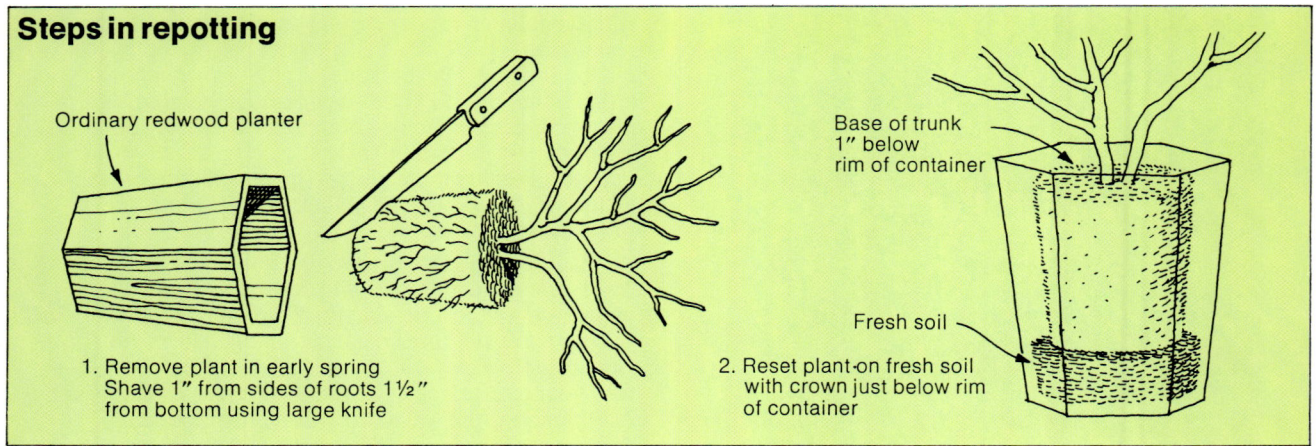

Watering containers

Again, judge watering by the behavior of your plant. It should never wilt, but it shouldn't stand in soggy soil either. If you check the soil occasionally by digging down an inch or two, you'll soon learn how much to water. The top inch may stay moist for a week in fairly cool weather, but in hot, windy weather you'll water often, even every day for a plant that needs repotting. That's why well-drained soil is so important. You can pour on the water without drowning the roots.

Mulch will help keep the soil moist and cool. Use a coarse organic mulch such as bark chips and pile it about 2 inches thick. In really hot weather, group your containers. They'll protect each other.

Don't count on rain to do all your watering, since plants in containers may act as umbrellas and shed most of the rain. Check the soil even when rainfall has been abundant. Of course you'll water less, since the moist air will keep water from evaporating.

It is important in any region to leach the soil occasionally. Leaching is long-soaking that dissolves any minerals or salts and flushes them out the drain hole. Well water, or any water that won't produce good soapsuds or leaves bathtub rings, is heavy with dissolved mineral salts and these deposit in container soil as water evaporates. Eventually you'll see brown leaf edges, then dead leaves, and finally a dead plant. To avoid disaster, put your garden hose in each container every couple of months and let it run slowly for about 20 minutes. It should run just fast enough that the water you add goes through the soil and out the drainhole. Letting it overflow won't add to the effect.

Also, for every watering in hard-water areas, fill the pot until water runs freely from the bottom, go on to other pots, then return and fill the pot a second time. This technique keeps salts to a minimum.

Vacation watering

When you leave home, group your containers near a water source and out of the afternoon sun. The grouping will help keep them moist, the shade will cut the need for water, and if they're near a hose, your vacation waterer won't miss any of them by accident. For large numbers of containers, you can buy water timers that will turn water on at regular intervals. Just hook up a system of small hoses that you place permanently in each container. Drip systems

Half barrels provide ideal homes for 'Southern Sweet' genetic dwarf peaches, leaving room for annual color below.

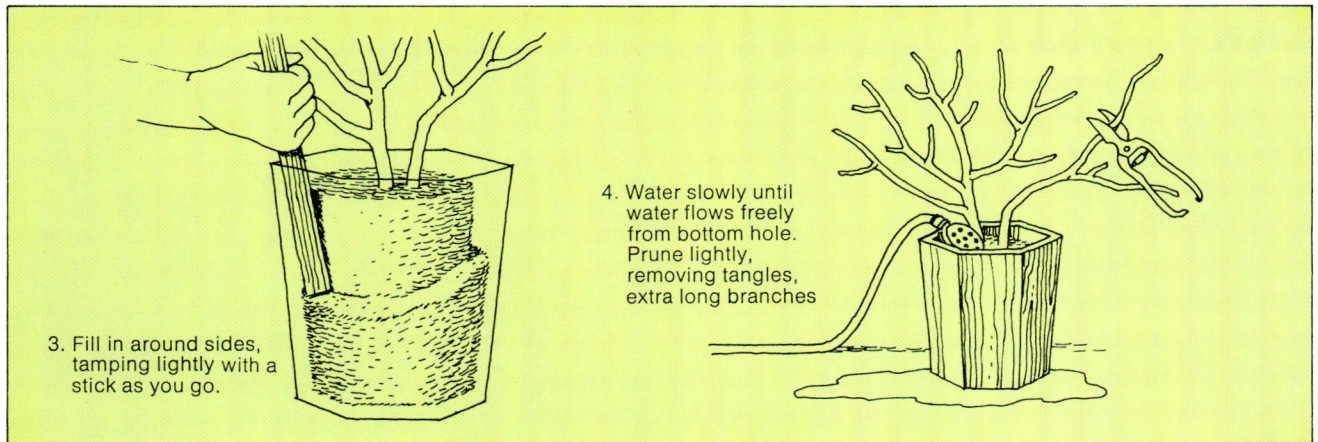

are effective here too, provided you filter the water before it goes into the system.

Potting and repotting

There are many successful potting methods, and gardeners have great success with methods you'll never see recommended in books. What we suggest here should work every time and keep your plants healthy.

You're aiming for a container soil that holds water but never gets soggy. Water should soak in immediately, never sitting on top, and it should run out just as fast. Choose a synthetic soil or a mixture of synthetic soil and garden loam. Moisten the soil until it's barely damp but not wet. You may find it best to sprinkle and stir the soil one day then pot your plants the next.

Be sure your pot or box has good drain holes. If you buy a container with one small hole, drill two or three more, or ask the nurseryman to do it for you. If you use a can for a season, punch a dozen holes around the bottom with a triangular punch can opener. Cover the holes with broken pieces of pot or broken glass segments, or bits of that old cracked cup you meant to throw out. DON'T fill the bottom with rocks or coarse gravel—they interfere with water flow. The mix should fill the pot from top to bottom.

Place enough soil mix in the pot, lightly tamped down, so the roots touch it when the crown of the plant is just below the pot rim. Hold your bareroot plant at that level and toss in enough soil to support it, tamping lightly as you go, then finish filling to about a quarter inch below the pot rim. The soil will settle, leaving you room to water. An evergreen plant, or any plant in a nursery container, can simply be placed on the first layer of soil. You then fill around it, but before covering the rootball, scratch it all around with a fork to rough up roots and get them pointing outward. Cut off any long, spiraling roots at the bottom.

The repotting technique is similar, and is described in the illustrations here. You repot because any plant tends to bunch feeder roots at the wall of the container. They dry out faster there and the plant lacks water and nutrients even when you care for it properly. When you shave off an inch of root and add fresh soil, the plant can grow healthy young roots and the empty soil around them holds a reservoir of moisture. You must always clip back the top a little when you shave the roots, so that the plant is balanced. New top growth will follow the new root growth.

After potting or repotting, soak the soil thoroughly.

'Washington' navel orange can spend winter indoors.

'Meyer' lemon has flowers, fruit year-round.

Dwarf and semidwarf

Dwarf trees are easy to prune, spray, thin, and harvest, and will often produce a crop years sooner than standard trees. Without the dwarf sizes, many landscape uses of fruiting plants would be difficult, with container plantings of tree fruit almost impossible.

Both the home gardener and commercial orchardist are finding more and more uses for dwarfed fruit trees. On the preceding pages we discuss these uses. Here, we would like to make clear just what the term 'dwarf' means.

Grafted dwarf and genetic dwarf

There are two distinct kinds of dwarf fruit trees; the grafted dwarf that is actually manufactured by the gardener or nurseryman; and the genetic dwarf that is small because of its genetic structure. Meaning, so to speak, it is born that way.

Grafting for small size

When a gardener sets out to create a grafted dwarf, he must first find a plant that will serve as a growth-limiting rootstock. The most extensive research on plants like this has been undertaken with apples, and the illustrations on page 13 will help you see what has been done so far.

The dwarfing part of a grafted dwarf usually consists of the root. The numbered Malling roots, if allowed to grow their own tops, would become slow-growing, shallow-rooted apple trees. When a well-known fruiting apple is grafted to one of these roots, the recalcitrant root doesn't nourish the top as well as ordinary roots might. And since the roots are relatively shallow and don't spread too widely, the mature size of the top is limited.

A propagator can accomplish somewhat the same result by grafting the numbered Malling plant to an ordinary root, then grafting a desirable variety to this trunk section. This is called an interstock graft and can be compared to a bottleneck. The ordinary root is vigorous, but the "slow-poke" interstock will only pass along a certain amount of nutrition and the top becomes dwarfed. Interstocks sometimes get very complex, with several kinds of tree making up a single trunk, but most of these three- or four-way grafts are experimental at the present time.

Grafted trees are precocious

The "stingy," dwarfing root or trunk has an important secondary effect on the top beyond dwarfing. A plant that doesn't receive enough nutrients not only grows slowly — it fruits young. Grafted dwarfs usually will have a little fruit on them in their second year.

Choosing a rootstock

Since most of the experimental work on grafted dwarfs has been done with apples, it's no surprise that you have a wide choice of size among apple dwarfs. The M27 rootstock is the most dwarfing, producing apple bushes 4 feet high, but it is not yet widely available.

The M9 root is the most dwarfing among available roots, excellent for containers and informal hedge training. Unfortunately, retail nurseries rarely label the root of a tree separately. You will see the variety name, such as

"If you have space for a rose bush, you have space for a dwarf apple tree," says Fay Paquette, retired horticulturist. "It's like propagating from cuttings, and something anyone can do. I start with two- or three-eye scions and graft them to very thin sections of dwarf root stock, six-inches to eight-inches long. Trees grown in this manner, and pruned back each year, develop short stocky branches and multiple-fruiting spurs. The tree in the photo was a graft of 'Red Delicious' on M.9 rootstock. It is three years old and produced 30 apples after thinning." If you would like to learn more about his grafting methods, you can write to:

Mr. Fay Paquette
2368 Barbara Drive
Camarillo, CA 93010

'Delicious' or 'Melrose' and then 'dwarf' or 'semi-dwarf.' Dwarf means relatively small, while semi-dwarf means relatively large. You can't be sure just what the mature plant will be like.

For containers or formal training it doesn't matter much. You add to the dwarfing effect by your treatment of the plant. For free-standing trees and informal training it can matter a lot, since a 'dwarf' might be a 9-foot M9 or a 15-foot M26. You can solve the problem by buying from a catalog dealer who lists his rootstocks separately, then propagating more rootstocks as needed. A method for doing this is described and illustrated on page 15.

A precaution

However you buy your dwarf trees, it is important never to bury the graft. You will see it on the lower trunk as a bulge with a round scar on one side, or possibly a change of bark texture. If you bury the graft, the top variety will root and grow to full size. The scar should be two inches above the soil. Some nurserymen help you to plant properly by grafting high, about 6 inches above the branching roots or crown. You can bury the lower 3 or 4 inches and still have the graft exposed.

The only exception to the rule of never burying a graft applies to harsh winter areas. Mulch both root and bud union deeply when all growth has stopped in fall, then pull back the mulch when spring growth begins.

Vigorous grafts and slow ones

Beginning on page 98, we discuss grafting techniques, so that you can create your own dwarf orchard from scratch. You can begin in two ways: Either buy grafted dwarfs and add varieties so each tree produces several kinds of fruit; or propagate rootstocks to graft single-variety dwarfs.

Either way, you must consider the vigor of the top varieties. If you mix vigorous and slow branches on the

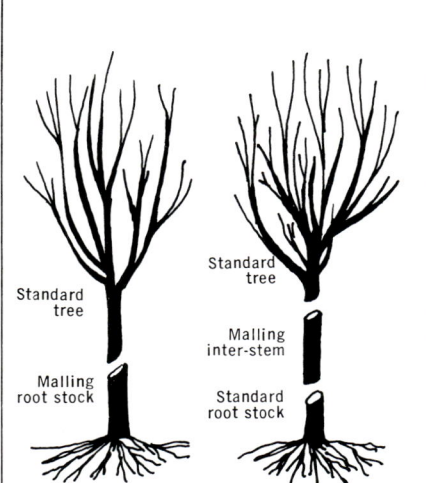

What's a dwarf tree?

A dwarf tree actually consists of 2 or 3 trees. In one type of dwarf, the Malling tree provides the roots, and the standard apple tree provides the fruit. In another type of dwarf, a full sized tree provides the roots, a portion of a Malling tree provides a section of the trunk (interstem), and the standard tree provides the fruit.

Apple tree size differences

To determine the correct spacing of dwarf trees, you should know the natural size of the variety as well as the dwarfing effect of the rootstock. The two charts will help you make this determination.

For instance, the Red Prince Delicious tree is naturally larger than Jonnee. If grown on the same rootstock, Jonnee can be planted closer together than Red Prince. Red Prince on MM 106 should be planted 14 feet apart, while Jonnee on MM 106 is planted at 12-foot intervals.

Or, if you are planting them together, Jonnee should be ordered on a larger rootstock to make best use of the spacing needed for the Red Prince. In this case, Jonnee on MM 111 would fit in the same space as the Red Prince.

Rootstock	% of natural size
Malling 9	40%
Malling 26	50%
Malling 7	60%
MM 106	70%
MM 111	75%

Actual tree size is determined by local climate and growing conditions. The sizes of these varieties are shown not by feet, but on a relative scale of 100.

The Malling and Merton Malling rootstock numbers determine tree size

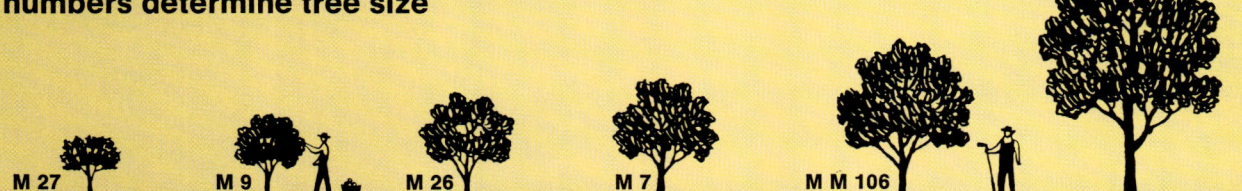

M 27 Very dwarfing. Mature trees reach about 4 feet. Hard to find; limited availability.

M 9—Most dwarfing root currently available. (About 9 feet.) Trunk section and root are brittle, so stake free-standing plants. Try to buy trees with bud 6 inches or more above the crown (where roots branch), and plant with bud 2 inches above soil for extra anchoring.

M 26—Less dwarfing than M9 (about 12 feet) unless used in formal espaliers, containers. Fewer suckers than M7.

M 7—Widely available semi-dwarfing root (about 15 feet). Trees budded high and planted deep will sucker less if you can find them. Suckers may be dug or layered for home grafting. Control size by training, pruning.

M M 106—Largest semi-dwarfing rootstock (about 18 feet). Trees can reach ¾ of full size. This root anchors well, suckers very little and resists wooly apple aphid. It is mainly a commercial root stock.

A hedgerow of apples on M9 roots are bent to 45° angle, summer-pruned to increase dwarfing effect of root (see pages 80 and 82).

same tree, the vigorous ones will try to take over. If you mix vigorous and slow varieties in a row of trained dwarfs, the vigorous will be much bigger, since the rootstock won't dwarf them as much.

The chart on page 13 compares a number of vareties on the same rootstock to give you an idea how growth habit changes the ultimate size. The spur varieties will grow the least, while a vigorous 'Cortland' or 'Mutsu' apple will grow perhaps 50 percent larger. The same will happen on a single tree with several grafts unless you match the vigor of the branches.

Wherever possible, we have mentioned the vigor of the varieties named in our variety lists. Before grafting, check to see whether the list gives equal ratings of vigor to the varieties you wish to use.

Other grafted dwarfs

Other major kinds of fruit can be dwarfed by grafting, but far less research has been done, so there are fewer kinds of rootstocks, and they are not always strongly dwarfing.

Pears are dwarfed on quince roots, and since some pears, ('Bartlett' for one) will not join well to quince, an interstock of 'Old Home' pear grows between root and top. Where fireblight is severe, you can sometimes grow a susceptible but tasty variety of pear by letting the 'Old Home' interstock form the whole trunk and the main branches (or scaffold). If a branch catches the blight, it will only die back to the 'Old Home' portion, since 'Old Home' is highly resistant. Finding the 'Old Home' scions to do this may be hard, but try a large wholesale nursery. They may be able to give you scions from their own grafting stock.

Peaches are dwarfed on several rootstocks, especially the Nanking cherry *(Prunus tomentosa)* and the St. Julien plum. Either root may shorten the life of a tree somewhat.

Plums are sometimes dwarfed on Nanking cherry root, while apricots go onto Western sand cherry *(Prunus besseyi)*. The plants that would normally grow from these roots are shrubby and small, thus their dwarfing effect with the various tops.

Any of these roots can be propagated by the method we describe on page 15, but you can also get more of the same by allowing root suckers to grow, then digging and replanting them during the dormant season. Apple roots don't often send up suckers from underground, but the various stone fruit rootstocks sucker frequently.

Genetic dwarfs are different

The plants called genetic dwarfs are small by nature. There are, however, many forms of them, somtimes more than one form for a single kind of fruit tree.

Among apples, the most common genetic dwarf grows into a fairly large tree. The so called 'spur' apple grows more slowly than the same variety of ordinary apple, produces fewer real branches, but produces many more fruiting spurs. The heavy crops slow its growth a bit more. Even so, a spur apple grows big unless you further dwarf it by grafting.

There is also a very small genetic dwarf apple that is not a spur tree. It is sold as 'Garden Delicious' and has fruit resembling 'Golden Delicious' or 'Mutsu.' In a container you might keep it to three feet, but in the ground it will slowly grow to six or eight feet.

Genetic dwarf peach on its 20th birthday.

Among peaches there is a wide range of genetic dwarfs all related to the Chinese dwarf peaches called 'Swatow' and 'Flory.' These plants grow almost no stem between leaf nodes, so the branches have a typical lumpy look. In the ground you can expect to see these dwarfs reach eight or nine feet, but it will take a while. They are all very decorative, with large, showy flowers; but are fairly tender. Nectarines also grow as short-stemmed dwarfs.

One variety of dwarf peach is a little different. It is a short-stemmed sport discovered in Washington on a 'Redhaven' tree and christened 'Compact Redhaven.' It is not quite as dwarf as the Swatow-Flory series, reaching about 10 feet, but it is quite hardy.

There is also a dwarf apricot and a dwarf sweet cherry. There are several good genetic dwarf sour cherries, including 'Meteor,' 'Northstar,' and 'Mesabi'—all of which are extremely hardy. 'Mesabi' has a sweet cherry among its ancestors, but its fruit is sour. All three grow to perhaps 10 feet under ideal conditions, but more often stay at 6 or 7 feet.

Among plums there are large numbers of natural dwarfs, but these are not plants that bear the familiar varieties. Rather, they are crosses with Western sand cherry or with true cherry and shrub plum. Most of them were developed for very cold climates and are easy to buy in the northern half of the country.

Genetic dwarfs are grafted

You may be surprised to see that your natural dwarf peach is grafted to a large and obviously different rootstock. The root here is not a means of dwarfing. Often it is very vigorous and sends out four-foot suckers almost overnight. Grafting to a rootstock is the only means of producing large numbers of plants for sale. Seed will be of mixed parentage and give a new kind of fruit, so grafting is the way to reproduce any fruit variety, dwarf or standard. However, the vigorous roots (of many kinds) used for dwarf peaches get impatient and grow on their own, so watch for a strange leaf above the normal foliage and tear suckers out at the base. Some nurseries use red-leafed rootstocks to make spotting these intruders easier.

What's better, grafted or genetic?

It's hard to determine whether grafted or genetic dwarfing is best. Neither is actually better, but there are definite advantages to grafting, which is why most of the work of plant scientists concerns rootstocks instead of natural dwarfing.

When you dwarf by grafting, the top can be any variety you like, a good old one, or a problem-solving new one. Scientists work constantly to breed hardy, disease-resistant, or larger, or better fruit, but the developments are slow and frequently disappointing. It simply complicates a difficult job to try to include a dwarf trait along with whatever else you want to see in the offspring. It's easier to work toward one thing at a time and then graft for small size.

The home gardener is also better off with grafted dwarfs in many cases, since his choice of varieties is not limited to fruit he doesn't know. Genetic dwarfs are distinct varieties, different from each other and from standard varieties.

Genetic dwarfs do have advantages. They require no pruning and their fruit tastes perfectly good, if not always top-notch. The peaches and nectarines have another plus: they descend from double-flowered ancestors, providing an extraordinary spring display of flowers. A border or hedge of peach dwarfs is quite a colorful sight during the flowering season.

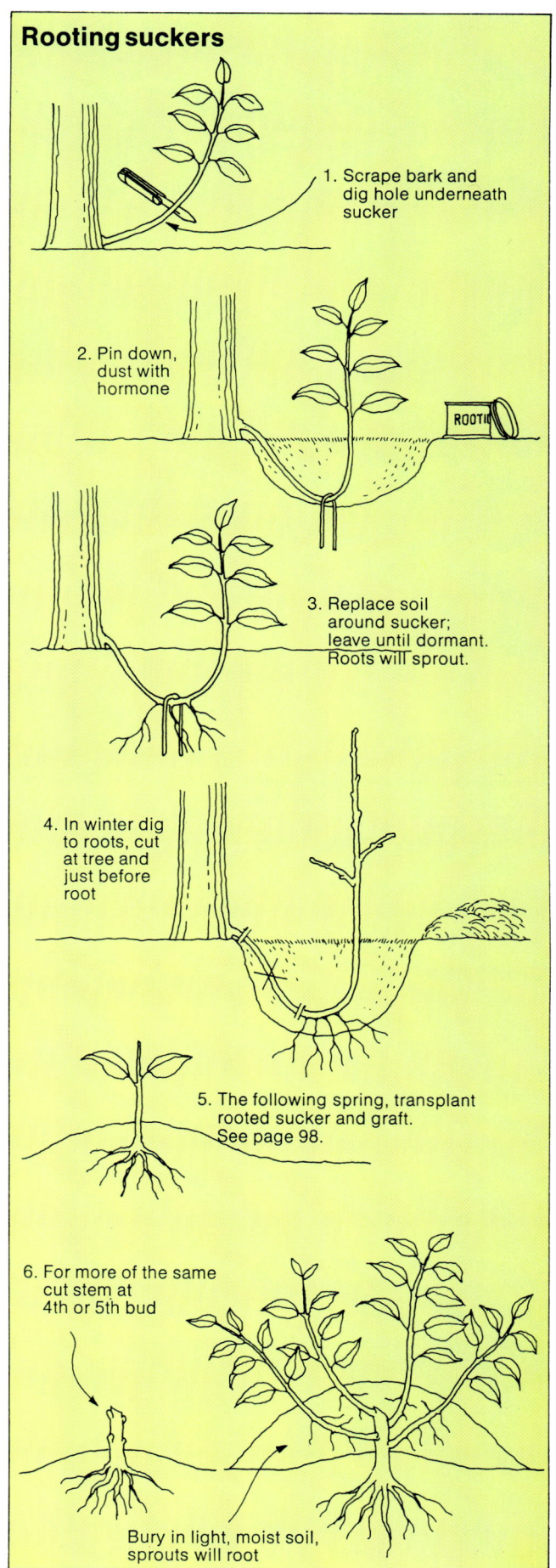

Rooting suckers

1. Scrape bark and dig hole underneath sucker
2. Pin down, dust with hormone
3. Replace soil around sucker; leave until dormant. Roots will sprout.
4. In winter dig to roots, cut at tree and just before root
5. The following spring, transplant rooted sucker and graft. See page 98.
6. For more of the same cut stem at 4th or 5th bud

Bury in light, moist soil, sprouts will root

Longer days and rising temperatures in early spring bring a release of buds from protective dormancy (apple blossoms).

Fruit climates of the West

We divide our maps on the following pages, with California separated from the other western states. The zone descriptions below are divided in the same way.

California

There are seven color zones on our California map. Each is a different fruit-climate region. White areas are too harsh for most fruit crops.

Zone 1. High slopes above Owens Valley and the Mojave. The growing season of 120 to 160 days permits you to grow many hardy fruits, but dwarf trees and small fruits will need heavy winter mulch to survive without damage.

Zone 2. The summer fog belt of coastal California is in many places a prime fruit area. Commercial growers around San Francisco Bay harvest European plums, Oriental plums, apricots, and sweet cherries. The coast north of the Bay may have enough summer fog to affect ripening of heat-loving crops such as peaches and grapes, so choose the hottest spot in the garden for these.

Zone 3. The interior valleys from the inner Coast Range to the Sierra Nevada include some of the finest fruit climates of the United States. Commercial orchardists grow peaches, plums, citrus, and strawberries, and almost all of California's wine and table grapes grow here. Central Valley heat limits your choice of apples and pears. Some good apples: 'Red Astrachan,' 'Gravenstein,' 'Golden Delicious.' Some pears: 'Bartlett,' 'Winter Nelis.'

Zone 4. This zone includes the hot inland region just behind the Southern California coast. It produces commercial citrus crops where building has not destroyed the groves. Heat-loving plants do well if they will stand some winter frost, but don't try the tender tropicals.

Zone 5. This is California's subtropical belt, with commercial groves of avocados. You can grow and harvest white sapote, cherimoya, and any citrus you like. Surprisingly, the hills just behind the coast are fine for many cool-climate fruits such as apples. Nurseries in the area carry any fruit you're likely to have heard of, and the low-chill dwarf peaches grow especially well.

Zone 6. The low desert is fine country for hardy heat lovers, and you'll do well with figs, pomegranate, and Oriental plums like 'Santa Rosa.' The winter cold and the wind make many fruit plants impossible to grow, and the summer heat rules out apples, pears, and cherries.

Zone 7. Intermediate and high desert gardeners don't get the worst of the summer heat and can grow fine apples and pears and many small fruits. The cold rules out tender plants.

Fruit climates in other western states

There are many prime areas for fruit growing, from the Pacific Northwest to the Salt Lake area and the Arizona desert.

Zone 1. This zone dots itself around our map. It is cold, but not nearly so cold as the related climate of zone 1a. Some influence of terrain (or water in Utah) lengthens the growing season and tempers the winter. Eastern Washington, for example, is prime apple country, with extensive commercial orchards, but it also produces fine peaches of the high-chill Elberta-type, and home gardeners can succeed with almost any temperate-zone crop. For tricky crops such as apricots and cherries, try the hardiest kinds.

The date when spring arrives changes from year to year, but the sequence of bloom is always the same (pear blossoms).

Zone 1a. Related to zone 1, but with a growing season up to 30 days shorter, this is still a mild enough climate for hardy varieties of most temperate-zone fruits. There is commercial fruit production in both Colorado and Montana. Protect trees in this zone by mulching the roots heavily in winter, holding the mulch in place with wire; planting on ground that has good air drainage, and establishing windbreaks.

Zone 2. The milder, warmer parts of southern Washington and western Oregon produce much of the nation's sweet cherry crop, some of the finest pears, and quantities of small fruits such as strawberries, raspberries, blackberries, blueberries, and so forth. The home gardener can plant almost any temperate-zone fruit, but summers are overcast and cool, so heat lovers like peaches and grapes must be carefully chosen for the region.

Zone 2a. Similar to zone 2 but with even cooler, wetter summers. The yellow 'Chehalis' apple was especially bred to ripen in this climate, replacing 'Golden Delicious.' The warning about heat-loving crops is even more important here. The 'Veteran' peach is an old favorite that does well, also the 'Wenatchee' apricot.

Zone 3. In the Phoenix area of Arizona, the climate corresponds roughly to the low desert regions of California, producing fine grapefruit and mandarins. Temperate-climate fruits like apples and pears won't do here.

Zone 4. The high desert of Arizona and New Mexico again corresponds roughly to the same terrain in California, and you'll find that hardy temperate-climate fruits like apples, pears, high-chill hardy peaches will do fine, but protect them in winter.

Key to the chart symbols

Chart symbols will help you to choose the varieties that suit your climate, and will suggest any special care they may need. Double symbols apply at extreme limits of a zone where the climate is at its warmest or coolest.

★ **(star).** The star symbol means that you can choose any of the varieties listed in the book.

H—hardy or high-chill. Choose cold-tolerant or cold-loving varieties developed for northern regions.

wp—winter protection needed. Use a heavy mulch over roots to protect them from freezing, or bury small fruits in mulch once early cold has stopped all growth. Tender plants such as citrus need plastic or burlap covers over and around them in winter when this symbol is used.

L—low-chill varieties only. Where winters are mild, you'll need special varieties of apples, peaches, and apricots. Standard varieties flower and leaf out erratically.

U—uncertain crops, possible plant damage. When the climate is too cold or too warm, some crops are erratic, doing well in one spot, poorly in another.

F—fog or cool summers may affect the crop. In coastal California the summer fog cover varies. Where it hangs most of the day, there will be insufficient heat to ripen a peach or apricot. Where fog gives way to heat in the early morning, the same crop will do well. In western Washington, rain and overcast have a similar effect.

(no symbol)—fruit type not recommended. Some crops should not be planted in the ground. There's little point in trying citrus in the mountains, for example. You can often grow these crops in containers that you shelter in winter. If heat is the limiting factor, as in the low desert, then you'll have to do without the plants that won't take it.

Fruit-climate zones for western states

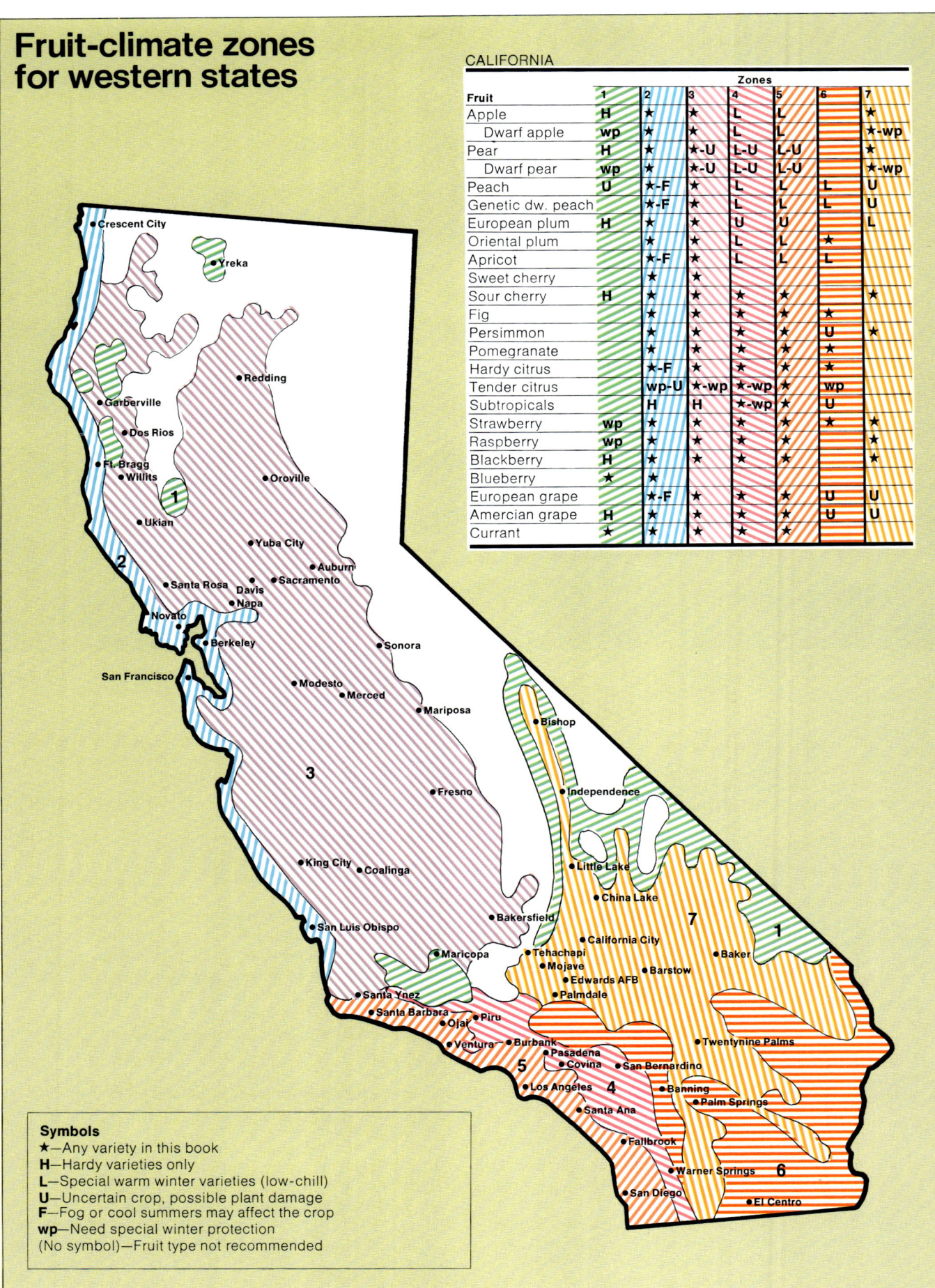

CALIFORNIA

Fruit	Zones						
	1	2	3	4	5	6	7
Apple	H	★	★	L	L		★
Dwarf apple	wp	★	★	L	L		★-wp
Pear	H	★	★-U	L-U	L-U		★
Dwarf pear	wp	★	★-U	L-U	L-U		★-wp
Peach	U	★-F	★	L	L	L	U
Genetic dw. peach		★-F	★	L	L	L	U
European plum	H	★	★	U	U		L
Oriental plum		★	★	L	L	★	
Apricot		★-F	★	L	L	L	
Sweet cherry		★	★				
Sour cherry	H	★	★	★	★	★	★
Fig		★	★	★	★	★	★
Persimmon		★	★	★	★	U	
Pomegranate		★	★	★	★	★	
Hardy citrus		★-F	★	★	★	★	
Tender citrus		wp-U	★-wp	★-wp	★	wp	
Subtropicals			H	H	★-wp	★	U
Strawberry	wp	★	★	★	★	★	★
Raspberry	wp	★	★	★	★	★	★
Blackberry	H	★	★	★	★		
Blueberry	★	★					
European grape		★-F	★	★	★	U	U
Amercian grape	H	★	★	★	★	U	U
Currant	★	★	★	★	★		

Symbols
★—Any variety in this book
H—Hardy varieties only
L—Special warm winter varieties (low-chill)
U—Uncertain crop, possible plant damage
F—Fog or cool summers may affect the crop
wp—Need special winter protection
(No symbol)—Fruit type not recommended

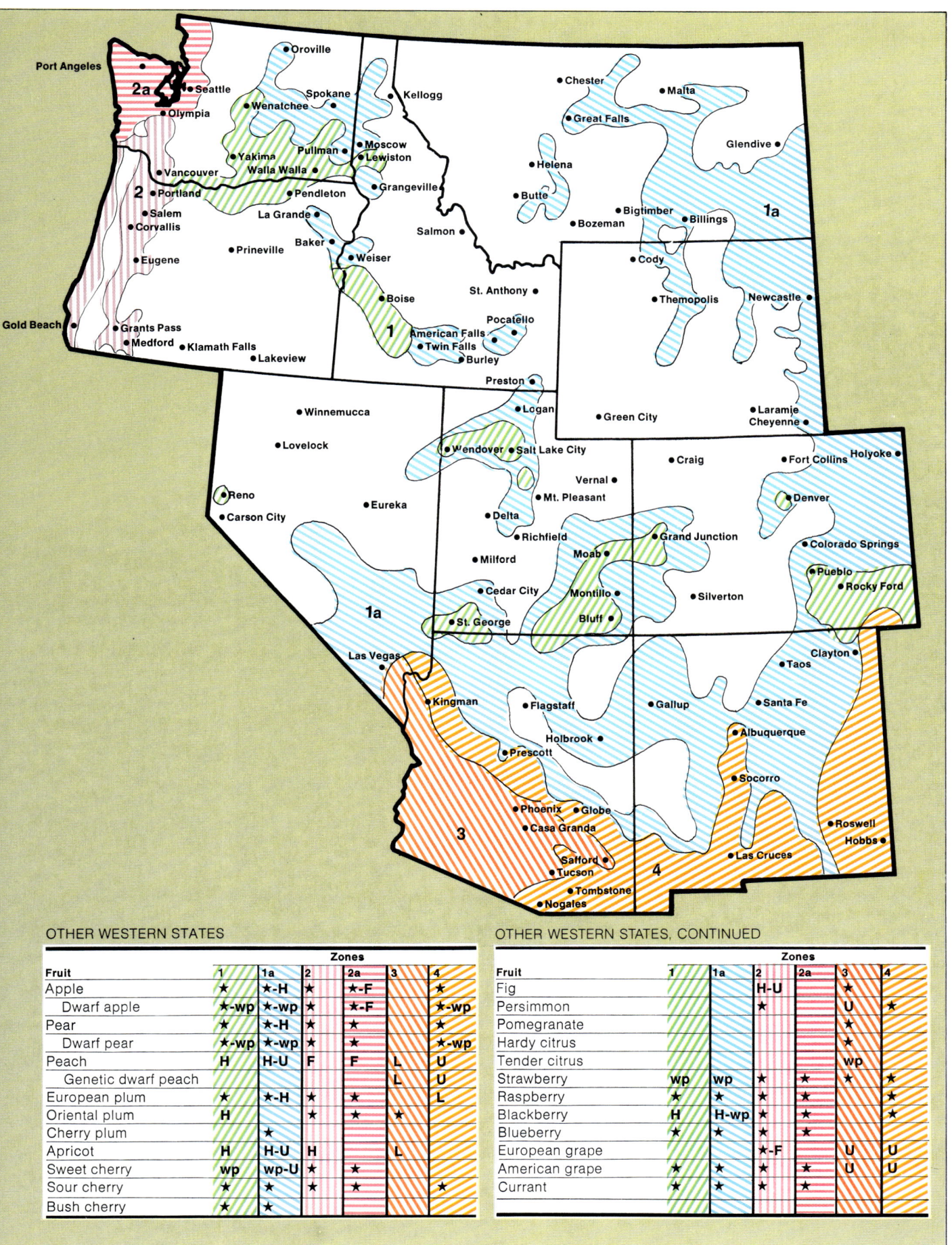

Tree fruits

**For the suburban garden or the high-rise patio terrace, there's a fruit tree to fit your needs.
You can forget the orchard these days and choose fruit for the living-space garden.**

The information in this chapter will help you choose the fruit tree that's right for you in every respect.

Using the introductions

Each variety list is preceded by an introduction. Use these paragraphs as a kind of expanded index to the rest of the book. We give you page references to the more detailed sections on landscaping, pruning, and grafting.

In the early paragraphs we tell you what sizes of plants are available, from standard through the various dwarfs, grafted or genetic. Following this, we discuss space-saving methods of planting and training.

Each kind of fruit bears its crop in a slightly different way, and you have to understand the where and how when you prune or train a plant. The discussion here includes sketches to help you find the fruiting wood on your own plants.

We also tell you how much pruning you can expect to do, and whether you should thin out the young fruit for a better crop.

The variety lists

The material under each variety name will give you a lot of information. Here's what you'll find.

1. The time of harvest: Fruits like apples, with varieties that bear over a very long season, are grouped under headings such as 'Early' or 'Midseason.' If all varieties fruit at nearly the same time, you'll find the information within the entry.

2. Place of origin of the variety: Many varieties are the result of modern plant-breeding experiments that suit them to a special climate. An apple or cherry developed by Minnesota breeders will take hard winters. We tell you if it does well in other climates too.

3. A description of the fruit: The entry mentions what it looks like, outside and inside, and many entries suggest the best uses, whether fresh, for cooking, or for canning.

4. A description of the tree: You'll find out whether the tree is especially vigorous or weak, productive, good-looking, or disease-resistant.

5. Best region for the variety: Some varieties are meant for special climates. The 'Red Baron' apple, 'Reliance' peach, and 'Moongold' apricot are for extreme winters and we say so. If the fruit is widely adapted you won't see a special mention.

6. Special information: Some peaches have big pink flowers that show off well in the landscape. We mention that, and we'll also mention anything special about pollination when one variety differs from the rest.

7. Availability: The numbers following each variety refer to our catalog list on page 111. You can order direct from many of these dealers, or ask your nurseryman to order from wholesalers. After some numbers you'll see a small 's' or capital 'D.' That means the dealer sells semidwarf or dwarf plants. If a variety is sold almost everywhere, we say merely that it is widely distributed.

Espaliers take little space, but provide lots of flowers and fruit.

◁

Small size is no indication of harvest, as the owner enjoys a bountiful crop of apples.

Apples

'Red Delicious'

For some people the only apple is a polished red one. Others must have a striped apple, or a golden, or a tart green apple for pies. Many remember a particular tree with some antique variety on its mossy branches. We've tried to satisfy these cravings and memories by presenting our varieties in a double list. First you'll find the more common fruits such as 'Delicious,' 'McIntosh,' and 'Jonathan' and the sports of these that vary mainly in color and bearing habit. Many apple varieties are really members of a group, with 'Delicious' alone counting many sports with redder fruit, more spurs on the branches, and larger fruit size.

In the same list you'll find the newest hybrids, just right for some special tricky climate, and recent imports such as 'Mutsu' from Japan.

A second list follows, under the heading Old Apples. These are fruits that have been around for hundreds of years, but are now less common in the nursery and commercial trade. One of them may be the fruit you remember from childhood.

The size of the tree

Plant scientists in England and elsewhere have done extensive work on dwarfing rootstocks for apples, so plant size ranges from a 4-foot bush to a 30-foot spreading tree. There is even a true, or genetic, dwarf these days that stays small on any rootstock. Since the subject is complex, you'll find a detailed discussion and silhouettes of comparative sizes on page 13 under the Merton and Malling heading.

Dwarfing rootstocks make it easy for a gardener to control size even further by special pruning and training. Apples can now grow in boxes, flat on a wall or trellis, as hedges, or in fanciful three-dimensional shapes. Look for training methods under the heading Space-Saver Training on page 79 and following.

Let us repeat here what we have said elsewhere about rootstocks. You may not be able to find labelled roots in your retail nursery. The nurseryman will say 'dwarf' or 'semidwarf.' The natural size of these trees covers the whole range of our silhouettes, but even the larger sizes can be successfully dwarfed still further by a container or a space-saver training method. It's good to know what root you have bought, but not absolutely crucial.

Small-space planting

Apples bear on long-lived spurs, so heavy pruning won't remove your crop. That means that any training method we mention in these pages will suit an apple variety. Put the young trees in the ground at a 45-degree angle and keep them pruned for a fruit-filled hedge, or have an orchard in boxes on your patio. Adapt the formal training described following page 78 and you can grow apples into the shape of a pergola or summerhouse and give tea parties behind apple walls.

Apples are also among the easiest fruit plants to graft, and a beginner can feel like an expert when he succeeds in producing a 10-variety tree on the first try. All methods are

Through the seasons this Gravenstein espalier needs care. For scale and scab, spray in winter and at bud break.

22 Tree fruits

'Jonnee,' a sport of 'Jonathan'

'Golden Delicious'

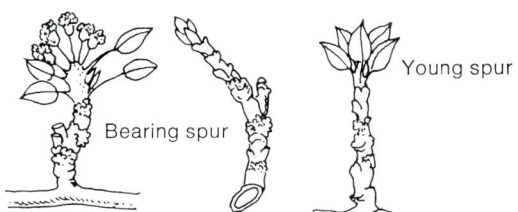

suitable, but for a tree that is fairly young, the T-bud and whip methods are the easiest. If you practice a little first, you can place buds along the trunk of a young whip and train them formally for a multiple-variety espalier. See the Space-Saver section for details, but instead of encouraging natural buds, add grafted ones.

Where does the fruit grow?

The sketch above will show you how an apple spur looks and bears. The fruit forms at the tip of last year's spur growth, and the spur itself then grows a bit more, off to the side of the fruit. Each spur bears for 10 years or more, so don't tear it off when you pick. For comparison, the straight spur at the right has not yet borne fruit.

You will hear about spur varieties. These are sports of a number of standard varieties, often of 'Delicious' or 'McIntosh' but there are others. They grow less each season, and their spurs are packed closer together on the branch. The less vigorous growth means that they are a kind of genetic dwarf, but they are still good-sized trees unless grafted to dwarfing roots. One caution: spur varieties are difficult to handle for the really formal training methods. If you buy spur varieties on dwarfing roots, use an informal training method that doesn't call for any particular form.

Pruning an apple

Pruning methods depend on how you grow the tree. For special training, turn to page 82. For general pruning of the larger dwarfed trees or standard trees, see the pruning pages.

Apart from special training, here are basic guides: The smallest dwarfs should be trained to branch very low, and if they are not otherwise supported they should be staked. Larger trees should be trained to a strong basic scaffold, and the oldest branches (usually dangling) should be pruned off when age or shade from upper branches cuts their production of fruit. Trim back to a more vertical branch.

Thinning the fruit

Thinning is crucial with many apple varieties. They overset, and the heavy crop can snap branches. Even more important, many apple varieties tend to bear every other year. If you leave too much fruit you encourage alternate bearing, and the following year you may find that your tree bears only a handful of apples.

There are many thinning methods, but the most direct is to wait for the natural drop of young fruit in June, then thin the remaining fruit so that there is a single apple every six inches along the branches. Each spur may have a cluster of fruit. A single fruit is less likely to become diseased so

Wait for petal fall to spray for codling moth. Thin the fruit at thumbnail size to one a spur.

Note the characteristic 'Delicious' shape.

'Tydeman's Red,' a 'McIntosh' type.

Great for cooking, this is 'Golden Delicious.'

'Cortland,' another 'McIntosh' descendant.

leave only the largest fruit on each spur. Thin carefully or you will damage the spurs.

Pollination
Apples are only partially self-fruitful, but many varieties set a good crop without a pollinator. Any two kinds that bloom together offer cross-pollination (with some exceptions listed below). If you plant only a very early and a very late variety, they will not cross-pollinate.

A few apples have infertile pollen. The following will not set a crop at all if you plant them together with no other source of pollen: 'Gravenstein,' 'Stayman' (and 'Stayman' sports such as 'Blaxstayman' and 'Staymared'), and 'Winesap.'

Winter chill
All apples need some cool winter weather, but there is an enormous range in this requirement, so varieties are available for any climate except subtropical and low desert regions.

Pests and disease
Apples are subject to attack by a good many organisms, but the gardener will have most trouble with codling moth and other fruit-spoiling pests, and then with the usual aphids, mites, scale, and so forth. See the pest and disease section for further details. A regular spray schedule is best. A fungicide will control diseases such as mildew and scab where they are a problem.

The variety list
Our list is divided by bearing season and further divided into two sections. First you will find the best of today's varieties, then a list of old apple varieties. Catalog numbers at the end of each entry include a small 's' where semi-dwarf trees are sold, and a 'D' for dwarf trees.

Early season
'Lodi.' Origin: Geneva, NY. A cross of 'Montgomery' and 'Yellow Transparent.' Fruit is medium to large, up to 3 inches in diameter. The skin is light green, sometimes with a slight orange blush. The flesh is nearly white, with a slightly greenish tinge, fine-grained, tender and juicy, and sour. The eating quality is only fair, but its kitchen quality is excellent. Use in sauce and for pies. An alternate bearer, 'Lodi' is noted for its tendency to overset fruit and must be thinned early. Widely available.

'Yellow Transparent.' Introduced from Russia almost 100 years ago, it is still valued by a discriminating, loyal following for quality as an early green cooking apple. Fruit is medium in size and shape. The skin is greenish-yellow and the flesh is white tinged greenish-yellow. It does show bruises readily and soon becomes overmature. The flesh texture is fine-grained, crisp, and juicy. Eating quality is good and kitchen quality is excellent for sauce and in pies. An annual bearer. Widely available.

'Summerred.' Origin: Summerland, British Columbia, Can. A cross of 'McIntosh' and 'Golden Delicious.' A medium-to-large apple, oblong-conic in shape. Skin has bright, solid red blush with many prominent dots. Flesh is fine in texture, soft, with a sharp, full, rich flavor. Good eating fresh and in sauce and pies. The tree is a strong upright grower, bears annually, requires thinning. Available: (7s), (10), (28), (43sD).

'Niagara.' Origin: Geneva, NY. A cross of 'Carlton' and 'McIntosh.' Fruit is of the 'McIntosh' type in appearance

'Prima,' is scab resistant.

Half 'Jonathan,' half 'Golden Delicious' equals 'Jonagold.'

'Melrose' resembles 'Jonathan' parent.

'Jonamac' shows 'McIntosh' influence.

and flavor. Ripens two weeks before 'McIntosh,' Tree growth habit and productivity similar to 'McIntosh'—Strong, very vigorous. Available: (28).

'Oriole.' Origin: Minnesota. Large, roundish fruit. Skin is orange-yellow in color, striped with red. Flesh is fine-grained and tender, juicy, and aromatic. Excellent for eating fresh and for sauce, or quartered for pies. Tree is medium tall, vigorous and rounded in shape. Available: (12), (43sD).

'Early McIntosh.' Origin: Geneva, NY. A cross of 'Yellow Transparent' and 'McIntosh.' Skin is a very good red. Excellent eaten fresh, for sauce, and for pies. However, the tree is very difficult for the average grower to thin and size. Available: (2), (25sD), (27), (34), (35sD), (48sD).

'Duchess.' An early bearer of red-striped, medium-size fruit. Flavor is tart. Good for sauce and quartered for pies. Available: (29), (32sD).

'Melba.' Origin: Canada. Very hardy, annual bearing, medium-to-large fruit. Skin is light green with red blush. Flesh is white, fine-textured, tender, and crisp. Available: (23D), (25sD).

'Puritan.' Origin: Massachusetts. A cross of 'McIntosh' and 'Red Astrachan.' Fruit is medium sized and uniformly round in shape. Skin is an attractive solid red. Flesh is white, tender, fairly soft, a bit tart but of very good quality. Tree is medium-sized, moderately vigorous, with wide crotch angles and well branched. Bears alternately. Available: (1s), (23), (44sD).

'Wellington.' Origin: Geneva, NY. A cross of 'Crimson Beauty' and 'Cortland.' Fruit is large, with red-striped, attractive skin. Essentially a sauce apple. Tree is upright, and spreading. Bears annually. Available: (32sD).

'Gravenstein.' Large, but not uniform fruit. Skin is red-striped with light green ground. Flesh is greenish-yellow, moderately fine-textured, crisp, firm, and juicy. Tree is strong and very vigorous, with an upright, spreading growth habit. An excellent variety for eating out-of-hand, for sauce, and quartered for pies. Bears alternately. Widely available.

Early to midseason

'Tydeman's Red.' Origin: England. A McIntosh type, ripening four weeks earlier than the 'McIntosh.' Fruits are almost entirely red from a very early stage. Shaped like a 'McIntosh,' they should be picked within a period of a few days for optimum dessert quality and distinctive flavor, and because they drop quickly at maturity. Fruits are of a good eating quality and keep in storage much longer than most early varieties. Its virtue is early ripening when few other varieties are being harvested. A drawback is growth habit—the branches are undesirably long and lanky and need to be controlled by pruning. For best results, should be grown on dwarf or semidwarf rootstocks. An annual bearer. Widely available.

'Paulared.' Origin: Michigan. This variety is rated high on several counts. It has eye appeal—a solid red blush with a bright yellow ground color. Excellent, slightly tart flavor, good for eating fresh and in sauce and pies. White-to-cream flesh is nonbrowning. The tree is everything an attractive tree should be—strong upright, with good branch structure. Ripens early, about two weeks before 'McIntosh.' Although it colors early, it should not be picked until nearly mature, for quality apples. An annual bearer, fruit holds well on the tree and is harvested in two pickings. Has long storage life. Available: (22D), (44sD).

Tree fruits **25**

'**Prima.**' This new variety is scab-resistant—a virtue that dramatically reduces the need for sprays. Fruit is medium-to-large, and round in shape. The skin is a medium dark red over bright yellow. Flesh is yellowish, firm, crisp, fine-grained, and juicy. Both a good eating and cooking apple. Bears a good crop every year. Fruits may hang on the tree and become overripe. Available: (12s), (34D), (44sD).

'**Jonathan.**' The standard 'Jonathan' is one of the top varieties produced by commercial growers in the Central States. The fruit is medium-sized, uniform. Skin is washed red and pale yellow, with firm, crisp, juicy flesh, with a rich flavor that makes it a good choice for snacks, salads, and all culinary uses. Widely available.

There are several new 'Jonathan' sports to consider. Among them are:

'**Jonagold.**' Origin: Geneva, NY. A cross of 'Jonathan' and 'Golden Delicious,' a beautiful large apple with a lively, yellow-green ground color partly covered with bright red stripes. Cream-colored flesh is crisp and juicy with good flavor. It is a dual-purpose apple—good for cooking, and eating quality is among the very best. Stores well. The trees are vigorous and annually productive; sturdy, with wide-angled branches. Available: (27s), (28), (32sD), (43sD), (48sD).

'**Jonamac.**' A 'McIntosh' type dessert apple. The eating quality is very good. Milder in flavor than the 'McIntosh.' Bears annually. Available: (28), (48sD).

'**Chehalis.**' Origin: Washington. Resembles 'Golden Delicious' but ripens in mid-September, 3 weeks earlier than 'Golden Delicious.' Fruit is large, crisp, juicy, and with high eating quality. A most important factor in its favor is its resistance to scab. Available: (43sD).

Midseason varieties

'**Wealthy.**' A hardy old variety. Good for eating and cooking. A long bloom period in midseason makes it a good pollinator for most varieties. Fruit is medium to large, uniform, rough. Flesh is white stained with pink, fine-textured, firm, tender, tart, and juicy. Eating quality is good and kitchen quality is excellent for sauce and good for pies, baking, and stewing. An alternate bearer. Widely available.

'**Wayne.**' Origin: Geneva, NY. A cross of 'Northwestern Greening' and 'Red Spy.' Fruit is large, solidly blushed and washed light scarlet. Excellent for sauce, or eaten fresh, and for desserts and salads. Tree is upright and spreading. Available: (2), (28), (32sD).

'**Minjon.**' Origin: Minnesota. A cross of 'Wealthy' and 'Jonathan.' Fruit is below medium in size. Skin is dark, solid red in color and the flesh is often pink or stained red. Tart in flavor, it is good eaten fresh, used for sauce, pies, and baking. Tree is very hardy and vigorous; requires thinning. Available: (12), (29).

'**Haralson.**' Origin: Minnesota. Fruit is medium-sized and round in shape. Skin is an attractive red with greenish dots. Flesh is white, firm, moderately tender, juicy, and tart. Good for eating fresh; also for sauce, pies, and baking. Stores well. Tree is hardy, vigorous, and upright-growing. Available: (12D), (13), (17D), (20D), (26), (29).

'**Macoun.**' Origin: Geneva, NY. This annual-bearing variety received a new burst of interest in the early 1970's because of its very excellent fresh eating quality. A cross of 'McIntosh' and 'Jersey Black,' the fruit is similar to 'McIntosh' but smaller. Skin is very dark red in color. Flesh is white, richly flavored, aromatic; high dessert quality. Tree is upright-growing, with long, lanky branches. Thinning aids in attaining good fruit size and annual cropping. Widely available.

'Cortland' is white under the red skin.

'**Empire.**' Origin: Geneva, NY. Cross between 'McIntosh' and 'Delicious.' Fruit is medium and uniform. Skin is dark red, striped, with whitish-cream flesh that is firm, medium-textured, crisp, and very juicy. Eating quality is excellent. One of its major faults is that it develops full color long before it has become harvest-mature, tempting the grower to harvest too early. Trees are moderately vigorous, upright-spreading in form, and annual-bearing. Available: (1s), (2s), (27s), (28), (32D), (44sD), (48sD).

Midseason to late

'**Newtown Pippin.**' A midseason-bordering-on-late variety. Fruit is medium in size with greenish yellow skin and crisp, firm flesh. Tree has a strong, very vigorous growth habit. Kitchen quality; good fresh, excellent for sauce, and pies. Widely available.

'**Delicious.**' A late-bearing variety. Medium-sized fruit that is long and tapering in shape. Skin is striped-to-solid red with yellowing, firm flesh that is juicy, sweet, and aromatic. The most important variety grown in the U.S. Hand thinning is usually necessary to produce apples of good size and dessert quality. Widely available.

'**Fireside.**' A late-bearing variety. Large fruit, up to 3 inches in diameter. Skin is medium red, lightly striped with darker red. Flesh is yellowish, medium coarse, tender, and juicy. An excellent variety for dessert purposes. Tree is vigorous and hardy. Available: (12D), (17), (29).

'**Idared.**' A cross of 'Jonathan' and 'Wagener.' Fruit skin is an attractive, nearly solid red, with a smooth finish. Fruit size is large and uniform, with white, firm, smooth-textured flesh. Excellent dessert and cooking quality. Long storage life. Tree is strong, vigorous, upright; very productive. Bears annually, late season. Widely available.

'**McIntosh.**' If you write down the attributes of a great apple—"medium to large fruits, white flesh, sweet, tender and juicy, very good eaten fresh, in sauce, in pies, or as a cider variety"—you would have the 'McIntosh.' The skin is yellow, with a bright red blush. The tree is an annual bearer, with a strong, very vigorous growth habit. Widely available.

'**Cortland.**' Origin: Geneva, NY. According to many apple growers, 'Cortland' rates "excellent" as a dual-purpose variety. "It's better than 'McIntosh,'" they say. Bears heavy annual crops of large red-striped fruit with white flesh which, when exposed to air, is slow to turn brown, making it especially suited for use in salads. The tree has a strong, very vigorous, spreading, drooping growth habit. Widely available.

'**Priscilla.**' One of the two new scab-resistant varieties

'Mutsu' descends from 'Golden Delicious.' From Japan.

and a good partner in the same orchard with 'Prima,' since it serves as a good pollinator. Fruit is large and slightly rounded. Skin has bright red blush over yellow ground. Flesh is white to slightly greenish in color, with a crisp, medium texture. It is good eating fresh, and will store up to three months. The tree has a moderately vigorous growth habit. Available: (2s), (34D), (44sD).

'Rhode Island Greening.' Still rated at or near the top as a cooking or processing variety after more than 200 years. Fruit is light green to yellow, firm-fleshed, crisp, and juicy. A top-quality cooking apple, good for sauces and baking. Generally a good cropper, but poor pollinator. Bears late, and in alternate years. Available: (23), (25sD), (27s), (28), (32sD), (44sD).

Late varieties

'Golden Delicious.' For a great dual-purpose, eating, and cooking apple, 'Golden Delicious' ranks as high as any. Fruit is medium-to-large and uniform in size. The skin is greenish-yellow with bright pink blush. Flesh is firm, crisp, juicy, and sweet. The eating quality is excellent fresh and in desserts and salads. It makes a very good grade of sauce. The tree is medium in height, moderately vigorous, upright, round-headed, with wide-angle crotches. It bears very young and ripens late in the season. Bears annually, if thinned. Widely available.

'Mutsu.' Origin: Japan. Cross of 'Golden Delicious' and the Japanese variety 'Indo.' This newcomer has gained the approval of both the grower and consumer. Large, oblong, greenish fruits develop some yellow color when mature. The flesh is coarse-textured, firm, and crisp. Excellent flavor (more tart than 'Golden Delicious') when eaten fresh. Rated high for sauce, pies, and as a baked apple. 'Mutsu,' unlike 'Golden Delicious,' does not shrivel in storage. The tree is a very vigorous, spreading grower. Bears crops annually. Available: (2s), (23D), (28), (32sD), (43sD), (44sD), (48sD).

'Rome Beauty.' "The world's best baking apple." Many red sports with a beautiful, solid, medium-dark red color. Fruit is large and round, with medium-textured, firm, crisp flesh. The tree is moderately vigorous, and a heavy annual producer. It comes into production at an early age. Fruit has a long storage life. Widely available.

'King.' Origin: North Carolina. A high-quality apple for eating fresh or for use in the kitchen. Fruit is very large and deep red. Flesh is pure white, firm, crisp, sweet, and juicy. Excellent for eating out-of-hand, and for use in pies and sauce. The tree is weak, slow-growing, and semidwarf in habit. Annual bearer. Available: (27s), (28), (32sD), (35D).

'Stayman.' Very late ripener. Where it can be grown, the 'Stayman' is good for cooking or eating fresh. The fruit is juicy with a moderately tart, rich, wine-like flavor. It is fine-textured, firm, and crisp. Skin is bright red. However, skin "cracking" is one drawback. Tree is medium-sized, and moderately vigorous. Annual bearer. Widely available.

'Granny Smith.' Apples of this variety have been shipped from Australia and New Zealand and sold in supermarkets here. Flesh is similar to 'Golden Delicious,' a bright glossy green, but more tart in flavor. Fruit size is medium to large. Customers rate it very good eaten fresh, in desserts and salads, as sauce, and quartered for pie. The tree is annual-bearing, strong, very vigorous, upright, and spreading. The big trouble in growing the variety is its late harvest date, even in the Willamette Valley. It won't ripen in the summer-cool areas of Western Washington. It has been grown in Washington's Okanogan and Columbia Valleys, and in the Lower Yakima Valley. Available: (7), (9sD), (10), (24s), (32sD), (35s), (44sD), (45).

'Northern Spy.' Trees are very slow to come into bearing; sometimes fourteen years elapse before they bear their first bushel. Alternate-bearing. Fruit is large, with skin of yellow and red colored stripes. Flesh is yellowish, firm, and crisp. Excellent quality fresh and quartered for pies. Fruit bruises easily. Trees are vigorous in their growth habit. Fruit has a long storage life. Widely available.

'Prairie Spy.' Origin: Minnesota. A late-bearing variety. Fruit is large. Skin is striped red, with crisp, juicy flesh. High dessert and culinary quality. Tree is hardy and vigorous. Available: (12), (17), (29).

'Redwell.' Origin: Minnesota. An annual-bearing variety. Fruit is medium-to-large in size; rounded shape. Skin is very attractive, bright medium-red over yellow, but tends to bruise easily. Flesh is cream-colored, mild, and tender; good for baking, dessert, sauce. Tree is medium-sized with strong framework; hardy. Available: (12).

'Red Delicious.' Everyone knows that 'Red Delicious' is the number-one apple in the supermarket. There is no question about the quality of 'Red Delicious' as a dessert and eating out-of-hand apple. Fruit is medium-to-large in size. Skin color is striped to full red and the flesh is moderately firm in texture. Your best choices are the red sports such as 'Wellspur' or 'Royal Red.' Tree tends to produce full crops every other year unless properly thinned. Widely available.

'Spartan.' Origin: Summerland, British Columbia, Canada. Cross between 'McIntosh' and 'Newton.' Fruit is medium size, uniform, and symmetrical in shape. Skin is a solid dark red color. Flesh is light yellow, firm, tender, crisp, and juicy. Strictly a dessert variety. Tree is strong, moderately vigorous, and well shaped. Must be thinned to assure good size and annual bearing. Widely available.

'Melrose.' Origin: Ohio. A cross between 'Jonathan' and 'Delicious.' Resembles the 'Jonathan' in color and shape, but is less tart. Rate it high as a home-orchard apple for eating out-of-hand, for use in sauce and pies, and for exceptional storage qualities. Fruit is large, uniform, and somewhat flat in shape. The skin is yellow with a bright red wash. Flesh is firm, tender, and crisp. Fruit won't polish like a well-grown 'Red Delicious.' On all counts, except color, it out-rates the 'Red Delicious.' The tree is medium in height, moderately vigorous, upright, and spreading. Available: (2s), (8D), (28), (32sD), (43sD), (44sD).

'Spigold.' Origin: Geneva, NY. A cross of 'Northern Spy' and 'Golden Delicious.' Fruit is very large, beautifully colored with bright red stripes on a golden yellow background. The flesh is crisp, delicately flavored, and most pleasing to the taste. An excellent variety for eating fresh and for desserts and salads. Tree grows more vigorously than most varieties and produces good crops at an early age, when grown as a semidwarf. Alternate-bearing. Available: (27s), (28), (32sD), (48sD).

'Monroe.' Origin: Geneva, NY. A cross of 'Jonathan' and 'Rome Beauty.' Fruit is medium to large, roundish, with nearly solid red skin. Flesh is yellowish, firm, crisp, and juicy. Used primarily for cooking. Tree is medium-sized, vigorous, upright, and spreading. A reliable annual bearer; very productive. Available: (28).

'Holly.' A heavy bearer of red, crisp fruit. Flesh is juicy and sweet. Available: (28).

'Northwestern Greening.' A producer of very large, green or yellow fruit. Good for sauce, and quartered for pies. Available: (1s), (12), (17), (29), (44sD).

'Red Duchess.' Producer of medium-sized, red fruit. Good for sauce, quartered for pies, and for jam and jelly stock. Available: (29), (32sD).

For Southern California
'Beverly Hills.' Early. This is a small-to-medium-sized apple, striped or splashed with red over a pale yellow skin. The flesh is tender, juicy, and tart. Overall, the apple resembles 'McIntosh.' Use it fresh, or cook it as sauce or in pies. The tree is suited mainly to cooler coastal areas. Heat spoils the fruit. Available: local nurseries.

'Winter Banana.' Midseason. The large fruit is strikingly beautiful. The skin color is pale and waxy with a spreading pink blush on the sunny side. The flesh is tender with a fine, special aroma and tangy flavor. 'Winter Banana' requires a pollinizer such as 'Red Astrachan' in order to set a good crop. Available: local nurseries.

In addition, you can plant the following from the main list: 'Bellflower,' 'Delicious,' 'Newtown Pippin,' 'Red Astrachan,' and 'White Pearmain.'

Old apples
The list below includes fine old varieties that are now rare in the commercial and nursery trade. We list the availability of plants by number, with numbers referring to our catalogue list, but you can also order scions for grafting. Write to the Worcester County Horticultural Society, 30 Elm Street, Worcester, Mass. 01608, for a descriptive list and order blank.

Early season
'Early Harvest.' Origin: Unknown. Tree is medium-sized, with an upright, spreading, roundish, and open growth habit. Fruit is medium-sized and nearly round in shape. Skin is pale yellow, smooth, and waxen. Flesh is white and has a soft, fine, tender-to-crisp texture. Excellent eaten fresh and for desserts and salads. Fruit is not a good keeper, and bruises easily. Bears alternately and annually, taking 4 to 6 years to the first crop. Available: (32sD).

'Red Astrachan.' Origin: Russia. A medium-sized tree, upright and spreading growth habit. Fruit is medium-sized and roundish in shape. Skin is yellow splashed dark red. Flesh is white, often strongly tinged red. An excellent cooking apple, and when fully ripe very desirable eaten fresh or for desserts and salads, though very perishable. Tree bears young, moderately, and sometimes annually. Available: (2s), (2sD), (10), (27), (28s), (32sD).

'White Astrachan.' Origin: Russia. A vigorous-growing tree, with a full, well-rounded crown, it needs moderate pruning. Bears medium-sized round fruit. Skin is green and yellow with pink stripes or blush. Flesh is white, crisp, and tart. A very good apple for all culinary uses. Bears annually, taking 7 years to the first crop. Available: (10), (15).

Midseason
'Chenango' ('Chenango Strawberry'). Origin: New York. A medium-sized tree, with an upright, roundish, and spreading growth habit. Fruit is medium to large. The yellow and white skin is striped red. Flesh is white, firm, tender, very aromatic, and juicy. Use for cooking and eating raw. Does not keep well in storage, having a tendency to lose color. Annual-bearing over several weeks. Takes 4 to 6 years to first crop. Available: (25sD), (27s), (28s), (32sD).

'Palmer Greening' ('Washington Royal'). Origin: Sterling, Massachusetts. Tree has an upright, spreading-to-roundish growth habit. Fruit is medium- to above-average-sized. Skin is waxy and greenish-yellow, shaded red. Flesh is

English 'Cox Orange' tastes fine fresh or cooked.

'Fameuse' from France should be eaten fresh from the tree.

white with a yellow cast, crisp, firm, tender, and quite juicy. Excellent for eating fresh and for desserts and salads. Available: (32sD).

'Red June.' Origin: North Carolina. Tree is medium height, growing upright and spreading. Bears small- or below-medium-sized apples, with a deep red over yellow or greenish skin. Flesh is white, fine, and tender. Excellent eaten fresh and for desserts and salads. Available: (10), (17), (20), (24s), (32sD), (35D), (36), (39).

'Summer Rambo.' Origin: France. Probably one of the oldest varieties known. Tree is a strong grower, very vigorous and hardy, with a semispreading growth habit. Fruit is very large and flat. Skin is greenish-yellow with bright red stripes. The tender flesh is juicy. An excellent apple eaten fresh and for sauce. Available: (1s), (2s), (24s), (27s), (32sD), (36D).

'Twenty Ounce.' Origin: Massachusetts. Tree is medium-sized, growing upright, eventually becoming roundish. It is vigorous, hardy, healthy, and long-lived, but produces only moderate crops. Fruit is large to very large, as the name suggests, with green skin that becomes yellow tinged red as it matures. Flesh is white, coarse, and juicy. Very good for most culinary uses, but not a good keeper. An almost annual bearer. Available: (24s), (27s), (28s), (32sD), (48sD).

Midseason to late

'Black Gilliflower' ('Sheepnose'). Origin: Connecticut. A large, upright, spreading tree which bears medium-to-large fruit. Its dark red skin turns somewhat purple as it matures, hence the name. The flesh is whitish or slightly tinged with yellow; firm and rather coarse texture. Sometimes used for baking, it is generally considered too dry and not sour enough for cooking. A reliable annual cropper. Available: (24s), (27s), (32sD).

'Blue Pearmain.' A very large, spreading tree, with a variable bearing habit. Not a reliable cropper. Fruit is medium to very large. Skin is yellow, washed and mottled with red. Flesh is firm, rather coarse, yellow, and juicy. Good as a dessert or salad apple, or for cider. Cooking quality is only fair. Available: (2s), (32sD).

'Cox Orange.' Origin: Bucks, England. Tree is medium-sized—sometimes larger—with a dense, upright growth habit. A heavy bearer of red and yellow medium-sized fruit. Flesh is yellow, firm, crisp, and tender. Very juicy and decidedly aromatic, it is an excellent dessert apple. It also processes very well. Tree bears regularly and productively. Available: (27s), (28s), (32sD).

'Fameuse' ('Snow Apple'). Origin: France. One of the oldest apple varieties. Tree is medium in height, with an upright, spreading growth habit. A heavy bearer of light, bright red fruit. Flesh is snow-white and crisp. The aromatic, sweet taste somewhat resembles the McIntosh, of which it is an ancestor. Excellent eaten fresh and for desserts and salads, but it is not a cooking apple. A biennial to variable bearer, it grows best at high elevations in well-drained, light soil. Available: (2s), (24s), (27s), (28s), (32D).

'Hubbardston Nonesuch.' Origin: Massachusetts. Tree vigor and fruit character vary considerably with different soil and climate conditions. A heavy bearer, with an erect-to-roundish spreading growth habit. Fruit is above medium to large. Skin is yellow or greenish. Flesh is white, slightly tinged yellow, medium-firm, fine-grained, and tender. The smaller and better colored fruit will be the better keepers. As an eating apple it is acceptable but does not cook well. An annual bearer, it takes 4 to 6 years to the first crop. Available: (2s), (28s), (32sD).

'Maiden Blush.' Origin: Unknown. A medium-sized tree with an open, spreading growth habit. Fruit is medium-sized, with pale lemon-yellow skin. Flesh is white with a very slight yellow tinge, fine to moderately crisp, and tender. Very juicy, with a sprightly flavor, it is an excellent drying apple, but not a good keeper. It bears biennially, almost annually, taking 4 to 6 years for the first crop. Available: (20), (32sD).

'Porter.' Origin: Massachusetts. A compact tree with desirable growth characteristics. Fruit is usually rather large, clear, bright yellow marked with red. Flesh is white, fine, crisp, and tender. Long a favorite of home fruit growers because it retains its flavor and form well when cooked and canned. It is also fine for eating raw.

'Hubbardston Nonesuch' was once the pride of Massachusetts.

'Twenty-ounce' is one of the really big apples.

An alternate bearer, taking 4 to 6 years for the first crop. Available: (32sD).

'Westfield-Seek-No-Further.' Origin: Massachusetts. A medium-to-large, slender tree, with a spreading, roundish growth habit. Bears light crops of medium-sized, deep yellow or greenish fruit, often shaded and splashed bright pink. Flesh is slightly tinged pale yellow; firm, medium-grained, and crisp. Excellent eaten fresh and in desserts and salads, but does not cook well. Available: (27s), (28s), (32sD).

'Wolf River.' Origin: Wisconsin. A large, strong, spreading tree valued for its hardiness. Bears medium crops of very large, yellow fruit, striped red. Flesh is firm, tender, and moderately coarse. Keeping quality is very short. Fair for eating and poor for cooking. A variable bearer. Available: (2s), (24), (29), (32D).

'Yellow Bellflower.' Origin: New Jersey. Tree grows medium to large, with an upright, spreading growth habit. Bears light crops of very attractive yellow fruit with a pinkish blush that improves in storage. Flesh is white, tinged pale yellow; firm, fine-grained, and crisp. Excellent for eating fresh and for desserts and salads, it also makes very good pies. A variable bearer. Available: (10), (32sD).

Late varieties

'Arkansas Black.' Origin: Benton County, Arkansas. A large tree with an upright, spreading, moderately vigorous growth habit. Bears medium- to below-average-sized fruit. Skin is yellow covered with purplish-red. Flesh is hard and crisp, tinged yellow. Excellent for sauce. An alternate bearer, taking 8 to 10 years to the first crop. Available: (10), (11), (15), (24s), (34s).

'Baldwin Woodpecker.' Origin: Massachusetts. A very large, vigorous tree, with an upright, spreading growth habit. Bears medium-to-heavy crops of medium-sized yellow or greenish fruit, striped red. Flesh is yellow and juicy. Texture is hard and crisp. Flavor is tart and mildly acid. Excellent for freezing, and good for sauce, jam, or jelly. A biennial, and sometimes triennial, bearing habit, taking 8 to 10 years to the first crop. Available: (2s), (4D), (6), (25sD), (27s), (28s).

'Ben Davis.' Origin: Tennessee. Tree is medium height, vigorous, hardy, with an upright, spreading growth habit. Fruit is medium to large with bright red skin. The flesh is exceedingly firm, crisp, and slightly acid in flavor. Has a tendency to turn mealy when over-ripe. A good apple for drying, fair for cooking, poor for eating. Annual-bearing and exceedingly productive, taking 4 to 6 years to the first crop. Available: (24s), (31sD).

'Esopus Spitzenberg.' Origin: Ulster County, New York. Tree is a slow grower with upright, moderately drooping branches. Should be planted with ample room and pruned to allow air and light in. Fruit is medium to large, bright red, and uniform in shape. Flesh is a rich, deep yellow, covered with bright red and has a mildly acid flavor. Texture is firm, crisp, and tender. A good all-round apple, except for baking. A moderate, biennial cropper taking 6 to 8 years to the first crop. Available: (2s), (24s), (27s), (28s), (32sD).

'Golden Russet.' Origin: Unknown. Tree varies from medium to large and has an upright, roundish, spreading growth habit. Fruit is nearly round, golden russet with a bronze cheek. Flesh is yellowish, fine-grained, crisp, and tender. Excellent for eating fresh and for desserts and salads. Only fair for baking. This hardy, vigorous tree bears early, produces small aromatic fruit almost annually. Available: (23D), (27s), (28s), (32sD).

'Grimes Golden.' Origin: West Virginia. Very probably a parent of the 'Golden Delicious.' Tree is medium to large, with a dense, spreading growth habit. Fruit has a golden yellow skin and yellow, tender, crisp, juicy flesh. Bears small fruit that is very good for eating and freezing, but poor for baking. An intermediate bearer, taking 6 to 8 years to the first crop. Widely available.

Apple families

We mentioned earlier that some apples are the heads of extensive families, varying in some detail of color or growth habit. These apple families come about in two ways: they are the result of breeding; or they are sports (natural genetic changes) of the original tree.

Sports may occur at any time. Often there is no apparent reason for them—suddenly one branch of a tree is different. Occasionally the odd branch results from mechanical damage, such as pruning. Sometimes experimenters purposely change genetic structure with chemicals or radiation. Most sports are without value, but some are valuable and are propagated to create new strains.

In breeding, each parent supplies half the heritage of the seedlings, but that half may be a set of characteristics that is partly or completely hidden in the parent. The seedlings are a mixed bag, and breeders must grow them to fruiting size to see what they have, so the work takes time and the seedlings may be inferior trees.

'Delicious.' The best known modern apple sprouted in an Iowa orchard in 1870. The owner, Jesse Hiatt, cut it down twice, but it resprouted, and finally he let it grow. It seemed to be a seedling of the Bellflower tree next to it. In about 1880 it bore fruit which Hiatt thought was the best he had ever tasted. The name 'Delicious' was given at a fruit show by C. M. Stark of Stark Nurseries. Stark didn't learn the name of the grower until 1894, but then 'Delicious' began its rise to fame.

Redder-colored sports include: 'Richard,' 'Royal Red,' 'Hi Early,' 'Chelan Red,' 'Red Queen,' and others. The original red sport was 'Starking.' Spur-type sports include: 'Starkrimson,' 'Redspur,' 'Wellspur,' 'Hardispur,' and 'Oregon Spur.' 'Delicious' is a parent of 'Melrose.'

'Jonathan.' The seedling sprouted in Kingston, N.Y., apparently from a fruit of an 'Esopus Spitzenberg.' A Judge Buel of Albany found the apple so good that he presented specimens to the Massachusetts Horticultural Society, giving it the name 'Jonathan' for the man who first showed it to him. 'Jonathan' was the primary variety before 'Delicious' took over.

Red sports of 'Jonathan' include 'Jon-A-Red,' and 'Jonnee.' Hybrid descendants include: 'Jonagold,' 'Jonamac,' 'Ida-red,' 'Melrose,' 'Minjon,' and 'Monroe.'

'McIntosh.' The apple came from the McIntosh Nursery in Ontario, Canada. John McIntosh discovered it about 1811, but did not propagate grafted stock until 1835 when the grafting technique was perfected. 'McIntosh' became widely known in about 1900.

A well-known spur variety is 'Macspur.' 'McIntosh' is frequently used in breeding, and well-known descendants include: 'Summerred,' 'Niagara,' 'Early McIntosh,' 'Puritan,' 'Tydeman's Red,' 'Jonamac,' 'Macoun,' 'Empire,' 'Cortland,' and 'Spartan.'

Other major apples with crowds of offspring include, 'Rome,' 'Golden Delicious,' 'Northern Spy,' and 'Winesap.'

'Hunt Russet' (Russet Pearmain'). Origin: Massachusetts. Tree is medium height, upright, and spreading. Fruit is medium-sized, golden russet with a red-russet cheek. Rather fine, tender flesh is whitish tinged yellow. Flavor is mild to bland. Good eaten fresh or for sauces, pies, jams, jellies, cider, or juice. A variable bearing habit. Available: (32sD).

'Lady.' Origin: France. Tree grows somewhat dwarfish. Fruit is small, with exquisite red and green coloring. Highly decorative, it is often used at Christmas time. Flesh is white, crisp, and firm. Its flavor is subacid, turning to very sweet. Excellent for a fresh dessert and also makes very good juice and cider. This is a very old variety, grown and enjoyed almost back to the Middle Ages. A biennial bearer. Available: (2s), (28s), (32sD).

'Northern Spy.' Origin: East Bloomfield, New York. Tree is medium to large. Bears large, roundish, bright red, striped fruit. Flesh is yellowish, firm, fine-grained, tender, and juicy. Still the standard for excellence in cooking and processing. It is an intermediate bearer, taking 10 to 14 years to the first crop. Tree is resistant to cedar rust. Widely available.

'Pumpkin Sweet' ('Pound Sweet'). Origin: Manchester, Connecticut. Tree is medium to large, with an upright, spreading growth habit. A reliable cropper of large to very large fruit. Skin color is first green—then turns clear yellow with greenish-yellow stripes. Flesh is yellow and has a peculiar, sweet flavor. Excellent for baking; poor for eating. Tree bears alternately, taking 6 to 8 years to the first crop. Plant in a wind-sheltered area as fruit is subject to windfall. Available: (2s), (32sD).

'Roxbury Russet.' Origin: Massachusetts. The most popular of the Russets. Tree is medium to large, with a spreading, flat growth habit. Fruit is above medium to large, greenish- to yellowish-brown. Flesh is tinged with yellow, and is firm, coarse, and juicy. A good apple for cellar storage and a favorite for blending in cider. Bears annually. Available: (2s), (28s), (32sD).

'Smokehouse.' Origin: Lancaster County, Pennsylvania. Large, dense, roundish trees bear above-medium-to-large fruit. Skin is yellow or greenish, mottled dull red. Flesh is tinged yellow, rather firm, and delicately aromatic. Good for eating fresh and for desserts and salads. A reliable bearer. Available: (1s), (24s), (27s), (32sD).

'Tolman Sweet.' Origin: Dorchester, Massachusetts. Tree is very hardy, long-lived, grows well, bears early and almost annually. Fruit is medium to large with a pale, clear yellow skin and firm white flesh. Flavor is rather dry and decidedly sweet. An excellent eating and baking apple. Keeping quality is short. Fruit is easily damaged so should be handled with care. A biennial bearer. Available: (23D), (28s), (32sD).

'White Pearmain.' Origin: Unknown. Large trees bear heavy crops of small to fairly large fruit. Skin is greenish to pale yellow shaded with brownish red. Flesh is white tinged yellow, fine-grained, crisp, tender, and firm. A juicy, pleasantly aromatic apple that is excellent eaten fresh and in desserts, salads, and pies. Also good for sauce, jam, jelly, cider, and juice. Keeping quality is very good. An annual bearer, taking 6 to 8 years to the first crop. Available: (10), (32sD).

In addition to the above, these old apple varieties are listed by the following sources:
'Gold Pearmain' (25)
'Red Pearmain' (32)
'Yellow Horse' (1)

'Rome Beauty' is a beauty, but not the best of the eating apples. Use it for splendid baked apples.

Pears

Pears are a good choice for the Western gardener. The trees are especially attractive, require little pruning, and their crop stores well without special apparatus. Of course, the pears of the Medford area in Oregon are among the finest in the world, but a gardener who chooses wisely can grow a good pear even in the central valley of California. Since winter cold is a must for pears, they don't do well in the Los Angeles-San Diego region, but most of the West is pear country.

At least one variety will produce its finest fruit only in the West. The Comice pear with its soft, juicy flesh and prime flavor is especially adapted to the cool summer regions of Oregon and the California coast.

Standard   Dwarf

The size of the tree
The standard and dwarf trees are shown here in silhouette, but no other fruit tree except the apple lends itself to small-space training like the pear. You can train it into formal espaliers and cordons, make a hedge with 45-degree-angle planting, even twist its trunk and limbs into fanciful curves and knots. A standard tree can be grown as a skyline specimen 25 feet tall and about as wide. A dwarf can come in closer as a small shade tree, about 15 feet across.

Small-space planting
Use pears as espaliers on fences and walls, prune them into hedges, or plant one tree with several varieties grafted on for a long season of harvest. There are pears for every month from late summer into winter. See the chapter on Space-Saver Training (page 79) for some ideas on landscape use.

Where does the fruit grow?
Pears bear on long-lived spurs, much as apples do. The spurs last many years if you're careful not to damage them during harvest.

Thinning the fruit
You don't need to thin, but if a very heavy crop sets, remove damaged or undersized specimens a few weeks before harvest.

Pollination
In the West, many pears are more or less self-fruitful, although it is always a good idea to graft or plant a second variety for really good fruit set. Bartlett is a poor pollinator for Seckel. A pollinator becomes more and more necessary toward the north, and is always necessary for Winter Nelis, and Winter Bartlett.

Pests and disease
Fire blight and codling moth are the most serious pests, although pear slug can spoil the looks of the foliage. See the pest and disease pages, page 74 and following.

Pear harvesting
Most fruits are best when picked ripe or nearly so. Pears are the exception. A tree-ripe pear breaks down and turns soft and brown at the core. Always harvest pears when they have reached full size but are still green and very firm. Hold them in a cool, dark place if you intend to eat them

'Seckel' is small and no beauty, but you won't find a finer aroma or flavor, for eating or cooking.

within a few weeks. For longer storage, refrigerate the harvested fruit, then remove it from cold storage about a week before you want to use it. Pears ripen faster if they are held with other pears in a poorly ventilated spot. For fast ripening, place several in a plastic bag together.

The variety list

Catalog numbers at the end of each entry includes a small "s" where semi-dwarf trees are sold, and "D" for dwarf trees.

Early midseason

'Clapp's Favorite.' A large yellow fruit with red cheek, resembling Bartlett. The flesh is soft and sweet, good both for eating and canning. The tree is of attractive shape and very productive, but highly susceptible to fire blight. Since it is very hardy, the variety is best in cold, late-spring zones. Available: (1), (2D), (4D), (6D), (14D), (23D), (25sD), (27D), (31D), (32D), (44sD).

'Moonglow.' Origin: Beltsville, MD. The large and attractive fruit is soft and juicy, nearly free of grit. The flavor is mild. Use it for canning or eating fresh. The very upright and vigorous tree is heavily spurred and begins bearing a good crop very young. It is resistant to fire blight, so use it where the disease is a severe problem. Available: (1), (2D), (4), (6), (8D), (10), (11), (14D), (18), (20), (27D), (32D), (34D), (44sD).

Midseason

'Bartlett.' The medium-to-large, thin-skinned yellow fruit is familiar to most people, since this is a major commercial pear. The flesh is very sweet and tender, fine for eating, but a good canner too. The tree form is not especially good, and the variety is subject to fire blight. It takes summer heat, provided there is adequate cold in winter. In cool climates it sets poorly without a pollinator (use any variety but 'Seckel'). This widely available pear is sold by most of our sources.

'Douglas.' A hybrid with sand pear. The smallish fruit is greenish-yellow with some acidity. The flesh is tender and contains grit cells. The tree is markedly resistant to fire blight, and although hardy does not need long winter chilling. Available: (10), (17), (26).

'Magness.' Origin: Beltsville, MD. The medium-sized oval fruit is slightly russeted. The flesh, nearly grit-free, is highly perfumed. The vigorous tree is very spreading for a pear. The variety will not set fruit without a pollinator (any other). It is highly resistant to fire blight. Available: (2D), (4), (13), (14D), (18), (24), (32D), (36).

'Max-Red Bartlett.' Origin: Zillah, WA. A bud mutation of 'Bartlett,' this is a cranberry-red fruit on the tree, changing to bright red when picked. The flesh is finer-grained and sweeter than 'Bartlett.' The tree form resembles 'Bartlett' but shoots and leaves have the reddish tinge of the fruit. Susceptible to blight. Needs pollination in cool climates (not 'Seckel'). Available: (10), (26D), (27D), (35).

Late midseason

'Anjou.' A French pear from the mild area near the Loire. The fruit is large and green with a stocky neck. The flesh is of a rather mild flavor, not especially juicy, but firm. Use it for eating or canning. It stores well. The upright and vigorous tree is susceptible to fire blight. Not a tree for hot-summer areas. Available: (1), (2), (7), (10s), (14D), (19), (25sD), (27D), (33D), (34D), (35s), (38D), (44sD), (45), (46D).

'Bosc.' A French pear. The long, narrow fruit is heavily russeted. The flesh is firm, even crisp, with a heavy perfume that makes some people consider it among the very finest pears. Good fresh or canned. A fine cooking pear as well. The very large tree is highly susceptible to fire blight.

A mixed harvest, including tiny 'Old Home,' a rootstock variety.

'Bartlett.' Green at left. Pick it like this, but eat it when it resembles center fruit. At right it's too ripe.

Don't place the fruit in cold storage. Available: (1), (2), (7), (10), (14D), (19), (23), (25sD), (32), (34), (35), (44sD).

'Seckel.' A small, yellow-brown fruit that is not especially attractive, but has the finest aroma and flavor of any home garden pear. Eat it fresh or use the small fruit whole for spiced preserves. The highly productive tree is very fire blight-resistant, but sets fruit best with a pollinator (not 'Bartlett'). Available: (1), (2D), (6D), (7), (10), (13), (14D), (20D), (23), (24), (25sD), (26D), (27D), (31D), (32D), (34D), (35), (36D), (40D), (44sD).

Late season

'Comice.' A French pear. The large round fruit is green to yellow-green with a tough skin. Of all pears, this is the finest for eating. It is sweet, aromatic, and juicy. Not for canning. The big, vigorous tree is slow to bear and moderately susceptible to fire blight. It sets better with a pollinator. This is the specialty of the Medford region in Oregon, but does well in home gardens along the California coast. Available: (7), (10s), (33D), (34), (35), (38D), (45).

'Kieffer.' A sand pear hybrid. The large yellow fruit is often gritty and poor for fresh use, but excellent for cooking and canning, and it keeps well in storage. The tree is especially recommended because of its high resistance to fire blight amounting to near immunity. It needs little winter chill but stands heat and cold well so its range is wide. Available: (2), (4), (10s), (11), (14D), (18), (20), (25sD), (26), (34), (36), (39), (40D), (45).

'Winter Nelis.' The fruit is small and rounded, green to yellow-green and russeted, rather unattractive, but of good flavor and it keeps well. The fairly vigorous tree is not very susceptible to fire blight. It is a good variety for hot-summer areas if there is enough winter cold. You must plant a pollinator. Available: (10s), (38), (45), (46D).

Peaches

Some of the greatest peach-growing country in the world is in the West: California alone produces 50 percent of the commercial peaches in the United States. The San Joaquin Valley in California and areas of eastern Washington have the climate to produce great peaches: 200 to 1000 hours of cold winter weather (around 45 degrees or below in December and January), warm and dry spring weather, and hot summers. Gardeners outside this prime area can grow satisfactory fruit by selecting the right variety for their own gardens.

The size of the tree

The silhouettes here can tell you a lot about what to expect when you bring home a young tree from the nursery.

Standard Dwarf Genetic dwarf

The standard tree on a peach rootstock grows to about 18 feet tall and 15 feet wide and then stays there because you prune it heavily each year to maintain that size and encourage lots of new growth along the branches. A semidwarf tree on Nanking cherry or St. Julien plum rootstock stays at seven to nine feet tall, and also needs the proper maintenance pruning to maintain size while encouraging new growth. The true, or genetic, dwarf peaches grow in bush shape to about four to six feet tall and require no pruning to maintain size or force growth. At most, you'll clip out tangles and remove broken twigs. See page 12 for more on genetic dwarfs.

Small-space plantings

You won't have any trouble fitting a peach to whatever space is available to you. Among commercial growers of standard trees, the trend these days is toward the hedgerow, a narrow wall of trees formed by training the young trees to a V-shaped scaffold, then pruning to hold all growth within the hedge shape. This means trimming a bit in summer as well as pruning in winter, but it's not hard. Just clip any runaways that shoot beyond the general hedge outline to about 8 to 10 leaves long. See page 82 for a trellis version of the same V-shape.

Semidwarf peaches are ideal for hedgerows and trellises and they lend themselves well to another simple technique that is the home gardener's specialty. Dig an extra big planting hole and set two to four varieties together with their roots almost touching. You'll get the effect of a single small tree with several kinds of fruit. Of course you can practice multiple planting with standards too.

The genetic dwarfs are great for patio container plantings. Put them in tubs on wheels and roll the dessert right up to the table after the barbecue.

Where does the fruit grow?

The sketch on page 35 shows you the most important thing about a peach tree: It illustrates where on the branch you'll find flowers and fruit. Notice that fruit is formed only on branch segments that grew the previous summer. New wood grows on beyond the fruit and will produce next year's crop. Once fruit is harvested, the section of branch

Many fruiting peaches have large, showy flowers.

on which it grew will never fruit again. That's why you need to encourage new growth for replacement branches.

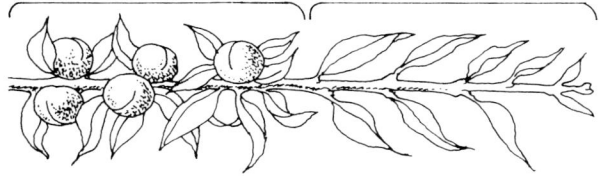

Last year's growth now bearing fruit | This year's growth now forming next year's buds

Pruning a peach
How do you encourage new growth on your standard or semidwarf trees? Pruning does it. You thin, head back, and remove weak branches. The tree responds with lush growth. See page 94 for details and a sketch of cuts to make.

Thinning the fruit
Once a crop sets on a peach tree, you may not even see the branch through the fruit. You can't leave it all for three reasons: It will be too small; it slows branch growth and cuts next year's crop; and it may snap branches. Thin it out when it reaches thumbnail size. For an early peach, leave six to eight inches of space between each fruit; for a late peach, thin after June fruit fall and leave four to five inches between each fruit. If a frost knocked off a lot of your crop, leave all the rest, even if they're clustered. The important thing is the ratio of leaf surface to number of peaches, so a sparse crop will do fine in singles or bunches.

Special advice
There's a pruning trick that bears repetition here, although you'll run into it again under Pruning. Peaches are twiggy trees, but the greatest number of flower buds form on sturdy new branches that made more than 10 inches of growth the previous summer. Keep these and thin the more anemic twigs. You can head the strong ones back by a third to a half if you want to keep the tree small. They'll bloom on the remaining half.

Pollination
Only a few peach varieties need a pollinator ('J. H. Hale' is one of the best known). Normally the trees are self-fertile, although bees are a big help in pollen transfer.

Winter chill
All peaches like a winter rest. Without it, they bloom late, open their leaves erratically, and finally die. Check the chart for varieties that suit your climate. Southern California peaches are listed as such.

Pests and disease
The universal peach ailment is leaf curl, but you control it with ease with a copper spray. See pages 74 to 77 for control methods. You will also probably meet the peach tree borer, gnawing the trunk at ground level. Brown rot attacks fruit but is controllable. For bacterial spot on leaves, check the list for resistant varieties.

The variety list
Here are some of the best peaches for the West.

The "s" and "D" after catalog numbers mean semidwarf and dwarf.

Very early
'Cardinal.' Origin: Georgia USDA field station. Ripens in Western Washington. Medium-sized cling with bright red skin over a yellow ground. The flesh is yellow, firm, and melting. Very slight fuzziness. The tree is moderately vigorous. Available: (15), (38), (45).

'Desert Gold.' Origin: Fresno, CA. For Southern California. The medium-sized, round fruit has yellow skin with a red blush. The flesh is yellow, firm, semicling. The tree is fairly vigorous and productive. Available: (34D), (38D), (45).

'Earlired.' Origin: Maryland USDA Exp. Sta. A medium-sized cling with yellow skin blushed red. The flesh is yellow, firm, and melting. Thin 'Earlired' heavily at thumbnail size. Moderately susceptible to bacterial leaf spot. Available: (7), (10), (35).

'Springcrest.' Origin: Fort Valley, GA. The small to medium-sized fruit has a bright red blush over a yellow ground. Fine, short fuzz. The yellow flesh is firm but melting. Semifreestone when ripe. The tree is of moderate vigor and productivity. Susceptible to bacterial spot. Showy flowers. Available: (38), (45).

'Springtime.' Origin: Ontario, CA. For Southern California. The small to medium-sized fruit has yellow skin with a high blush and abundant short fuzz. The flesh is white and semifreestone. Available: (10), (45), (46).

'Sunhaven.' Origin: Michigan. For Western Washington. A medium-sized to large freestone with bright red skin on a golden ground and short, soft fuzz. The yellow flesh is flecked with red. It is firm, fine-textured, and nonbrowning. The tree is vigorous and productive. Available (7).

'Tejon.' Origin: Riverside, CA. For Southern California. The medium-sized fruit is yellow with a red blush over half its surface; light fuzz. The yellow flesh is semicling. The tree bears very well. Available: (10), (45).

Early
'Blazing Gold.' Origin: Merced, CA. The skin is blushed, and the yellow, freestone flesh has reddish streaks near the pit. Flavor is slightly acid. The vigorous and productive tree bears regularly. Somewhat showy flowers. Available: (10), (38), (45).

'Fairhaven.' Origin: South Haven, MI. For Western Washington. The large fruit is bright yellow with an attractive red cheek and light fuzz. The freestone flesh is yellow with red at the pit, firm and melting. Good freezer. Showy flowers. Available: (7), (35).

'Gold Dust.' Origin: Merced, CA. For Southern California. The yellow fruit is mottled and streaked red. The freestone flesh is yellow. The large and vigorous tree is upright, hardy, and productive. Available: (10), (38), (45).

'Golden Jubilee.' Origin: New Jersey. This old standby is a medium-to-large freestone. The skin is bright red and mottled. The yellow flesh is coarse-textured and firm. The tree sets heavily but is often self-thinning. Wait for fruit drop to thin. Very hardy. Available: (7), (10), (19D), (33D), (35).

'Herb Hale.' Origin: Yakima, WA. For Western Washington. The very large fruit is bright red over half of surface. The skin is thick and tough with medium fuzz. The orange-yellow freestone flesh is juicy, firm, and melting with fine texture. The tree is vigorous with showy flowers. Available: (7).

'Nectar.' Origin: Bakersfield, CA. The large fruit is blushed pink to red. The freestone flesh is white tinged

'Early Elberta' resembles namesake, ripens a week sooner. 'Springtime' an early white peach for mild climates.

with red, juicy, and aromatic. Susceptible to brown rot. The tree is vigorous and heavy-foliaged. Available: (10), (38), (45).

'Ranger.' Origin: Maryland. Ripens in Western Washington. The medium-to-large freestone is greenish-yellow to yellow-gold, mottled with red. The yellow flesh is flecked with red, firm and medium- to fine-textured. The tree is resistant to bacterial spot. Good for canning and freezing. Available: (10), (45).

'Redhaven.' Origin: Michigan A.E.S. Medium-sized freestone. Widely recommended and widely available. One of the finest early peaches. Skin deep red over yellow ground. Flesh yellow, firm, melting, nonbrowning. Fruit sets heavily, thin, is good for freezing. Tree is spreading, vigorous, highly productive. Resistance to bacteriosis. NOTE: 'Early Redhaven' is nearly identical, but two weeks earlier. Available: (7).

'Redtop.' Origin: Fresno, CA. Will grow in Southern California. The large fruit is nearly covered with an attractive blush and light fuzz. The yellow, freestone flesh is unusually firm, good canned or frozen. The tree is moderately vigorous and somewhat susceptible to bacterial spot. Showy flowers. Available: (7), (38).

'Reliance.' Origin: New Hampshire. Winter hardy to —25 degrees. For coldest mountain, intermountain gardens. The large fruit is dark red over a yellow ground. The freestone flesh is bright yellow and firm, but slightly stringy. Showy flowers. Available: (17D), (20D), (22), (23), (26), (27), (28), (32), (33D), (34D), (44sD).

'Robin.' Origin: Ontario, CA. For Southern California. The medium-to-small fruit is yellow with a high blush and thin, tender skin, very fuzzy. The freestone flesh is pale yellow with few fibers and strong aroma. The tree bears well, has showy flowers. Available: (10), (38), (45).

'Veteran.' Origin: Ontario, Canada. Favorite in Western Washington, Oregon. The medium-to-large fruit is yellow splashed with red with medium fuzz. The nearly freestone flesh is yellow, melting, and soft. The tree is vigorous and highly productive. One of the very best in cool Pacific climates. Available: (7), (10), (28).

Midseason

'Babcock.' Origin: Berkeley, CA. For Southern California. NOTE: The name 'Babcock' is often applied to a range of early white peaches, especially in the market. The small-to-medium fruit is light pink, blushed red with little fuzz. Skin peels easily. The nearly pure white flesh is red near the pit, tender, juicy, and of mild flavor. The medium-to-large tree is spreading and vigorous. Available: (10s), (15), (38D), (45), (46D).

'Bonita.' Origin: Riverside, CA. For Southern California. The medium-to-large fruit is light yellow with a deep, attractive blush. The yellow flesh is dark pink at the pit, freestone, with some fiber. The tree produces well. Available: (10s), (45).

'Early Elberta' ('Gleason Strain'). For Western Washington. Origin: Kaysville, UT. The fruit resembles 'Elberta,' but the yellow, freestone flesh is of better flavor. Excellent for canning and freezing. It ripens 10 days before 'Elberta.' Available: (6D), (7D), (10s), (19D), (33D), (35D), (45).

'Elberta.' The standard commercial freestone in much of the country. The large fruit is deep gold, blushed red. The firm yellow flesh is excellent for canning, freezing. Fruit tends to drop when ripe. There is a touch of bitterness near the pit. Resists brown rot. Available: wide distribution.

'Fay Elberta' ('Gold Medal'). Old variety that resembles 'Elberta' but is more colorful. It ripens at about the same time. Be sure to thin well. Showy flowers. Available: (7), (10), (38), (45).

'Halberta' ('Halberta Giant,' 'Hale Berta'). Origin: Xenia, IL. The very large fruit is mottled and blushed red over a yellow ground, with little fuzz. The golden yellow freestone flesh is red at the pit, firm and melting. The vigorous tree is a light producer. NOTE: Pollinate with an 'Elberta' type. Available: (10).

'Halehaven.' Origin: Michigan. The medium-to-large fruit is dark red over most of the surface. The yellow freestone flesh is red at the pit, firm, and melting. The tree is vigorous and productive. Susceptible to brown rot. Available: wide distribution.

'Indian Free.' The large, round fruit is yellow. The yellow-to-red flesh is deep red at the pit, freestone, very acid until fully ripe. Good freezer. NOTE: Pollinate with any peach except 'J. H. Hale.' Available: (10), (45).

'J. H. Hale.' The very large golden yellow fruit is overlaid with brilliant red. Little fuzz. The yellow freestone flesh is not stringy. Once a top commercial peach, although tree is not vigorous. NOTE: Pollinate with any midseason peach except 'Halberta.' Available: wide distribution.

'July Elberta' ('Kim Elberta'). Origin: Sebastopol, CA. For Willamette Valley. The medium-sized fruit is greenish-yellow blushed and streaked with dull red. Very fuzzy. The yellow flesh is of high quality. The vigorous tree is highly fruitful but susceptible to bacteriosis. Available: (34), (38), (45).

'Redglobe.' Origin: Maryland. For Western Washington. A very adaptable variety with medium-to-large yellow fruit blushed bright red. The freestone flesh is yellow, firm, and of fine texture, good for canning and freezing. The tree is dependably productive, with large, showy, deep pink bloom. Available: wide distribution.

'Redskin.' Origin: Maryland. The medium-to-large fruit maintains its size even with a heavy crop. It is deep red over yellow with light fuzz. The nonbrowning flesh is freestone, yellow. The spreading, vigorous tree is very productive. Large, showy flowers. Resistant to bacteriosis. Available: (7), (10).

'Redwing.' Origin: Ontario, CA. For Southern California. The fairly large fruit is unsymmetrical with thick, tough yellow skin and moderate fuzz. The yellow-white flesh is fairly firm with few fibers. A freestone. The medium-to-large tree is vigorous and productive. Needs coolest S. Cal. climate. Available: (10).

'Rio Oso Gem.' Origin: California. A peach that excites adoration among its admirers. The larger fruit is very red. The firm yellow freestone flesh is melting and fine-textured. Disappearing as a commercial peach, but pickers were said to prefer it to any other. Very showy flowers. The tree is susceptible to bacterial spot. Available: wide distribution.

'Suncrest.' Origin: Fresno, CA. The large, round fruit is yellow, two-thirds covered with bright red. Light fuzz. The yellow flesh is firm but melting, freestone. The vigorous tree is productive, has showy flowers. Susceptible to bacterial spot. Available: (7), (45).

'Ventura.' Origin: Riverside, CA. For Southern California. The small fruit is yellow with a wine-red blush. The yellow flesh is firm, freestone, of fair quality. The vigorous tree is upright. Very low chilling requirement, for warmest areas. Available: (10s), (38D), (45), (46D).

'Ventura' is a fine low-chill peach for warm winters.
Genetic dwarf 'Bonanza' bears full-sized fruit.

'Veteran' is dependable where summers are cool, damp.

Nectarines

The nectarine is simply a fuzzless peach. Peach trees sometimes produce nectarines as sports, and nectarines will produce fuzzy peach sports. Therefore, the two plants are nearly identical, but the nectarines are generally more susceptible to brown rot. In climates where spring and summer are warm and moist, both blossoms and fruit must be sprayed to control it. Otherwise, nectarines require the same care as peaches.

Early season

'Independence.' Origin: Fresno, CA. The medium-sized oval fruit has brilliant cherry-red skin. The freestone flesh is yellow and firm. The tree is productive and moderately vigorous with showy flowers. Will take warm winters. Available: (10), (18), (38), (44sD), (45).

'John Rivers.' Origin: England. The earliest nectarine variety, with greenish-white flesh that is nearly freestone, and both tender and juicy. The tree must have chill during the winter or it is subject to delayed foliation. The blossoms are showy. Available: (10), (38), (45).

'Silver Lode.' Origin: Ontario, CA. The skin of the fruit is red. The freestone flesh is white and sweet, of good texture. The tree requires little chilling and produces in southern zone 4. Available: (10), (46).

Midseason

'Fantasia.' Origin: Fresno, CA. The fairly large fruit has bright yellow skin covered up to two thirds with a red blush. The freestone flesh is yellow, firm, and smooth. The tree is vigorous and productive with showy flowers. Requires little winter cold. Available: (2), (7), (10), (15), (38), (44sD), (45).

'Flavortop.' Origin: Fresno, CA. The large oval fruit is mostly red. The freestone yellow flesh is firm and smooth. The tree is vigorous and productive with showy flowers. Needs moderate winter cold. (2), (7), (44sD), (45).

'Garden State.' Origin: New Bruswick, NJ. The large fruit has a rounded oval shape. The skin is greenish yellow, almost completely covered with red. The firm and juicy yellow flesh is freestone. The vigorous tree is spreading with large showy flowers. Available: (2D) (7D), (8), (35D).

'Gold Mine.' An old variety. The large white fruit is blushed red. The juicy white freestone flesh has an excellent flavor. It ripens late in July or early in August and requires little winter chill. Available: (10), (38), (42), (45).

'Le Grand.' Origin: Le Grand, CA. The large fruit has yellow skin with a light red blush. The clingstone flesh is firm and yellow. The large spreading tree is productive, with large showy flowers. Available: (10s), (35), (38D), (45).

'Panamint.' Origin: Ontario, CA. The fruit has a high red skin. The freestone flesh is yellow. The vigorous and productive tree needs little winter chilling. Available: (10), (38), (46).

'Pioneer.' Origin: Ontario, CA. The fruit has a thin red skin. The freestone yellow flesh is of a rich and distinctive flavor with red near the pit. The tree requires little chill and has large, showy bloom. Available: (10s).

'Sun Grand.' Origin: Merced, CA. The large fruit has greenish-yellow skin with a red blush. The freestone flesh is yellow, of a firm, melting texture. The large spreading tree is productive with large flowers. Available: (10), (38), (45).

Late season

'Freedom.' Origin: Le Grand, CA. The very large fruit has a highly blushed skin. The golden yellow freestone flesh is firm and juicy, good for canning or dessert. The medium-sized tree is spreading and productive and the flowers are large and pink. Available: (45).

'Stanwick.' Origin: an old variety. The large pale green fruit has red cheeks. The white, freestone flesh is juicy and of fine flavor. Use it for drying, canning, or freezing. Fruit tends to drop before it is fully ripe. The tree has large flowers. Available: (10), (38), (45).

Genetic dwarf peaches and nectarines

The genetic dwarf peaches and nectarines form dense bushes with the long leaves trailing in tiers from the branches. In spring, the branches are entirely hidden in bloom, usually semidouble and very showy. Even in winter the bare plants are interesting. Fruit of all these plants is of normal size, sometimes large.

In containers, the plants can be kept to about three feet tall, but in the ground they will eventually reach six to eight feet and spread widely. They can be used as ornamentals and require little care beyond spraying for the usual maladies of peaches.

Most require little winter chilling for good bloom, and none are blossom-hardy in really cold places, but they can be grown in containers and protected until the warm season. If you try this method in the coldest northern regions, you may have to pollinate the flowers yourself with an eraser, touching it first to pollen, then to stigma of a different flower.

These dwarf plants were created by breeding numerous varieties together, but they all probably share the common heritage of the Swatow peach or the Flory peach, naturally dwarf Chinese varieties.

Peaches

'Bonanza.' Origin: California. This is one of the oldest, widely known dwarfs. The medium-sized fruit has a moderately red skin. The freestone flesh is yellow and ripens early. The tree needs moderate winter chill. The flowers are pink and semidouble. Available: (14), (23), (46).

'Compact Redhaven.' Origin: Orondo, WA. Not the same background as other dwarfs. This peach is a chance sport that is like 'Redhaven' in everything but size. It grows with leaf nodes close together to about 10 feet tall. Will take more cold than other dwarfs, and grows where 'Redhaven' grows. Available: (22), (34).

'Empress.' Origin: Le Grand, CA. The medium-sized fruit is bright red over yellow. The freestone flesh is yellow, firm, and very well flavored. The tree is productive with large leaves and flowers. Ripens late midseason. Available: (10).

'Garden Sun.' Origin: California. A medium-sized, yellow-fleshed freestone that ripens early. Available: (38).

'Golden Gem.' Origin: California. The fruit resembles 'Rio Oso Gem,' and has yellow, freestone flesh that is firm and of good flavor. The plant is low and spreading with pink bloom. Available: (32), (45).

'Golden Glory.' Origin: Le Grand, CA. The rather large fruit is yellow, mottled orange-red with moderate fuzz. The freestone flesh is yellow, red near the pit, and soft. It ripens late. The flowers bloom late, have red anthers. Available: (6), (10).

'Southern Flame.' Origin: California. A large yellow fruit overspread with red. The freestone flesh is firm and melting. Low chill, ripens midseason. Available: (10).

'Southern Rose.' Origin: California. The large yellow fruit has a red blush. The yellow, freestone flesh is firm and good fresh. Very low chill, ripens late. Available: (10).

Nectarines

'Garden Delight.' Origin: California. The medium-sized yellow freestone ripens midseason, later than 'Garden King.' Available: (38).

'Garden King.' Origin: California. The medium-sized, yellow-fleshed clingstone ripens in midseason. Available: (38).

'Golden Prolific.' Origin: Le Grand, CA. The large fruit has yellow skin, mottled orange. The freestone yellow flesh is red near the pit and soft, of fair to good quality. Needs considerable winter chill. Showy flowers. Available: (6), (10).

'Nectarina.' Origin: California. The medium-sized fruit is yellow, blushed red. The yellow, freestone flesh is red at the pit, of good quality. Ripens mid- to late July, needs little chilling. Available: (46).

'Southern Belle.' Origin: California. The very large fruit is freestone, with yellow flesh. It is very prolific, very low chill, ripens late. Available: (10).

'Sunbonnet.' Origin: California. The large red fruit has firm yellow flesh. It is clingstone. Low-to-moderate chilling requirement, very productive, ripens in midseason. Available: (10).

Harvesting and storing tree fruits

Each tree fruit demands different treatment when you harvest and store it. Stems should break free easily.

Apples. When apples reach full size, check color. Reds should be bright, but ground color (background) still greenish. Greens and yellows should be green. Taste a fruit. It should be juicy with some tartness remaining. Bend upward to snap fruit loose. Store with good ventilation to retard further ripening, or place in cold storage for long keeping.

Pears. Tree-ripened pears will break down at the core. Harvest when full-sized but still green and crisp. Taste for sugar. Hold in a cool place with good ventilation or place any pear but 'Bosc' in cold storage.

Peaches. Peaches should be tree-ripe for fresh use. Taste one to see if flesh is soft, juice runs freely. For jam or canning, a firm ripe fruit is best, but it should be nearing full ripeness.

European plums. For fresh use or cooking, these plums should be fully colored and just beginning to soften. If you want to dry them, wait until they are dead-ripe and about to drop. In dry climates, spread a sheet and let them fall for drying.

Japanese plums. Be careful, they color early. A ripe fruit is soft, sweet, and very juicy. Taste before harvest.

Apricots. Pick dead-ripe fruit for fresh use, or pick them firm but sweet for jam or canning. For drying, they should be very ripe but not mushy-soft. Cut in two and sulfur the fruit to retard spoilage.

Cherries. Only fully ripe cherries are good, but don't let them go too far. They should be firm but very juicy. Even sour cherries for canning must be tree-ripened for best flavor. Don't break the spurs. Hold cherries in cold storage even if you mean to use them soon or they may soften and shrink.

Figs. An underripe fig oozes white latex from the stem when you pick it. For drying, let figs get limp on the tree. In dry summer climates you can spread a sheet to catch windfalls.

Nectarines are smooth skinned sports of regular peaches.

Nectarines also grow as genetic dwarf trees.

Plums

Of all the stone fruits, plums are the most varied. Some variety will suit any climate or soil. The variety list will help you to choose, but in general the European-type fruit suits cooler climates, while the larger Japanese plums are for mild climates. For very rigorous climates there are a number of American native plums available. Trees bear for 15 years and more.

The size of the tree

European and Japanese plums grow to perhaps 20 feet tall and spread wider than the height. As the silhouettes show, dwarf trees are about half as big.

Standard Dwarf

Where is the fruit?

European plums bear on long-lived spurs. Japanese plums bear on spurs and also on new wood of the previous season.

Pollination of plums

Check the variety list for pollinators. Some plums, such as 'Green Gage' and 'Italian Prune' are self-fruitful, or partly so, but many need a second variety nearby.

Pruning and thinning for good crops

European and native plums need little pruning or thinning beyond clearing out tangles. They should be trained to a vase shape (see page 91). Japanese plums send out long whips that must be cut back (see page 94), and they overbear, so you must thin to one fruit every four to six inches when fruit is thumbnail sized.

Space-saver planting

Plums lend themselves best to a three-in-one-hole planting, rather than formal training. Choose a mix of varieties that pollinate one another.

Pests and disease

Brown rot is a major concern. See details on page 76.

The variety list

Check especially for pollination requirements. The "s" and "D" after catalog numbers mean semi-dwarf or dwarf trees are sold.

European plums

The fruit tends to be small, and most varieties are egg-shaped. The flesh is rather dry and very sweet. Prunes are the sweetest, easiest to dry. The plants are fairly hardy but do well where winter is mild.

Midseason

'Green Gage' ('Reine Claude'). (Best: any region.) Old European variety. The greenish-yellow fruit has amber flesh and is good fresh, cooked, or preserved. Trees are medium-sized. Pollinator: self. Ripens: mid-July, later North. Available: wide distribution.

'Sugar.' (Best: California.) A very sweet, dark blue fruit, fairly large and excellent for home drying and canning. The trees bear in alternate years with light crops in off year. Pollinator: self. Ripens: after July 15. Available (10), (45), (46).

'Damson.' (Best: any region.) An old plum from Europe that is included in a different species than other European plums. The smallish blue fruits are best for jam, jelly, and

'Italian Prune' (Fellenberg), a typical European plum; note the egg shape.

preserves. There are several improved varieties, such as 'Blue Damson,' 'French Damson' (large), and 'Shropshire Damson.' The trees are small. Pollinator: self. Ripens: end of August or September. Available: wide distribution.

'**Yellow Egg.**' (Best: West, South.) The golden yellow fruit has a thick skin and yellow flesh. The round-topped, vigorous tree is hardy and productive. In the West, the fruit is planted in Washington. Pollinator: self. Riptns: late August. Available: (2), (35).

Late

'**French Prune.**' (Best: California.) The small fruit is red to purplish-black, very sweet with a mild flavor. This is the main prune variety in California. The tree is large and long-lived, often remaining when orchards become housing tracts. Pollinator: self. Ripens: late August to September. Available: widely in California.

'**Italian Prune**' (Fellenberg). (Best: Pacific Northwest, North.) The dark blue fruit is very sweet, good for dessert, canning, or drying. In eastern areas, 'Stanley' is taking over from 'Fellenberg' but it is still the major plum of the Washington-Oregon areas. Pollinator: self. Ripens: late August, September. Available: wide distribution where adapted.

Japanese (Oriental) plums

The fruit is relatively large, soft, and juicy. The plants are the least hardy of the various kinds of plum, although selected varieties are grown in the milder northern regions.

Early

'**Beauty.**' (Best: California.) Origin: California (Luther Burbank). The medium-to-large fruit is bright red, and the amber flesh is tinged red. Use it fresh or cooked. The tree is strong and vigorous. Pollinator: self or 'Santa Rosa.' Ripens: early June in California. Available: (4D), (6D), (25sD), (36D), (44sD).

'**Bruce.**' (Best: South, Southwest.) Origin: Donley County, TX. The large fruits have red skin and red flesh. The flavor is good. The fruit matures early. The trte bears young and heavily. Pollinator: 'Santa Rosa.' Ripens: June. Available: (10), (14), (45).

'**Santa Rosa.**' (Best: any region.) Origin: Santa Rosa, CA (Luther Burbank). Widely popular large plum with a deep crimson skin and flesh that is purplish near skin and yellow, streaked pink near pit. For dessert or canning. Pollinator: self or any early or midseason plum. Ripens: California: mid-June; North: late. Available: wide distribution.

Early midseason

'**Satsuma.**' (Best: California.) Origin: California (Luther Burbank). A blood plum with red juice. The meaty fruit is small to medium with a dull, dark red skin, red flesh, and small pit. Flavor is mild and good. Use for dessert or preserves. Pollinator: 'Santa Rosa,' 'Wickson.' Ripens: after 'Santa Rosa.' Available: wide distribution.

'**Wickson.**' (Best: California.) The large and showy yellow fruit turns reddish when ripe. The flesh is firm and of good flavor. Keeps well, good in cooking. Pollinator: 'Beauty,' 'Santa Rosa.' Ripens: late July. Available: (10), (15), (45).

Midseason

'**Burbank.**' (Best: any region.) Origin: Santa Rosa, CA (Luther Burbank). The large red fruit has amber flesh of excellent flavor. The trees are fairly small and somewhat

Blue is European plum color.

drooping. Use the fruit for canning or dessert. Pollinator: 'Early Golden,' 'Santa Rosa.' Ripens: early August in Northwest; mid-July in California. Available: wide distribution.

'**Duarte.**' (Best: California.) The medium-to-large, dull red fruit has silvery markings. The flesh is deep red. Fruit keeps well, is tart when cooked. Pollinator: 'Santa Rosa,' 'Satsuma.' Ripens: late July. Available: (7), (10), (35D).

'**Eldorado.**' (Best: California.) Origin: California (Luther Burbank). The medium-large fruit has very dark skin and firm, rather dry, amber flesh. It holds its shape well for canning or slicing into pie. Pollinator: 'Santa Rosa,' 'Wickson.' Ripens: late July. Available: (15), (38D).

'**Formosa.**' (Best: California, North.) Fruit is early in California. The large fruit is greenish-yellow overlaid with red. The flesh is cream-colored, firm and juicy with somewhat clinging pit. The tree tends to bear in alternate years. Pollinator: 'Santa Rosa,' 'Wickson.' Ripens: June in California; early August in New York, Michigan. Available: (1), (28).

'**Frontier.**' (Best: California, North.) Origin: Fresno, CA. The fruit is a large, blue-black freestone with red flesh. The tree is vigorous. Pollinator: 'Burbank,' 'Santa Rosa.' Ripens: about July in California; mid-August in Michigan. Available: (39), (45).

'**Howard Miracle.**' (Best: California.) Origin: Montebello, CA. The fruit is yellow with a heavy red blush when ripe. The flesh is yellow with a distinctive, very good flavor, recalling pineapple. Rather acid plum. The tree is very vigorous. Pollinator: self. Ripens: after July 15. Available: (10), (45), (46D).

'**Laroda.**' (Best: California.) Origin: Winters, CA. The large, round fruit is deep reddish-purple with light amber flesh, reddish near the skin. The tree is vigorous with numerous spurs. Pollinator: 'Santa Rosa.' Ripens: after July 15. Available: (15), (19), (32), (35), (38D), (45).

'**Mariposa.**' (Best: California.) Origin: Pasadena, CA. (Also called 'Improved Satsuma.') The large round fruit has maroon skin and flesh. The tree is medium to large and needs little winter chill. A good Southern California choice. Pollinator: 'Santa Rosa,' 'Late Santa Rosa.' Ripens: mid-July. Available: (10), (38D), (45).

'**Nubiana.**' (Best: California.) Origin: Winters, CA. The large flattened fruit is a deep reddish-blue with light amber flesh. The vigorous tree is very productive. The fruit turns red when cooked. Pollinator: self. Ripens: late July. Available: (10), (32), (35).

Late

'**Elephant Heart.**' (Best: California, North.) Origin: Sebastopol, CA (Luther Burbank). The large, thick-skinned fruit is mottled purple and green. The flesh is blood red. Trees are strong and hardy. Fruit ripens over a long period. Pollinator: 'Santa Rosa.' Ripens: late July, August. Available: (10), (15), (32), (34), (45).

Apricots

Apricots bloom early, and like the mild spring of California's coastal valleys. But there is a variety for all but the harshest and mildest of western climates.

The size of the tree
Under ideal growing conditions, even dwarfed apricots on special rootstocks are fair-sized trees. But any apricot can be controlled to a large extent by heavy pruning and still bear a heavy crop. Standard trees spread wide if left to themselves, and you can train them to a high-branching shape that lends itself to lawn planting as a shade tree. In lawns they need an occasional extra-deep watering. A genetic dwarf is available for container culture.

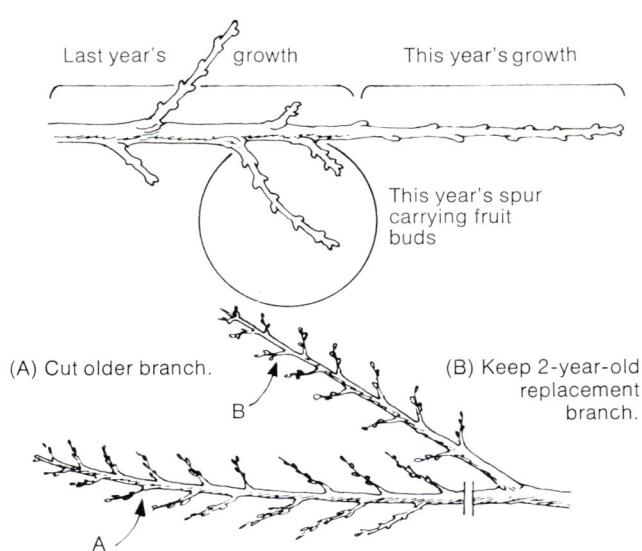

Where is the fruit?
Apricots, like plums, bear mainly on spurs that form on two-year-old branches. See the sketch above right. The spurs last about three seasons and should then be replaced with new growth. Fruit may form in the first year after planting, but real crops come after three to four years. The trees bear well for 20 to 30 years if well cared for.

Pollination of apricots
Many are self-fruitful, but see the variety list. The 'Riland' and 'Perfection' types need pollination.

Pruning and thinning for good crops
See pruning details on page 94. Mainly, you head back new wood and cut away the oldest spurred branches. You need not thin, but it is best to remove the smallest young fruits, leaving at least two inches between the remaining ones.

Space-saver planting
Use two or three trees in one hole for pollination or choice of fruit. Apricots are poor subjects for confined spaces. However, apricots will take plum scions as grafts, so try several kinds of fruit on the same tree.

Pests and disease
Brown rot and bacterial gumming are serious problems. See page 74 to 77.

The variety list
Check especially for climate adaptation in harsh or mild climates, and for pollination wherever you live.
The "D" after variety numbers mean dwarf trees are available.

Apricots grow in landscape settings, but require deep watering to thoroughly soak roots.

'Earligold.' Origin: Ontario, CA. This is a medium-sized fruit with rich golden skin and juicy flesh. The tree is a heavy producer. The variety requires little winter chill and ripens beginning in mid-May. For Southern California. Available: (45).

'Chinese' ('Chinese Golden,' 'Mormon'). Large, smooth-skinned fruit is orange-yellow with a red blush. The flesh is sweet and juicy. The tree and blossoms are about as hardy as the peach, and the variety bears well in late frost areas. Available: (6D), (10s), (40D).

'Moongold.' Origin: Excelsior, MN. A hybrid with 'Manchu' as one parent. The same cross produced 'Sungold' (below) and the two must be planted together for pollination. The fruit is orange with tough skin. The flesh is orange-yellow and of very good quality. The tree is a spreading, medium-sized plant. Fruit ripens in Minnesota in late July before Sungold. Available: (12), (14D), (17), (20), (26), (27), (31), (33).

'Moorpark.' Origin: Hertford, England (1760). The variety is considered by many to be the standard of excellence among apricots. The large fruit is orange with a deep blush, sometimes overlaid with dots of brown and red. The flesh is orange, of excellent flavor and with a pronounced and agreeable perfume. Ripening is uneven, with half the fruit still green when the first half ripens. This is unimportant in the home garden since the gardener can wait until the second half ripens to eat the fruit fresh. For canning, half the fruit is either too firm or too soft. The tree does well in all but the most extreme climates. Available: Wide distribution.

'Newcastle.' For Southern California. The fruit resembles 'Earligold' with medium-sized golden fruit. The tree requires little chilling and bears in June. Available: (10).

'Perfection' ('Goldbeck'). Origin: Waterville, WA. The fruit is very large, oval and blocky, light orange-yellow without blush. The flesh is bright orange and of fair quality. The tree is vigorous and hardy, but blooms early and so is uncertain in late-frost areas. Since it requires little winter chill it will grow in mild-winter areas. The variety needs a pollinizer. In Southwest, use another early variety. Available: (7), (10), (19D), (33D), (35D).

'Reeves.' Origin: Burbank, CA. A medium-sized, yellow-orange fruit of good flavor that ripens in early June. Low winter-chill requirement, but it must have a pollinizer. Available: (10).

'Riland.' Origin: Rock Island, WA. The fruit is large and rather flat. The light yellow skin is covered over half the fruit by a deep blush. The flavor is rich and plumlike, but texture somewhat coarse. The tree is vigorous and upright. Requires a pollinizer. Available: (7), (35).

'Royal.' (This is identical to 'Blenheim'). The fruit is yellow to yellow-orange with thick, aromatic flesh of a sprightly flavor. It should be thinned to reach its largest size. This is the preferred commercial fruit in California, excellent for canning and drying. The tree is large and somewhat spreading. Available: (10s), (15), (32), (46D).

'Scout.' Origin: Morden, Manitoba. A seedling from seed sent from a Manchurian fruit experiment station. The flat, bronzy fruit is medium to large with deep yellow flesh. It is good fresh and can be canned or used in jams. The tree is tall and upright, both vigorous and hardy. Fruit ripens from late July. Available: (17).

'Stella.' A hardy Russian apricot. The fruit is golden yellow and of good quality. The tree succeeds where a peach will grow. Available: (2), (14D).

'Sungold.' Origin: Excelsior, MN. A selection from the same cross as 'Moongold' and must be planted with 'Moongold' for pollination. The fruit is rounded and of medium size with a tender, golden skin blushed orange. Flavor is mild and sweet, and the fruit is good fresh or preserved. The tree is upright and vigorous, of medium size. The fruit ripens somewhat later than 'Moongold.' Available: (12), (17), (20), (26), (27D), (31).

'Tilton.' Similar to 'Royal' but somewhat inferior. The medium-to-large fruit is a little less susceptible to brown rot than 'Royal.' Should be thinned for best size. Sometimes bears alternately. Available: (7), (10s), (15), (19D), (33D), (34), (35D), (38D), (45), (46D).

'Wenatchee.' The fruit is large in the form of a flattened oval with orange-yellow skin and flesh. The tree does well in the Pacific Northwest. Available: (7), (19), (33D), (35D).

Pick heavy crops firm and ripe and try drying them for winter.

Cherries

Cherries come in four distinct forms, with many varieties in each. The sweet cherry sold in markets is planted commercially in the coastal valleys of California and widely in the Northwest, especially Oregon. In the home garden it is tricky, but try it wherever summer heat and winter cold are not too intense. The sour cherry such as 'Montmorency' is more widely adapted, and is good in cooking and canning. The Duke cherries (hybrids) share sweet and sour characteristics. In areas with extremely cold winters, try the Hansen bush cherry, a group of selections from the Nanking cherry, *Prunus tomentosa*. All cherries are long-lived and productive where adapted.

The size of the tree
Recently a number of genetic dwarf cherries have been propogated, such as 'Garden Bing,' 'Compact Stella,' and others. These will do well where sweet cherries grow. Among sour cherries try the dwarfs, 'Meteor' and 'Northstar.'

The semidwarf sweet cherries and all sour cherries are of peach or apricot dimensions; then come the enormous standard sweet cherries than can rival oaks.

Where is the fruit?
All cherries bear on spurs, and those on tree types can produce for more than 10 years. The spurs begin to form on two-year-old wood. Count on your first crops in the second or third year on dwarfed trees and sour cherry trees, a year or two later on sweet cherries.

'Montmorency' is common pie cherry with scarlet skin.

Pollination of cherries
All sweet cherries need a pollinizer, with the exception of the new variety 'Stella,' but not any pair will work. If you plant 'Napoleon' ('Royal Ann'), 'Bing,' and, 'Lambert,' none

Standard   Sour   Semi-dwarf   Bush   Genetic Dwarf

will be pollinated. Add 'Corum,' 'Van,' or 'Black Tartarian' and you get the right mix. Sour cherries will often pollinate sweets and are self-fertile, although in some regions the bloom periods don't overlap well, and sour cherries are not usually recommended pollinizers for sweet, although they work in California gardens.

Use grafts as pollinators for sweet cherries, since the trees are so large. You can also plant two in one hole. The genetic dwarf cherries are self-fertile.

Pruning and thinning
Cherries of any kind need no thinning and little pruning. Train young trees to wide crotches (see page 92) and give sweet cherries space to spread. Sour cherries are especially subject to weak crotches that snap, so use spreaders in training the young trees.

Small-space planting
A cherry espalier is possible, since the spurs are productive for so long, but crops are small. Use grafting and multiple planting to increase choice of fruit and for pollination. Use the dwarf trees for screen plantings or in containers.

Pests and disease
Birds are the main nemesis of cherries and only netting over the tree is really effective, but sometimes birds are discouraged if you throw strands of cotton string over the tree in many directions. It tangles in their wings. Bacterial gumming is bad on some sweet cherries in humid areas. 'Bing,' for example, is not recommended for the Northwest. Other pests, such as cherry slug and cherry fruit fly, need control. See pages 74 to 77 for details.

The variety list
Check sweet cherries for the right pairs of pollinizers, and all cherries for climate adaptation.

Early
'Black Tartarian.' This medium-sized black cherry is fairly firm when picked, but softens quickly. The trees are widely planted since this is one of the earliest cherries and an excellent pollinator for many others. Trees are erect and vigorous. Pollinator: any sweet cherry. Available: wide distribution.

'Sam.' Origin: Summerland, B.C. A medium-to-large, black-fruited cherry that is firm and juicy, of good quality. The fruit resists cracking. The tree is very vigorous, and bears heavy crops. Pollinator: 'Bing,' 'Lambert,' 'Van.' Available: (1), (7), (35), (44sD).

Midseason
'Bing.' The standard for black sweet cherries. The fruit is very deep mahogany-red, firm and fleshy, and very juicy. The tree is spreading and produces heavy crops. 'Bing' is subject to cracking and doubling of fruit, and the tree

suffers from bacterial attack in humid climates. Not easy to grow but a favorite of many. Pollinator: 'Black Republican,' 'Sam,' 'Van,' 'Black Tartarian.' (NOT 'Royal Ann' or 'Lambert.') Available: wide distribution.

'Chinook.' Origin: Prosser, WA. A 'Bing'-type fruit, it is large and heart-shaped with mahogany skin and deep red flesh. The tree is spreading and vigorous with good production, and slightly more hardy than 'Bing.' Pollinator: 'Bing,' 'Sam,' 'Van.' Available: (7), (33), (35).

'Corum.' Origin: Eugene, OR. The variety is the recommended pollinator for 'Royal Ann' in the Pacific Northwest. It is a yellow cherry with a blush. The flesh is thick and sweet, quite firm. It is moderately resistant to cracking and is a good canning cherry. The tree is fairly vigorous. Pollinator: 'Royal Ann,' 'Sam,' 'Van.' Available: locally in Pacific Northwest.

'Garden Bing.' A 'Bing'-like dark red fruit on a genetic dwarf plant that remains only a few feet high in a container, but grows to perhaps 8 feet in the ground. It is self-fruitful. Available: (38).

'Rainier.' Origin: Prosser, WA. In shape, the fruit resembles 'Bing,' but this is a blushed yellow cherry, very attractive with firm, juicy flesh. The tree is vigorous and productive, spreading to upright-spreading. Particularly hardy. Pollinator: 'Bing,' 'Sam,' 'Van.' Available: (7s), (9sD), (19), (28), (35).

'Royal Ann' ('Napoleon'). Very old French variety. This is the standard for yellow, blushed cherries. It is the major brining cherry, appearing in commerce as candy and maraschino cherries. The firm, juicy fruit is excellent fresh and good for canning. The tree is very large and extremely productive, upright, but spreading widely with age. It is relatively tender, although the buds tolerate some cold. Pollinator: 'Corum,' 'Van' (NOT 'Bing' or 'Lambert.') Available: wide distribution.

'Stella.' Origin: Summerland, B.C. The first true sweet cherry that is self-fertile and needs no pollinator. The fruit is large, of 'Lambert' type, dark in color and moderately firm. The tree is vigorous and fairly hardy and bears early. Pollinator: none needed, but 'Stella' can be used on any other sweet cherry. Available: (7), (9sD), (28).

'Van.' Origin: Summerland, B.C. A large, dark fruit with some resistance to cracking, on a tree that is very hardy. 'Van' is especially good in borderline areas since it has a strong tendency to overset and therefore may produce a crop when other cherries fail. It bears from one to three years earlier than 'Bing.' Pollinator: 'Bing,' 'Lambert,' 'Napoleon,' any other. Available: wide distribution.

Late

'Black Republican' ('Black Oregon'). The fruit is firm and very dark with some astringency. The tree is quite hardy, but tends to overbear heavily, producing small fruit. In borderline areas it may produce where others fail. Pollinator: any sweet cherry. Available: (7s), (9s), (10), (35).

'Lambert.' The fruit is large and dark, ripening later than 'Bing' but similar to it. The tree is more widely adapted than 'Bing' but it bears erratically in many eastern areas and is more difficult to train and prune. The strongly upright growth produces weak crotches if left untrained. Pollinator: 'Van,' 'Rainier.' (NOT 'Bing' or 'Royal Ann.') Available: wide distribution.

Sour cherries (pie cherries)

The following varieties are all self-fruitful. They will pollinate sweet cherries in mild climate areas. There are two types: the amarelle with clear juice and yellow flesh, and the morello with red juice and flesh. In the coldest northern climates the amarelle is the commercial cherry.

'Early Richmond.' An amarelle that is especially hardy. The fruit is small, round, and red, excellent for pie, jam, and preserves. It is astringent when eaten fresh. The tree is small, reaching 15 to 20 feet. Available: (2), (4), (14), (18), (20), (25), (26), (34), (36), (40).

'Meteor.' An amarelle. Origin: Excelsior, MN. A genetic dwarf that reaches only about ten feet tall. The fruit is bright red and large for a pie cherry, with clear yellow flesh. The tree is especially hardy, but does well in milder climates too. An ideal home garden tree for all cherry climates. Available: wide distribution.

'Montmorency.' An amarelle. The standard sour cherry for commercial and home planting. The fruit is large and brilliant red with firm yellow flesh. It is strongly crack resistant. The tree is medium to large, vigorous and spreading. Various strains have slightly different ripening times and fruit characteristics. Available: wide distribution.

'Northstar.' A morello. Origin: Excelsior, MN. Developed with 'Meteor,' this is a genetic dwarf, excellent for the home garden. The fruit is red with red flesh and is resistant to cracking. The small, attractive tree is vigorous and hardy. It is resistant to brown rot. Fruit ripens early but will hang on the tree for up to two weeks. Available: wide distribution.

Duke cherries

The Dukes are hybrids between sweet and pie cherries. They have tart, acid fruit like the pie cherries, but are large, fairly upright trees like the sweet cherries.

'May Duke.' A medium-sized, dark red fruit of excellent flavor for cooking or preserves. In cold climates, use an early sweet cherry for pollination. In mild climates it is self-fruitful. Available: (35).

'Late Duke.' A large, light red fruit that ripens in late July. Use it for cooking or preserves. In cold climates it requires a sour cherry pollinator. In mild climates it is self-fruitful. Available: (35).

French 'Royal Ann' or 'Napoleon,' popular yellow cherry.

Figs

Although the fig is generally thought of as a subtropical plant suited mainly to the mild winters and heat of California and the desert regions, there are varieties that will bear even in the milder climates of the Northwest. If a freeze knocks down the plant, it sprouts again quickly.

Figs are a satisfactory fruit for gardeners who don't want to fuss with spraying and pruning, but like to see a big crop on their tree. In warm regions the fig bears big juicy fruit in early summer, then sets a heavier crop of small fruit, perfect for drying, in fall. It lives for many years, loves heavy soil, tolerates drought, and needs next to no attention. You have a choice in warm regions of red-fleshed dark fruit, or bright pink-fleshed greenish yellow fruit.

The size of the tree

In the Northwest, figs grow as many-stemmed shrubs, reaching perhaps 10 feet in a series of warm years. In warm climates, the trees grow on one or several trunks and reach 20 to 25 feet, spreading wide. You can easily cut them back or confine them if you wish.

Where is the fruit?

Figs are not quite fruits. They are a collection of inside-out flowers with all the important parts accessible to the outside world through a hole at the base. The first crop "blooms" on new wood of the previous season, and the second crop appears on new wood of the current season. When a tree is cut back to confine it, you usually lose most of the first crop. You also lose it in cold regions where winter does your pruning.

Pollination of figs

Since figs are not strictly fruit at all, most need no pollination, which is lucky, because the pollinizing process is very complicated. The commercial 'Calimyrna' fig does require pollinizing from a separate male tree called a caprifig. Fruits of the male contain larvae of a tiny wasp. They are picked and hung in a female tree and the winged wasps emerge and enter the female fruit. There is also a spray that sets seedless fruit, but the flavor is changed when spray is used.

Pruning and thinning

No thinning is needed. Prune the young tree to an open shape in the first two years, then remove suckers at the base when you think about it. Pull—don't cut—them off.

Space-saver planting

You can prune a fig to a five-foot spreading shrub if you like, or flatten it on a wall as discussed on page 83.

Pests and disease

Figs are rarely subject to any serious pest or disease damage. You may find some chewed leaves in spring.

The variety list

Favorites are 'Mission' and 'Brown Turkey,' but you may want a variety that appears less frequently in the market.

'Adriatic.' The fruit is green-skinned with a strawberry-colored pulp. In hot areas, the second crop has a paler pulp, and in cool-summer areas the fruit of both crops is larger. This is principally a drying fig. The tree is vigorous and large. Recommended for California. Available: (45).

'Brown Turkey' ('Turkey,' 'Southeastern Brown Turkey,' 'San Piero,' 'Black Spanish'). A large-fruited variety for fresh use. The first crop is large and dark brown, the second crop smaller. The pulp is light strawberry. The tree is small and can be pruned heavily to cut the crop. Recommended for Southeast and Southwest. Available: (2), (10), (15), (18), (36), (38), (39), (45), (46).

'Celeste' ('Blue Celeste,' 'Celestial,' 'Sugar,' 'Malta'). Bronzy fruit with a violet tinge. The pulp is amber with rose tones. 'Celeste' is the most widely recommended fig in the Southeast, but also grown in the West. An especially hardy plant. Available: (2), (10), (36), (39).

'Conadria.' Origin: Riverside, CA. One parent 'Adriatic.' The fruit is thin-skinned and white with a violet blush, white to red flesh that resists spoilage. The tree is vigorous and precocious, producing two crops. Recommended for hot valleys of California. Available: (10), (45).

'Kadota' ('Florentine'). Fruit is tough-skinned and greenish-yellow, and the first crop has a richer flavor. This is principally a canning and drying variety. The tree is strong growing. Recommended for hot California valleys. Available: (10), (15), (38), (45), (46).

'King' ('Desert King'). The fruit is green with flecks of white, the pulp is violet-pink. The tree comes back from the roots after a freeze and bears in fall. Recommended for Oregon fig climates. Available: (15).

'Latterula' (White Italian honey fig). A large greenish-yellow fig with honey-colored pulp on a very hardy tree. It bears two crops. Recommended for Oregon fig climates. Available: Local nurseries or cuttings

'Mission' ('Black Mission'). Two heavy crops of black fruit with deep red pulp. First crop has larger fruit. The tree is large and vigorous. Second crop can be dried. Recommended for California and desert regions, also grown in warmer Southeastern zones. Available: (10), (15), (38), (45), (46).

Check local availability of 'Granata,' 'Negronne,' and 'Neveralla' in Oregon; and 'Genoa' ('White Genoa') on the California Coast.

The elegant form of the fig tree has stood the test of time in this landscape plan.

First crop 'Mission' fig ripens as second crop appears.

Persimmons

The large Oriental persimmon could be far more popular than it is if more gardeners realized the great value of both tree and fruit.

The tree grows well in any well-drained soil, and makes a fine medium-sized shade tree with large leaves that turn a rich gold in fall. A heavy crop of orange fruit holds on until winter, decorating the bare branches.

Two kinds of fruit exist. The large, pointed kind sold in markets must be fully ripe and very soft before you eat it or it is astringent. It is excellent in cooking, adding its spicy flavor to fruit breads, cakes, puddings, and pies, and if you peel it and dry it when firm-ripe, the flavor is extraordinary. A smaller, flattened fruit is eaten firm.

The size of the tree
Persimmons are often allowed to grow naturally, forming globe-shaped trees to 25 feet high. They grow slowly and can be pruned back in spring to keep them smaller.

Space-saver planting
Since the persimmon is slow it takes well to espalier training. Train it informally against a flat surface, or use a trellis to form a persimmon hedge.

Where does the fruit grow?
Fruit forms on growth of the current year, and on naturally shaped trees it tends to set on the outer portions of branches. An espaliered plant will set fruit throughout.

Pruning a persimmon
Little pruning is necessary. Train the young tree to three widely spaced scaffolds and let it alone thereafter, or control its size by cutting each year to strong lateral branches, removing as much growth as needed to maintain the size you want. In pruning an espalier, cut off enough of the previous year's growth to expose the interesting lines of the plant.

Thinning the fruit
Thinning is completely unnecessary. If a ripening crop seems to threaten a branch or two, remove firm, ripe fruit, picking it with a bit of stem. Then peel it, leaving the green calyx that covers the top, and string it up in branches by the stem to dry in the sun. Use dried fruit like prunes or apricots.

Pollination
The Oriental persimmons set fruit without pollination.

Winter chill
Oriental persimmons stand winter temperatures to about zero degrees, but they need only a short period of chill to fruit well.

Pests and disease
In the West, the persimmon has no serious pests. In the East, a flat-headed borer may attack the trunk and can be removed by hand.

The variety list
Numbers refer to the catalog list on page 111.

'Chocolate.' A Mexican variety with dark flesh. The tree is very large. Fruit must be fully ripe for fresh eating. Available: (10), (15).

'Hachiya.' A Japanese variety, planted mainly in California. The large, pointed fruit must be fully ripe and soft for eating. Dry it when firm-ripe. Available: (10), (15), (38), (45), (46).

'Fuyu.' A Japanese variety. The fruit is the shape and size of a medium-sized tomato and of reddish-yellow color.

Brilliant 'Fuyu' crop brightens December branches.

The color of persimmons in autumn.

48 *Home garden specialties*

It can be eaten when still firm. Available: (10), (15), (38), (45), (46).

'Tamopan.' A Japanese variety. The very large fruit is turban-shaped. Mainly planted in California, not widely available. Available: (10).

'Tanenashi.' A Japanese variety. The recommended large-fruited persimmon for the South. Let it ripen completely before eating, or dry it when firm-ripe. The tree is small and somewhat weeping. Available: (6), (39).

Pomegranate

The pomegranate, with its shiny leaves and fleshy orange flowers, is one of the most ornamental fruiting plants. The young leaves have a reddish tint in spring, and in fall turn bright yellow. Against this background, the large red fruits are most attractive.

Pomegranates stand winter temperatures to about 10° but ripen their fruit best in very hot climates. They are ideal plants for the desert Southwest since they also stand considerable drought, but you can harvest edible fruit in much milder climates.

Many people who admire the pomegranate as an ornamental shrub or tree seem to have trouble eating it. The edible portion is the juicy scarlet flesh around the abundant seeds. If you score the skin just down to these seeds in about six places, cutting from stem to flower, you can open the fruit and expose all the seeds at once. They are good in fruit salads and make an excellent syrup when cooked with sugar and a little water. The syrup is sold commercially as grenadine.

The size of the tree

You can grow pomegranates as fountain-shaped shrubs, as multiple-stemmed trees, or train them to a single trunk. They reach about 10 to 12 feet tall under ideal conditions but often remain smaller. A shrub can spread to six or eight feet across. Since they fruit on new growth, you can prune them back heavily without loss of flowers or fruit.

Training a pomegranate

To train a plant to a single trunk or just a few trunks, begin in the first year by selecting the strongest stem or stems and cutting others to the ground. Then remove all suckers, watersprouts, and stem growth as it appears. You will have to do this for several years, until the tree is well established, or it will revert to a shrub.

Where does the fruit grow?

Blossoms form on the current year's growth, and as the fruit grows heavier, it pulls down the slender new branches, making a decorative, weeping effect. Although the plant will stand drought, the fruit will split if a tree is allowed to dry out completely and is then watered. For a good crop, keep the moisture level even.

Pruning a pomegranate

See training, above. You can prune as you like to shape the plants, but no pruning is necessary if you choose to allow it to grow naturally. It still blooms and fruits.

Thinning and pollination

Neither is necessary. An excess crop is very decorative if left on the tree.

Pests and disease

Normally there are none.

Variety

The variety 'Wonderful' is the only fruiting pomegranate you're likely to see in the nursery. Details are described in the text above.

Pomegranate flowers last for weeks.

Fruit grows to three times this size, turns bright red.

Citrus for mild climates

In much of the West there's nothing unusual about an orange tree outside the front door, bearing its juicy load of golden fruit. But even where winter cold makes it impossible to put citrus in the ground, a smart gardener may manage some of the pleasure of the perfumed flowers and bright fruits.

Citrus varieties can be grouped in two ways in relation to climate. First, for the gardener whose winter temperatures drop to 15° or 20° the question becomes: Is the plant hardy enough? Where temperatures are even lower, you can grow many dwarfed varieties in containers and haul them off to shelter for the winter.

Hardy citrus for borderline gardens include the 'Nagami' kumquat and the calamondin. They will take 20° without serious damage. If your temperatures stay above that, or you can offer temporary frost protection on bad nights, you can branch out to the 'Meyer' lemon with rather sweet, perfumed fruit, and the mandarin oranges. In Portland or Seattle, where tub planting is the only way to go, be sure to use a very well-drained container mix as discussed on page 9. The tubs go out in the warm season, then move in to a well-lighted spot under roof in winter. After all, Louis XIV of France kept tubbed oranges at Versailles with great success.

A second climate grouping is determined by whether citrus fruit develops sugar. Inadequate summer heat means sour fruit, so even in areas where the plants grow outdoors, a cool summer may make your mandarins very puckery. That doesn't matter at all for sour fruit such as lemons, Rangpur limes, and so forth, and a sour mandarin is just as pretty on the tree and produces fine juice for drinks. The most climatically limited fruit is the grapefruit. The plant does fine in protected Northern California gardens, but the rind is thick and the fruit sour and dry. If you want to eat grapefruit from the garden, you need desert heat.

Never avoid a plant because of climate. Citrus is a pleasure to look at and to smell, whether your crop is of market quality or not, and there are many surprising successes. We know a gardener who grows a tubbed Mexican lime where snow falls every winter. She rolls it into her bright, south-facing kitchen and admires it more than if it grew outdoors.

Planting citrus

All citrus is touchy about its roots and lower trunk. The plants need a soil with constantly available moisture, but wet soil and poor drainage will be fatal in a short time. Warm-season gardeners should set their young plants high, as discussed on page 108, for burlap-wrapped plants. A thick mulch over the roots holds moisture and keeps temperatures down. If the subsoil is especially dense, you should raise the plants even more with a raised bed. Container plants need the very light mix mentioned above, so that you can water frequently without drowning the plant. Don't forget to feed heavily watered plants at least monthly with a food containing iron and zinc.

Whether in containers or in the ground, never bury the lower trunk of the plant. It should dry out immediately after watering. And if the plant is trimmed so the trunk is exposed to the sun, paint it with white interior latex paint to prevent sunburn.

In watering citrus, it is especially important not to wet the trunk and crown. Plant high and keep your watering basin at least a foot away from the crown.

Characteristic of navel orange—it peels without effort.

The size of the tree
Standard trees can reach 30 feet tall and wide. Dwarfed trees are a lot more manageable. A dwarfed navel orange grows to perhaps 10 feet tall, a mandarin about six feet, and a kumquat to about four feet.

Where is the fruit?
Trees flower and fruit in the leaf nodes along newer growth, so the tree is decorated over the entire surface with bright orange, yellow, or yellow-green fruit. Since fruit will hang for months on many kinds of citrus, the fruit and bloom often occur together.

Pollination
Citrus requires no attention to pollination. All kinds are self-fertile, and some need no pollination at all, forming seedless fruit without it.

Pruning and thinning
Don't worry about thinning fruit unless you think a branch is about to break. Pruning should consist of removing any damaged branches (cut off winterkilled branches only

Orlando tangelo combines mandarin, grapefruit.

50 Tree fruits

Green on 'Valencia' skin does not mean fruit is unripe.

'Tarocco,' a blood orange has flesh ranging from scarlet to orange.

after new growth is sturdy), and clipping off dead twiglets inside the tree. Sometimes an extra vigorous shoot suddenly sprouts beyond all the other branches. Reach in and break it off at the base. This will remove other buds that may do the same.

Dwarf citrus may sprout suckers from the rootstock, often a plant called trifoliate orange. Break these at the base as soon as you see them.

Small-space planting
Although citrus is sometimes flattened into espaliers and hedges, a natural shape takes less fussing, and dwarfs of similar size can be grown as attractive screen plantings. You can also play with grafting citrus. Use the bud grafting method described on page 100, inserting the bud just before rapid growth begins in spring. You can mix several kinds of fruit on a single tree. Combinations are listed on page 99.

Pests and disease
Stringent laws against transporting citrus from one commercial growing area to another help to keep disease at a minimum. The worst thing a gardener has to face is root and crown rot caused by poor planting, poor soil, and standing water. Proper planting in light soil helps you to avoid this.

Using the variety list
Check for hardiness, and prepare to protect tender plants by moving them in winter or covering them. Otherwise, experiment with any plant listed here.

All plants listed are available from the following wholesale sources. They can supply your nurseryman if he does not carry the plant you want.

Four Winds Growers
P.O. Box 616
Mission San Jose, CA 94538

Dwarfed trees a specialty. Instructional booklet available to the home gardener.

Ponto Nursery
656 West Quarry Road
San Marcos, CA 92069
Wholesale only. No direct sales or catalog.

Pear shape identifies 'Minneola' tangelo.

'Dancy' tangerine appears at Christmas time.

Tree fruits 51

'Eureka' lemon likes California's south coast.

'Meyer' lemon tastes sweet and aromatic, tolerates light frost.

The variety list

Navel orange
The navels have relatively thick skin that peels easily, and, except for 'Trovita,' all have a folded protrusion (the 'navel') at the blossom end. They are poor choices for desert regions, but ripen with less heat than the other oranges listed. Standard trees reach 25 feet tall, dwarf trees about eight feet with considerable spread.

'Robertson.' Ripens in November. Very productive tree a little smaller than 'Washington.'

'Summernavel.' Ripens into summer months. More open tree with larger leaves than 'Washington.'

'Trovita.' Smaller, navelless fruit needs the least heat for ripening. Ripens in spring.

'Washington.' The standard navel fruit, available in markets from December to February.

Juice orange
The fruit is thin-skinned and hard to peel, but the flesh is juicier than navels. Needs heat. The standard is 'Valencia' but desert gardeners use 'Dillar' and 'Hamlin.'

'Dillar.' Small-to-medium fruit is very juicy. Ripens in late fall. Tree is vigorous.

'Hamlin.' Similar to 'Dillar' but less hardy.

'Valencia.' Standard commercial fruit ripens in summer, needs heat. Very full and vigorous tree. There is a seedless form.

Other orange varieties
'Shamoudi.' An import from Israel that somewhat resembles navel fruit, but grows on very decorative trees, spreading very wide.

'Tarocco.' A blood orange. The flesh ranges from scarlet to orange with scarlet spots. Develops sugar without too much heat and is redder in the cooler growing areas. Very open tree.

Tangelo
This is a mandarin-grapefruit cross with loose skin and

'Kinnow' mandarin bears large fruit.

'Clementine' tangerine needs less heat than 'Dancy.'

'Mexican' lime or 'Key' lime needs mildest climate.

'Bearss' lime, a Persian type, is hardier than 'Key.'

the sugar of a mandarin but not the same aroma or flavor. Tangelos require cross-pollination from other citrus.

'Minneola.' Cross of 'Dancy' tangerine and 'Duncan' grapefruit. A large fruit with prominent neck, tender flesh with much juice. Ripens in late winter.

'Orlando.' Same cross as 'Minneola.' Tender and juicy, ripening early.

'Sampson.' Not a commercial variety. More like a grapefruit than other tangelos. Best in cooler areas.

Mandarins

The mandarin is the small, loose-skinned fruit sometimes called tangerine or satsuma. The plants are very hardy, but the fruit needs high heat or it is sour.

'Clementine.' Needs pollinator. Fruit is fairly large with few seeds, ripens in late fall then hangs on for months. Needs less heat than other types.

'Dancy.' The standard commercial fruit. Rather seedy but good for desert regions. Ripens in winter.

'Kara.' Large fruit is slightly tart, ripens in winter in desert, spring elsewhere. Tree is spreading and drooping.

'Kinnow.' Medium-sized fruit with rich flavor, ripens from winter into spring. Tree is columnar. Good in any mild climate.

'Owari.' (Owari Satsuma). Extremely hardy plant. The fruit is loose-skinned with delicate flavor. Ripens from October until winter. Small trees are spreading. Not for desert.

Tangor

Hybrids of tangerine (mandarin) and orange that need very high heat to ripen fruit properly.

'Dweet.' The large, juicy fruit ripens in spring. It is as large as an orange and seedy. Will not take desert conditions, but needs high heat.

'King.' A complex hybrid with large, bumpy fruit. Plants sunburn in desert. Ripens in spring.

'Temple.' The best known commercial fruit. Good in the low desert. The orange-sized fruit ripens in spring and is deep orange in color. Spreading, thorny tree.

Another mandarin variety, 'Honey.'

'Encore' mandarin, a newer variety not yet widely available.

'Eustis' is a kumquat and lime hybrid for warm regions.

Another limequat, 'Lakeland.'

Lemon
Lemons can't stand excessive heat, but they are very tender. Grow them in southern coastal areas or mildest northern areas with frost protection.

'Eureka.' The commercial fruit. It ripens the whole year. The new growth is an interesting purplish color. Somewhat thorny.

'Lisbon.' Takes more heat and cold than 'Eureka,' and is good in desert. Most fruit in fall, but some all year. Thorny.

'Ponderosa.' A conversation piece with enormous fruit. The tree is small and bears very young. Fruit ripens in winter.

Lime
The lime that appears in markets and is used in mixed drinks is the 'Mexican.' It is extremely tender. All limes need the mildest winters and high heat.

'Bearss.' The hardiest. It grows where oranges are good. The fruit is lemon-sized, yellow when ripe, ripens mainly in winter. Tree is thorny. Derived from South Pacific variety.

'Mexican.' The small, round, green fruit of markets. It will not take cold. The small tree is upright.

Grapefruit
Grapefruit is best in the desert, although it ripens fairly well in any high-heat region. In cool areas it is thick-skinned and pithy, but decorative.

'Marsh.' A seedless white-fleshed variety that takes 18 months to ripen, finishing in winter and spring in the desert. Beautiful large plant is ornamental even if fruit is of poor quality.

'Ruby.' A pink-fleshed fruit. Needs desert heat to color well.

Limequat
A hybrid between the kumquat and the 'Mexican' lime, with edible peel and a limelike flavor. It is quite tender, although less so than the true lime.

'Eustis.' Fruit is rather more elongated than lime, and small. The tree is open and shrubby, good in a container.

The calamondin grows well in containers, stands cold.

A dwarf grapefruit bears well even outside best climate.

Pomelo 'Kao' stands more cold than grapefruit cousin.

To eat a pomelo, peel the tough skin around segments.

Other popular home-garden fruit

The following are special-use fruits, either hybrids, plants related to citrus, or mainly decorative.

Calamondin. Good as a container dwarf. It covers itself with tiny mandarinlike fruits that have very sour juice and a sweet rind. The plant is among the most hardy with a decorative columnar shape. You can use it for juice or marmalade, and it is excellent for areas that normally cannot grow citrus since you can protect it indoors during the worst cold, but won't lose it to early, mild frost.

'Etrog.' A citron, used for candied peel. The plant has attractive leaves, and the fruit is somewhat lemonlike.

Kumquat. Not a citrus, but a member of the related genus *Fortunella*. It has tiny round-to-oval fruits with sour flesh and sweet rind. The foliage is attractive and the tree is small even on standard roots. Use it for preserves or eat it fresh, skin and all.

'Meyer lemon.' A roundish yellow fruit with a rather sweet, aromatic peel and flesh. It is not quite a lemon. It tends to bloom and fruit constantly and is much hardier than lemon, good for coastal gardeners. The plant is small even on standard roots. Most plants carry the quick-decline (tristeza) virus and are not permitted in Arizona, but virus-free stock is becoming available.

'Otaheite orange.' Not an orange, but a tiny genetic dwarf plant that produces decorative but insipid fruit that is deep orange and small. A good pot plant.

Pomelo. A grapefruit relative that has large fruits, much bigger than any other. You eat it by peeling both the rind and the skin of each segment. May be hard to find in nurseries. Common variety is 'Kao.'

'Rangpur lime.' Really a very sour mandarin on an attractive plant that is easy to espalier. Use it for juice, but don't expect any lime flavor. It bears heavy crops and is very hardy, good in coastal areas.

Sour orange. Used as a rootstock for many other citrus fruits. It lends itself to pruning as a hedge or screen, or you can grow it as a 30-foot tree. The small fruits are bitter, but many people like them in marmalade or in mixed drinks for a touch of bitter flavor.

'Marsh' seedless grapefruit needs high heat to ripen.

Pink-fleshed 'Ruby' resembles 'Marsh.'

Tree fruits 55

Subtropical fruits

The fruiting plants listed below are all considered subtropical. None of them will tolerate much frost. However, six of those listed will stand up to cold weather well enough to be planted throughout much of California. The four others will only grow in the mildest regions of the south coast. We do not include a few plants that are regularly or occasionally offered by nurseries, since the fruit crop is usually poor. Among these are bananas, papaya, litchi, and mango. These are chancy, but fun if you have room.

Hardy
These plants can take light frost for short periods, and will grow around San Francisco Bay.

Avocado
The two avocado varieties 'Bacon' and 'Zutano' will fruit in cool regions, especially if they have protection from wind and a good exposure. 'Bacon' is preferred. In milder regions, from Monterey Bay to the mildest San Diego region, you can plant the black-fruited 'Hass,' the green 'Fuerte' and other tender varieties.

Carissa (natal plum)
The beautiful but thorny plants range from tall shrubs to ground-cover dwarfs. They produce single, white, very fragrant flowers and plum-colored, cranberry-flavored fruit. They are widely available as ornamentals and survive around San Francisco Bay.

Feijoa (pineapple guava)
Tall shrubs or small trees, these hardy plants have silver-backed leaves and striking flowers with sweet and edible petals. The fruit needs heat to be good. It is small, oval, and yellow, good fresh or in jam. A good variety is 'Coolidge.'

Jujube
An attractive and fairly hardy tree, the jujube produces a round or pear-shaped fruit that is good fresh or will dry on the tree. Dried, it resembles a date, hence the common name Chinese date. There are two varieties: 'Lang' is pear-shaped; 'Li' is round.

Kiwi (*Actinidia chinensis*)
In the supermarket the furry egg-sized fruit looks like it might mew and lick your fingers. Inside is emerald-green flesh with an odd but delicious flavor. This "stuffed-animal" fruit comes off a sturdy vine that grows even in snowy climates, but is most tender when the young growth sprouts in spring. That's the time for night protection. You must have both a male and female kiwi for fruit, and you prune and train them like spur grapes. Try 'Hayward,' 'Monty,' or 'Bruno.'

Loquat
Usually an ornamental tree, but named varieties produce delicious fruit if there's enough heat. The big leaves are striking and the tree is hardy and drought-tolerant. Try 'Champagne,' 'Gold Nugget.' Fire blight can kill it quick.

Tender
Don't try the following anywhere north of Santa Barbara and hope to keep them long. They're for the south coast.

Cherimoya
The fruit looks like pine cone *manquée* with its large bumpy scales. Inside is spicy white custard. You have to pollinate by hand if you want a good crop. (Cold-climate gardeners can try the related fruit called pawpaw, from eastern North America.) If you can find a named variety, buy it. Most are seedlings. Tree grows to 15 feet.

Guava
There are two real guavas (genus *Psidium*). The strawberry guava is the more common in nurseries. It will grow

Passion fruit juice adds to drinks, sherbets.

Feijoa tastes good fresh or in jams and fruit salad.

to 10 or 15 feet; has red or yellow fruit with red more common. The yellow or lemon guava is larger with white, pink, or yellow-fleshed fruit to three inches long.

Passion vine
Only the *Passiflora edulis* gives you fruit, and then only where it gets heat. The vine survives well north of its fruiting region. Passion fruit is delicious, especially when crushed for juice.

White sapote *(Casimiroa)*
A big, big tree to 50 feet, and hardy enough to live where tender avocados do. Leaves are divided into fans of three to seven leaflets. The three- to four-inch fruits are odd but pleasant, of a papaya consistency.

In Hawaii
Jaboticaba *(Myrciaria cauliflora)*
Attractive in form and foliage amenable to pruning and clipping as a hedge, this large shrub or small tree deserves a place in the home landscape regardless of the added interest of its spectacular fruiting habit. The grapelike fruits are borne singly or in twos or threes on the trunk and larger branches.

The fruit has a thin tough skin. The flesh is white, juicy, gelatinlike with a few small seeds. It has a pleasant, sprightly grape flavor when ripe and freezes well. It is used for making a superior jelly, for juice, and for wine making.

Jak-fruit *(Artocarpus heterophyllous)*
Giant-sized fruit on a modest sized tree. Fruit ranges from 12 to 20 inches long, 6 to 8 inches thick, weighing 20 to 30 pounds. Handsome, dark green, glossy foliage. The whitish pulp of the fruit is edible but nothing to get excited about. The fruit pays its way with its numerous nutlike seeds which when roasted are a much relished delicacy throughout the tropics.

Lychee *(Litchi chinensis)*
A handsome evergreen that will grow to 40 feet in height to form a symmetrical, dense, rounded canopy. Fruits are borne in clusters of 3 to 20 at the ends of twigs. When ripe they look like clusters of strawberries. Beneath the rough brittle shell you find the whitish flesh with the texture of firm gelatin. It is sweet and mildly acid. The pulp encloses one shiny, dark brown seed. After ripening the fruit can be stored in polyethylene bags in the refrigerator for 2 or 3 weeks. Fruits can be frozen, dried, or canned in syrup.

Mango *(Mangifera indica)*
Following years of testing, the University of Hawaii has introduced 3 superior varieties of Mango: 'Pope' in 1960, 'Momi K' in 1964, 'Gouveia' in 1968. The 'Gouveia' is an attractive, medium-sized tree worthy of a place in the home garden. Its fruits are classed as "highly flavored" rather than "mild." In comparative tests, 'Gouveia' outscored the standard varieties 'Haden' and 'Pirie' in flavor, texture, size and shape, and proportion of seed to flesh.

Papaya *(Carica papaya)*
Technically it's a giant herb growing as a small tree to about 20 feet. Most types do not branch but form huge leaves with hollow stems at the top of the hollow trunk. A well-grown tree will begin to bear fruit a year after planting. Improved variety selections 'Solo,' 'Sunrise' and 'X-77' are generally available. 'X-77' has the most attractive form.

Surinam cherry *(Eugenia uniflora)*
This evergreen shrub has enjoyed popularity as a handsome and useful landscape plant. With the introduction of varieties with improved fruit qualities, its value as a fruiting plant has been recognized. The fruit is used in making jams and jellies, syrup, compote, wine, and sherbets.

Tender strawberry guava makes fine jellies.

Very tender soursop needs near-tropical climate.

The small fruits

A little sunlight and a pot is all you need to grow luscious breakfast strawberries, and many of the other small fruits offer rich rewards for a small investment of time and space.

The small-fruited plants return bumper crops with only a minimum of effort on your part, and several of the shrubby or vining plants also add beauty to the ornamental landscape.

In considering small fruits, space and the number of plants needed for a reasonable supply of fruit are factors to be worked out. If the plants are right for your climate and are given excellent care, the number of plants for a family of five would go something like this:

- Strawberries: 25 (20 to 30 quarts)
- Raspberries: 24 (20 to 30 quarts)
- Blackberries: 12 (9 to 15 quarts)
- Blueberries: 6 (9 to 15 quarts)
- Currants: 2 (6 to 12 quarts)
- Gooseberries: 2 (6 to 12 quarts)

Strawberries are without question the easiest to work into any space you may have available. Even on a south-facing apartment terrace you can produce a crop in containers such as strawberry jars or a moss-lined wire strawberry tree. An ideal plant for containers where you can find it is the European wild strawberry or *fraise des bois*. This plant won't make runners. It grows in a clump, so a container planting stays put instead of trying to invade the living room. You'll have to do some detective work to find a source for the plants.

The cane berries, raspberries and blackberries, take more space, although you can grow a few in large containers. Train them carefully along a fence or trellis and keep them pruned, and they won't take very much space, but they *will* produce heavy crops of fruit that you just can't buy, since the finest flavor disappears when farmers and greengrocers transport and hold the berries.

Blueberries, currants, and gooseberries make extremely ornamental shrubs, filled with bloom in spring and with decorative fruit in later seasons. Blueberries require light, acid soil and constant moisture, so try them where you would grow azaleas. Currants and gooseberries are an interim host to a serious disease of five-needle pines, so in some areas you're not allowed to plant them. Where they are permitted, nothing takes less care, is more decorative, or gives a more useful crop.

Grapes, of course, are among the best landscaping plants with their lush foliage, fall color, and interesting vines. Use them on arbors, against walls, as fences, or freestanding shrubs. Do choose varieties recommended for your climate, since grapes are touchy about the amount of heat they get.

Strawberries

If you have grown strawberries for any length of time, you know that flavor and yield are not exactly predictable. They vary from year to year depending upon spring growing conditions. Also, if you have gardened in several locations, you learn that what is the best variety in one place may only be fair in another. A good nurseryman is a big help, since he'll keep abreast of developments in plant breeding and offer plants that should succeed. Your County Agricultural Agent can help too, especially if you've had trouble in other seasons.

'Sequoia' may fruit at Christmas on the West Coast.

◁

Top left: 'Olallie' blackberries are a good California crop.
Top right: Strawberries grow anywhere if you pick the right kind.
Bottom: 'Olallie' berries in a neat wooden frame.

Planting and care

Strawberries can be grown in either the matted-row or the hill system.

There are two types of matted rows. In one, all runners are allowed to grow; in the other, only the earliest to form remain, spaced about eight inches apart. The latter, spaced-runner system gives you larger berries, easier picking, and larger total yield. See the illustration for the arrangement of runners. The rows should be spaced three to four feet apart when you plant.

In the hill system, plants are 12 inches apart in the row and all runners are picked off. The rows are spaced about 12 to 15 inches apart in groups of three. Each group is separated by an aisle 24 to 30 inches wide so that you can walk among the plants to pick or care for them.

To encourage vigorous growth of regular varieties, remove blossoms that appear the year the plants are set. The year that everbearing kinds are set, remove all blossoms until the middle of July. The later blossoms will produce a late-summer and fall crop.

Plant strawberries in soil with good drainage, and mound the planting site if you're not sure. See the illustration for proper planting depth. The new leaf bud in the center of each plant should sit exactly level with the soil surface.

Gardeners who grow strawberries in containers in a disease-free soil mix don't have to worry about verticillium wilt and red stele (root rot). Both are caused by soilborne fungus. When growing strawberries in containers or in garden soil, ask for plants that are certified as disease-free.

Mulching in winter

Winter protection is needed where alternate freezing and thawing of the soil may cause the plants to heave and break the roots. Low temperatures also injure the crowns of the plants. Straw is one of the best mulch materials.

Place straw three or four inches deep over the plants before the soil is frozen hard. Remove most of the mulch in spring when the center of a few plants shows a yellow-green color. You can leave an inch of loose straw, even add some fresh straw between rows.

Western planting techniques

Take a look at the maps on pages 18 and 19 to see which climate zone you live in.

In the coldest areas of zone 1 (California) and zones 1 and 1a (Great Basin to Colorado) plant as early in spring as possible since there is good moisture in the soil to start the plants. If soils are usually too mucky, protect a mounded bed with plastic to keep it friable.

In the Northwest, especially the coolest areas of western Washington, plant early in fall so plants can become established before real cold sets in, or wait until early spring. Watch for washouts from heavy fall rain. Weed carefully in spring, so weeds don't compete.

In California, plant in fall in cold-winter zones 2, 3, and 7, but get the plants in early in zone 7. In mild-winter zones 4 and 5, use chilled plants (stored at 34 degrees for a short period) and set them out in October and November. The low desert is a chancy area for strawberries, but October planting may give results.

Anywhere in California, the berries will do better with a plastic mulch, which increases winter soil temperature and holds water well.

The variety list
Rockies and Great Basin

'Cyclone.' Early. Iowa. Large berries of very good flavor and good for freezing. Plant is winter-hardy and resistant to foliage diseases. Available: (4), (20).

'Olympus' is Pacific Northwest home and commercial crop with very large fruit on vigorous plants.

'Dunlap.' Early to midseason. Illinois introduction, 1890. Medium-sized. Skin is dark crimson and flesh is deep red. Fruit is too soft to ship well but it's a good quality home-garden fruit. Plants are hardy and adapted to a wide range of soil types. Available: (12), (13).

'Gem' ('Superfection' and 'Brilliant' are considered to be nearly identical to 'Gem'). Small, glossy, red, tart fruit of good dessert quality. Available: (2), (6).

'Ogallala.' Berries are dark red, soft, and of medium size. Good flavor and good for freezing. Vigorous grower and hardy. Available: (5), (6).

'Ozark Beauty.' Berries are large, sweet, and of good flavor. Bright red outside and inside. Production on mother plants, but not on runner plants during summer and fall. Available: (2), (6).

'Sparkle.' Midseason. Productive plants. Bright red, attractive berry, fairly soft, good flavor. Berry size is good in early picking, but small later. Available: (2), (5), (6).

'Trumpeter.' Late. Minnesota, 1960. Medium-sized berries, soft and glossy and of very good flavor. Winter-hardy and productive home-garden variety. Available: (17).

Western Washington and Oregon

'Hood.' Midseason. Corvallis, OR. Fruit held high on strong upright clusters. Berry large and conic, bright red

Plastic mulch helps retain water, warm soil.

and glossy. Good fresh or in preserves. Plant is resistant to mildew, but somewhat susceptible to red stele. Available: (3), (14), (37).

'Northwest.' Late midseason. Puyallup, WA. Fruit is large at first, then smaller with crimson skin and red flesh. It is firm and well flavored, good fresh, for preserves, or freezing. Very productive plant is resistant to virus diseases and can be planted where virus has killed other varieties. Available: (3), (14), (37).

'Olympus.' Late midseason. Puyallup, WA, 1965. Fruit is held well up on arching stems. Bright red throughout it is tender and firm, of medium-to-large size. Plants are vigorous but produce few runners. Resistant to red stele, tolerant of virus diseases, somewhat susceptible to *Botrytis* infection. Available: (14), (37).

'Puget Beauty.' Midseason. Puyallup, WA, 1965. The large, glossy, very attractive fruit has light crimson skin. Flesh is highly flavored, excellent for fresh use and good for freezing and preserves. The plants are large and upright with moderate runner production. Resists mildew, somewhat susceptible to red stele. Available: (14).

'Quinault.' An everbearer with moderate early crop, heavier July-September. The fruit is very large and soft with good color. The plant produces good runners. Available: (3), (14).

'Rainier.' Late midseason. The large firm berries are of good quality. The plants are very vigorous with large leaf blades but moderate runner production. Available: (3), (14), (37).

'Shuksan.' Midseason. The very large, firm berries are bright red, glossy, broad wedge-shaped. The plants are vigorous. Good for freezing. Available: (3), (14), (37).

California

'Fresno.' Midseason. California, 1961. The large and uniform fruit is a light red, sometimes wedge-shaped. Very good fresh. The plant is very vigorous, producing many runners. Tolerant of salinity. Good for Southern California. Available: (10), (14).

'Salinas.' Midseason. Davis, CA, 1959. The skin is red with a bright finish. The flesh is light to bright red, firm, with excellent flavor. The medium-sized plant is productive with profuse runners. Resistant to verticillium wilt. Recommended for the central coast. Locally available.

'Sequoia.' Early. It may bear in December. California, 1968. The exceptionally large fruit is dark red, tender, with soft

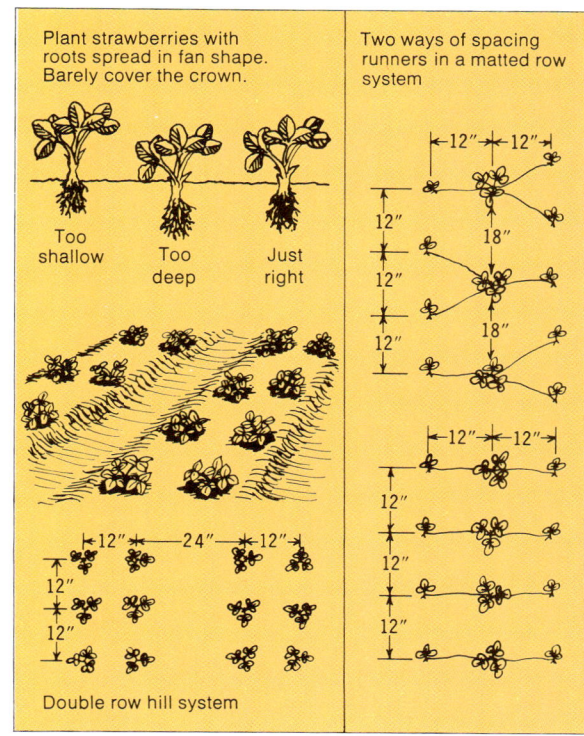

flesh and excellent flavor. Harvest frequently for best quality. The plant is erect and vigorous with low chilling requirement, many runners. Recommended for winter planting along central and south coast. Available: wide distribution.

'Shasta.' Midseason. Davis, CA, 1945. The large fruit keeps its size through the harvest. It is bright red and glossy with red firm flesh, good for freezing or preserves. The fairly vigorous plant produces moderate numbers of runners. Some resistance to mildew and virus diseases. Available: (10), (14), (15).

'Tioga.' Early. Davis, CA, 1963. The fruit is conic to wedge-shaped, medium-red, glossy, with firm flesh that is fine for preserves, freezing. The plant is vigorous, moderately resistant to virus, but highly susceptible to verticillium wilt. Fairly tolerant of salinity. Good for late summer planting. Available: (10), (14), (15).

'Torrey.' Early. California, 1961. The large, uniform fruit is wedge-shaped, with dark red skin and firm flesh. The vigorous plant produces numerous runners. Low chill requirement, good for Southern California. Tolerates salinty and virus. Available: (14).

Permanent bird protection saves your crop the easy way.

Screen plants before the fruit ripens.

Small fruits 61

Raspberries

Raspberries are the hardiest of the cane berries, and a very worthwhile garden crop, since market prices are high, and the fragile fruit suffers in handling and transport. Home-garden fruit can be picked and eaten at its peak.

Unfortunately for California and Arizona gardeners, the plants do not like spring and summer heat, so only the red raspberries will grow, and they are recommended only for coast or mountain regions. The prime berry country in the coastal states is western Washington around Puget Sound (zone 2a) and the Willamette Valley of Oregon. Good berries grow throughout zones 1 and 1a, but may need winter protection in the coldest regions.

What is a raspberry?

A raspberry is a raspberry because the fruit pulls free of its core when you pick it. Other bramble fruits take the core with them when you harvest. The real raspberries come in a variety of colors: red, yellow, purple, and black. Plants of reds and yellows trail and need a trellis. The plants of purples and blacks are stiff and can stand alone.

A warning: Don't try both red and black raspberries in the same garden. Reds sometimes carry a virus that they can tolerate, but that kills blacks. Virus-free stock won't give you this trouble, but you have to be sure.

Planting raspberries

Cut the nursery plants to 6- to 12-inch stubs and plant them about two to four feet apart, and two inches deeper than they grew in the nursery row. Rows should be six or seven feet apart.

Where is the fruit?

On most raspberries the fruit forms on side shoots along canes that grew the previous year. One group of red or yellow raspberries produces some fruit at the top of current season canes in fall, then a second crop on the rest of the cane in the following year.

Pruning raspberries

See page 97 for instructions on pruning. New canes should be laid carefully along the rows until time to prune away old canes, then lifted and trained. Pull out suckers of red raspberries that sprout between the rows.

When you pick a raspberry the core stays on the plant.

Pests and diseases

Raspberries are subject to many troubles, but verticillium in the soil rules them out altogether. Try to obtain virus-free stock where possible.

Propagating raspberries

If you want to enlarge a planting, it's important to know the difference between black and red raspberries. Blacks and purples arch their canes to the ground and root at the tip to form new plants. If you want more, leave a few canes unpruned and in late summer pin the tip to the ground. Throw on a little soil if you like. Then dig and separate the new plant in spring.

Red raspberries send up root suckers. You can dig and replant them just before spring growth begins. Take a piece of root and cut back the top.

The variety list

Single-crop and everbearing raspberries may be red or yellow. They require trellising.

Single-crop

All fruit is borne on laterals that sprout from the year-old canes. Crops come in late spring, early summer.

Blackcaps produce abundantly on erect plants.

Ripe blackcap raspberries ready to pick.

'Canby.' Midseason. The large, firm berries are good for freezing. For light soils in Northwest. Semithornless. Available: (3), (14).

'Cuthbert.' Once the leading commercial fruit, and still unexcelled for dessert, canning, or freezing, but the plants are low-yielding, and difficult to pick. No problem in home gardens. Locally available.

'Fairview.' Large-to-very-large berries are fairly light red. The tall, branched canes are moderately hardy. A good plant for Western Washington. Available: (3), (10), (14).

'Newburgh.' (sometimes spelled 'Newberg.') Berries are large and firm, must be ripe to pick. The bushes spread, branch in the first years. An old variety. Available: (3), (7), (10), (14), (15).

'New Washington.' Excellent coastal variety into California. The late ripening berries are moderately firm, sweet, deep red. Locally available.

'Puyallup.' Late-ripening large berries that are somewhat soft. Recommended for light soils in the Northwest. Available: (14).

'Sumner.' The medium-to-large fruit is firm and sweet with intense flavor. Some strains crumble badly. The plants do well in heavy soil and are recommended for Western Washington or down the coast to California. Available: (14).

'Willamette.' Berries ripen in midseason, are large, round and firm, good for freezing or canning. A widely planted and vigorous commercial variety. Available: (3), (14), (15).

Everbearing

In California the second crop may succumb to heat prostration. In the Northwest, these may produce a little fruit throughout the spring and summer.

'Heritage.' The medium-sized, firm fruit ripens in July and September. The plants are vigorous and stiff-caned, need little support. If you mow all the canes in late winter, you'll get a single August crop and save pruning. Available: wide distribution.

'Indian Summer.' Berries are dark, rather crumbly, and soft. The very aromatic flavor is good. Plants are vigorous and productive, resist mosaic. Available: (3), (4), (6), (10).

'Ranere' ('St. Regis'). Small, bright red berries of only fair quality, but dependable for a second crop except in the warmest areas. Locally available.

Black (blackcap)

Blackcaps need cold, and they do poorly in Western Washington, although they are planted in the Willamette Valley and elsewhere in Oregon.

'Bristol.' A midseason variety that is medium to large and of good flavor. Excellent for canning and freezing. Available: (2), (6), (14).

'Cumberland.' An old timer that produces large, firm berries of good quality. The stiff plants need no support. Available: wide distribution.

'Morrison.' A midseason variety with large berries. The total crop is light, less than on 'Bristol.' Available: (13), (14).

'Munger.' The medium-sized fruit is of good quality. The plants are especially recommended in western Oregon. It's worth a try in Western Washington, but may succumb to disease. Available: (3).

Use a double-wire trellis for the woven method of training.

Make the crossbar sturdy to hold weight.

The lowest wires help protect growing canes.

Use your trellis to protect crop from birds.

Small fruits 63

Blackberries

Blackberries are almost a Western exclusive. Of course, all but the coldest northern regions grow something like a Western blackberry, but the most succulent kinds find the climate congenial to them along the Pacific coast.

Choosing a variety

In the list at the end of this section, you will see that we have divided the varieties into three groups: The Pacific Northwest, the Interior, and California. The groups overlap to a large extent, but here are the basic distinctions.

Berries for the Pacific Northwest like mild winters and cool summers. If you try them elsewhere, the climate should approach that mix, as it does along the northern California coast. California berries take a bit more summer heat and even milder winters. Berries for the interior are of a different kind with stiff canes. They are hardier in cold winters.

Planting blackberries

Prune the dormant plants to six-inch stubs and set them at about the level they grew in the nursery, and from four to eight feet apart, depending on the training method you choose (see below). Rows should be six to nine feet apart. If you build a support structure, do it at planting time.

Where is the fruit?

Blackberries fruit on twiggy side branches growing on canes of the previous season. The canes fruit only once and must be removed every year.

Pruning and training

Pruning and training methods are numerous, and practically anything reasonable will work. See page 97 and the photograph on these pages for some ideas. More trellis ideas are shown on page 63.

Here is some general information that will help you to choose your training method. Blackberry canes of the trailing type are very vigorous and usually thorny. If you arrange new canes along the ground as they grow, you will suffer less when time comes to pick them up for training. A four-wire trellis lets you train new canes *as* they grow, on the bottom wire one year, the top the next.

Canes fruit on laterals, but laterals are produced mainly after you pick up the new canes and train them. The horizontal position discourages side growth. Therefore early training, in August, probably means better crops.

If you daub some white paint on the bases of canes in January, it will be easier to figure out which should be cut away after harvest.

'Olallie' is mild-climate berry, best in California but sometimes grown in Gulf Coast climate as well.

'Logan' is popular trailing berry everywhere.

Pests and diseases

There are so many that it's hardly worth worrying. Spray for blackberry mite, and you'll avoid those berries with hard bits in them that never mature.

A word of warning

More than any other cultivated plant, blackberries can be troublesome. If you plant them, keep suckers pulled between rows and keep them trained. Abandoned, they quickly turn into a deep and thorny carpet, strangling everything else, and any tiny root piece will sprout a new plant, so it's hard to eradicate a wild patch.

The variety list

These varieties are not limited only to the region indicated, but they do well there. You will have more success with them if your climate resembles the one indicated.

Pacific Northwest

By this heading, we mean the mild coastal climates, not the eastern areas.

'Aurora.' Very early. Fruit is large and firm, of excellent flavor. The canes are very pliable and easy to train, and they are most productive on the bottom five feet, so they can be planted closely and headed heavily.

'Boysen' ('Nectar'). See California. Good in Clark County, WA. Available: wide distribution.

'Cascade.' A hybrid with Pacific native berries among the parents. The flavor is unsurpassed, fresh or preserved. The plant is vigorous and productive, but tender. Available: (3), (7), (37).

'Marion.' Midseason. The fruit is medium to large, and longer than wide. Of very good flavor. The plants send out few but long and vigorous canes, to 20 feet and very thorny. This berry was the subject of an experiment by Arden Sheets of Oregon, proving that August-trained plants planted only two and a half feet apart are more productive than with wider spacing. Available: (3), (7), (33), (37).

'Thornless Evergreen.' A top commercial berry in Oregon. Fruit is large, firm, and sweet. Plants are vigorous but very tender, produce heavily. A training experiment suggests that pinching canes at 24 inches may increase productivity by encouraging more canes and laterals. There is a thorny form. Available: (3), (10), (15), (37).

'Thornless Logan.' A large, reddish, acid fruit that is best in pie or preserves. It is adapted to the Columbia River area of Washington, the Willamette Valley, and the central coast of California. There is a thorny form. Available: (3), (10), (33), (37).

The Interior

The following will grow in eastern Washington, and throughout zones 1 and 1a where cold is not too intense. They are stiff-caned, from rigid to somewhat trailing.

'Bailey.' Introduced in 1950 from New York. The fruit is large and firm, of good quality. The plant is reliably productive. Available: (13), (20).

'Darrow.' Introduced in 1958 from New York. The berries are very large and irregular. The flavor is mildly subacid, flesh firm. They ripen over a very long season, sometimes into fall. The bush is very hardy and reliable. Available: (2), (6), (20).

'Ebony King.' A purplish-black berry of unknown origin with sweet, tangy flavor, ripening early. The upright plant is hardy and resists orange rust. Available: (4), (20).

'Smoothstem.' From Maryland, 1965. A late variety with large, jet-black fruit that is firm and good. The canes are thornless and tend to trail, reaching eight to ten feet unpinched. Plants productive and somewhat tender. Available: (2), (13), (14).

California

The cool north coast suits the Northwest berries too. Mountain and high desert gardeners may need berries from the Interior list.

'Boysen.' Identical to 'Nectar.' Early crop from May 20 to June 20, depending on area. Second crop in some areas extends picking through August. A large berry of excellent flavor and aroma, but covered with dusty bloom.

'Marion' is a fine Washington berry for close planting.

Good fresh or processed. Very vigorous plants. For Central Coast, Valley, South Coast. Available: wide distribution.

'Himalaya.' A late berry that is grown in limited quantities in Northern California. Locally available.

'Ollalie.' The prime California berry, although introduced in Oregon. The large berries are shiny, black, firm, and sweet, high quality. Very productive and thorny canes, low-chilling requirement. Resists verticillium wilt and mildew. Best for Southern California. Available: (10), (15).

'Young.' Earlier than 'Boysen.' It originated in Louisiana and does well in Southern California. The large fruit is very sweet, the canes thorny and few. Available: (10), (37).

Trailing berries need support such as this woven trellis.

Blueberries

Blueberries demand just the right climate and planting soil, but take very little care if you provide the conditions they like. They are about as hardy as a peach, but need a fair amount of winter chill, and will not grow well in mild-winter climates.

Blueberries belong to the heath family, and count azaleas, rhododendrons, mountain-laurel *(Kalmia),* and huckleberries among their cousins. If any of these grow naturally near your garden, or if you have prepared an artificial site that suits them, then blueberries will do well too.

Blueberries like soil rich in organic material such as peat, and very acid, but extremely well drained. Soils such as these are usual in areas of high rainfall, which is lucky, since the berries need constant moisture, even though they will not tolerate standing water.

You'll find major commercial plantings of blueberries in New Jersey, especially Burlington and Atlantic Counties; in Michigan in favored areas of the lower peninsula; in Washington and Oregon; and to a certain extent in New York, Massachusetts, and Indiana.

Planting blueberries

The soil must be both acid and well drained. You will have to plant in raised beds if there is any chance of water standing around the roots for even a day. For both drainage and acidification, add large amounts of peat moss or other organic material to the planting soil; up to three-quarters peat moss by volume for soils that tend to be heavy. Never add manure; it is alkaline.

Dig the planting hole somewhat broader and deeper than the roots of the young plant. Never cramp the roots into a small hole. Spread them in a wide hole and press soil firmly over them.

Set high-bush blueberry plants about four feet apart, and at the same level as in the nursery. Plant two varieties for better crops.

Do not feed plants the first year. In succeeding years, use cottonseed meal, ammonium sulfate, or any commercial fertilizer prepared for camellias, azaleas, or rhododendrons.

Care after planting

Blueberries require constant light moisture in the soil, and you can damage their shallow roots by cultivating. For both of these reasons, mulch the plants heavily. Use any organic material such as straw, leaves, peat moss, or a combination, and renew it regularly to keep it about six inches deep. Some materials will use nitrogen as they decay, and you will have to compensate with extra feeding.

Pruning blueberries

The technique is simple, and you don't have to be too precise. Leave the plants alone for two or three seasons, trimming only tangles or broken twigs. Then, to cut back a little on the extremely heavy crops of small berries, remove some of the oldest canes and clip out the weakest twigs. For the largest berries, clip off the outer third to half of the fruiting twigs you retain.

If you never prune you will still get fruit, but it will be small, and eventually decline in quantity.

Pests and disease

Blueberries suffer from very few difficulties, but birds will take them all unless you net the plants. Nurseries carry suitable netting.

Harvest

It's best to taste blueberries before picking, since they tend to be a bit tart up to harvest.

The variety list

Approximately the same varieties are used throughout the country, since the conditions for growing them are so similar.

Early season
'Weymouth.' From New Jersey. The large, round berry has a dark blue skin, little aroma. Best for cooking, but it ripens

Harvest high-bush blueberries from Washington to North Carolina. This cluster grew on 'Dixi' variety.

All those in the pail didn't come from one plant, but blueberries give a good return in small space.

very early. The bush is very productive, erect, and spreading, not vigorous. Available: (2), (4), (31).

'Earliblue.' New Jersey, 1952. One of the best for all areas. The fruit is large, light blue, and firm. The picking scar is small, so fruit keeps well and is resistant to cracking. The plants are upright and comparatively hardy. Available: (2), (6), (7), (14), (36).

'Northland.' Michigan, 1968. A very hardy variety for colder regions. The fruit is medium-sized and round, moderately firm and medium blue. The flavor is good. The plant is spreading, reaching only four feet at maturity. Available: (14), (22).

Midseason

'Collins.' New Jersey, 1959. The fruit is large and light blue, firm and sweet. It resists cracking. The plants are erect, well shaped, and fairly hardy, but not consistent in production. Available: (14), (36).

'Bluecrop.' From New Jersey, 1952. Recommended in all areas. The fruit is large and light blue, rather tart, but an excellent keeper, good in cooking. The fruit stands cold well which recommends the plant for the shortest Michigan growing seasons. The plant is upright and medium hardy. Available: wide distribution.

'Bluehaven.' Michigan, 1968. The fruit is large and light blue, ripening over a long season. The flesh is firm, aromatic, and does not crack. The plant is tall and upright, fairly hardy and consistent. Locally available.

'Blueray.' New Jersey, 1959. The fruit is very large, firm, and sweet. The plant is upright and spreading. A recommended variety in Washington. Available: wide distribution.

'Berkeley.' New Jersey, 1949. The very large fruit is pale blue, firm, resistant to cracking. The bush is fairly upright, moderately hardy. Recommended along the West Coast into Northern California. Available: wide distribution.

'Stanley.' New Jersey, 1930. A widely recommended variety. The medium-sized fruit is firm, with good color and flavor. The bush is hardy, vigorous, upright. Since there are few main branches, pruning is easy. Available: (2), (4), (7), (14), (31).

Late season

'Coville.' New Jersey, 1949. An inconsistent variety with large light blue fruit that remains tart until near harvest. The plant is medium hardy. Available: wide distribution.

'Dixi.' New Jersey, 1936. The name is not an affectionate term for the South. It means "I have spoken" or loosely, "That's my last word." It was given by the developer, F. V. Coville upon his retirement. The fruit is large, aromatic, and flavorful, good fresh. The picking scar is large, so the fruit keeps poorly. The plant is productive, recommended in most areas. Available: (7).

'Jersey.' New Jersey, 1928. Large fruit in a long and loose cluster on a vigorous and spreading plant. It is a preferred commercial variety in Michigan and is recommended on the West Coast. Available: wide distribution.

Birds and kids leave these berries alone until they're ripe.

Grapes

The West is grape country, wherever you go, and yet many gardeners are disappointed in the fruit they harvest from their vines. The problem is usually a poor choice of varieties. Grapes, more than any other fruit, demand the right climate and amount of heat to produce well.
Too many gardeners buy vines because they like the fruit in the market, or because they know a famous name.

Grape climates

In general, Western grape climates are divided in three. The first includes all of the West except California and the Southwestern desert. Gardeners in these cool regions should choose an American grape of the 'foxy' flavored species, *Vitis labrusca*. The most highly recommended appear below under the heading Northwest. One famous name often sold by nurserymen in the cool regions is not successful in western Washington and Oregon—that is 'Concord.' It requires more heat.

In California the cooler coastal areas and coastal valleys are suited to American grapes, and to selected European varieties with a low-heat requirement. 'Concord' does well, but the popular 'Thompson Seedless' will almost always disappoint a gardener. The variety named 'Perlette' is similar, but was developed for the low heat of this climate.

In the hot inner valleys of the Coast Range there are major commercial vineyards growing all the renowned European wine varieties. The Napa-Sonoma wine region is well known, but there are wine grapes in newer plantings in southern Santa Clara County, San Benito County, near Salinas, and north of Santa Barbara.

'Perlette' grows in any California climate and desert.

The very hot central valley climate is perfect for the European table grapes that you see on your grocer's counters. 'Thompson,' 'Ribier,' and 'Emperor' all do well.

The low and high deserts are not really good grape country. The earliest-maturing European varieties stand the best chance of producing a worthwhile crop.

Soil and site

Grapes root very deeply if they can, although good grapes grow on shallow and heavy soils. Improve very heavy clay with organic material. The soil should drain fairly quickly to prevent root damage. Grapes often do well on sloping and hilly ground, because of exposure and air and water drainage. The vines must have moisture available at all times. A mulch will help to ensure cool and moist soil.

Planting, training, and pruning

See pages 95 and 96 for sketches and instructions. There are two kinds of grapes, each pruned differently. In general the Americans need cane pruning, in which long canes with 10 or more buds on each remain to fruit after pruning; and the Europeans need spur pruning, in which permanent arms or cordons are developed and canes along these are cut back to two buds. There are some exceptions.

Wine grapes are often trained to a head; that is, they are freestanding, with the fruiting stubs, or spurs, selected early, about four per vine, then clipped back each year until the leafless plant looks like a caveman's club.

Feeding grapes

Grapes need only nitrogen, and may not always need that. If the leaves yellow and there is little growth in the early part of the season, they definitely need feeding. If you're not sure, try a feeding to see the result. Late feeding during the ripening period can force excessive growth and spoil the fruit.

Harvest

Harvest grapes by taste and appearance. When you think the bunch looks ripe, taste a grape near the tip. If it's good, cut the bunch.

Sometimes grapes never taste sweet, no matter how long you wait. That simply means that you have planted the wrong variety for your area. Either switch to another variety, or replant the one you stubbornly insist on in a hot spot against a south wall or in a westward fence corner.

The variety list

We list the varieties by region. The inland Northwest and parts of Utah, Colorado, and Idaho can also use 'Concord' and 'Niagara' from the Coastal California list. A list of well-known wine grapes appears without full description at the end if you would like to attempt a small vineyard.

Northwest

'Buffalo.' New York origin. Ripens in midseason. Good grape for wine or juice. The fairly large cluster holds reddish-black berries with a heavy bloom. Slipskin with foxy Concord flavor. The vine is vigorous and hardy. Cane pruning. Available: (2), (6), (13), (14).

'Interlaken Seedless.' New York. The fruit ripens early with medium clusters of small, seedless berries. The

American and European table grapes. You will find at least one variety for any climate except the warm-weather South. There, gardeners use muscadines or selected warm-winter bunch grapes, southern specialties.

Cabernet Sauvignon

Carnelian

Chardonay

Twelve of the best new and old California wine grapes are pictured above and below. You will have more success with any of these if your garden is near a commercial vineyard that grows the grape you select.

greenish-white skin adheres. The flesh is crisp and sweet. Resembles 'Thompson Seedless' but has interesting flavor overtones. Vine fairly hardy. Cane pruning. Available: wide distribution.

'Ontario.' Canada. The white berries form in fairly loose clusters. The vines are vigorous, productive, and fairly hardy, and prefer quite heavy soils. Cane pruning. Available: (6), (14), (32).

'Seneca.' New York. An early to midseason grape with small-to-medium berries resembling European grapes. They have tender, golden skin, and a sweet and aromatic flavor. The vine is hardy. Cane pruning. Available: (2), (32).

'Schuyler.' New York. Midseason ripening. The berry has a flavor without foxiness, resembling European grapes. It is soft and juicy with a tough skin. The vine is fairly hardy and disease-resistant. Spur or cane pruning. Locally available.

'Van Buren.' New York. Ripens early. The small-to-medium clusters of medium-sized jet-black berries are well filled. The flavor is sweet and foxy, very good fresh. The juice holds the flavor less well than 'Concord.' The vines are fairly vigorous and hardy, subject to downy mildew. Available: (2).

California coast

'Cardinal.' California. Ripens very early. The medium-sized fruit clusters are extremely abundant, to three per cane, but irregular. The large, dark red berries have firm, greenish flesh. The vine can be rampant. Use it to cover an arbor or summerhouse. Spur pruning. Available: (10), (15), (45).

'Concord.' Massachusetts. Ripens midseason to late. 'Concord' is the typical foxy American grape, so well known in juices, jellies and other commercial products that it needs little description. The juice holds its flavor better than any other grape, but the clusters ripen evenly. It doesn't like high California heat, nor the coolest Northwest summers, but does well anywhere in between. Cane pruning. Available: wide distribution.

'Delight.' California. Ripens early. The well-filled clusters of large, greenish-yellow berries have firm flesh with a distinct, muscatlike flavor. Spur pruning. Locally available.

'Niabell.' California. Ripens midseason. The well-filled clusters of large, black berries have a good flavor fresh, or can be used for juice. The vigorous vines can be pruned to long canes. The large leaves resist powdery mildew. Cane pruning. Available: (10), (45).

'Niagara.' Ripens midseason to late midseason. This is the most widely planted white American, good for wines, juice, or eating. It is more productive than 'Concord.' The vine is vigorous, good for arbors. Cane pruning. Available: wide distribution.

'Perlette.' California. Ripens early. Needs some thinning. The large clusters are very compact. The berries are white to yellowish, very tender and juicy with mild flavor. Stands high temperatures, but ripens where overall heat is fairly low. The vine is vigorous and very fruitful. Spur pruning. Available: (10), (45).

'Pierce.' If 'Van Buren' is the *cool* summer 'Concord,' then this is the *hot* summer 'Concord.' Grow it in the

Rubired

Sauvignon Blanc

Semillon

70 *Small fruits*

Flora

Gamay

Pinot Noir

warmer regions of Central California where you want a foxy black slipskin. Very vigorous vine. Cane pruning. Available: (10), (45).

Hot Climates, California Valleys

'**Cardinal.**' See above.

'**Emperor.**' Ripens late. This is a large red grape with flesh so firm it seems to crunch. It is adapted to the hottest part of the valley. Cooler valley regions can obtain a similar fruit by planting 'Tokay.' Cane or spur pruning. Available: (10), (15), (45).

'**Muscat of Alexandria.**' Ripens late in midseason. The large green berries in somewhat loose clusters are not very pretty, overlaid with splotchy amber. However, there is no flavor to match this. It is musky and rich, as the names implies. It loses this aromatic flavor if held too long, so it's a good fruit for the home garden. Spur pruning. (Muscats are often used in a sweet dessert wine. If you can find the nonfortified muscat wine, made by two or three vintners, it is a real treat with desserts or fruit. Since the wine is fragile, tending to ferment in the bottle, you might see it in a refrigerated case.) Available: (10), (15), (45).

'**Niabell.**' See above. A juice grape. Locally available.

'**Perlette.**' See above. Try this one in low desert regions as it is resistant to sunscald. Locally available.

'**Red Malaga.**' Ripens in early midseason. The large clusters are loosely filled with large pink-to-reddish-purple berries with little flavor. Spur pruning, or cane pruning with thinning of flowers. Available: (10), (15), (45).

'**Ribier.**' Ripens early midseason. A beautiful dessert grape with very large jet-black berries. They tend to soften quickly in storage and lose their very mild flavor. The vines are overproductive. Use spur pruning and thin the flowers for best fruit. Available: (10), (15), (45).

'**Scarlet.**' Ripens midseason. The compact clusters hold jet-black berries with abundant bright red juice that is sweet and richly flavored. There is a mild foxy flavor. The vines are vigorous and leaves turn dark red in fall. Ideal for arbors. Cane pruning. Locally available.

'**Thompson Seedless.**' The top commercial seedless green grapes. They ripen in early midseason. The clusters are well filled with rather long green grapes of mild flavor. Only for hot climates. Go to 'Perlette' or 'Delight' if you're not sure. Cane pruning. Available: (15), (45).

'**Tokay.**' Ripens late midseason. A large, very firm red grape in large clusters. Splendid to look at but little flavor. It does well in the Lodi area, the cooler valley climates. Use 'Emperor' in hotter climates. Spur pruning.

Wine grapes

The list includes three of the best-known varieties. They change character over short distances, so unless you know that professionals grow them near you, don't count on getting the best quality. Other well-known but hard to find California wine grapes are pictured on this page.

'**Cabernet Sauvignon.**' The little black Bordeaux grape with the claret flavor. Available: (10), (15), (45).

'**Pinot Noir.**' The small, black Burgundy grape, used in the very finest French wines. Difficult to handle. Available: (15).

'**Zinfandel.**' A California specialty for red wine. You can probably grow this better than any other as it seems to make drinkable wine in a variety of climates. Available: (10), (15), (45).

Sylvaner

White Reisling

Zinfandel

Small fruits 71

Currants and gooseberries

As you can see from the photographs here, currants and gooseberries are among the most beautiful of the small fruits, but they are good home-garden shrubs for other reasons as well.

You won't often see fresh fruit in the market, since crops from the limited commercial plantings go to processors for commercial jellies and canned fruits. But since the plants are ornamental, easy to care for and productive, northern gardeners can tuck a few among other shrubs—for the bloom, fruit, and fall color. The crop can be used for jelly and pie, or just fresh eating for those who like a tart fruit.

We discuss only the red and white currants of the species *Ribes sativum,* and the gooseberries, *Ribes grossularia* and *R. hirtellum.* The black currant, *Ribes nigrum,* so aromatic and rich in vitamin C, is unfortunately banned almost everywhere, since it is part of a disease cycle of five-needle pines. The other Ribes species also take part in transferring this disease (the white pine blister rust), and they too are banned in some areas. Ask your nurseryman, and do not transport or plant any currant or gooseberry from outside your region without checking with your Cooperative Extension Office.

Planting

Fall or winter planting is a good idea, since the plants leaf out early. In cold climates, plant right after the leaves drop and the roots will establish before winter. Space the plants about four feet apart, or set them closer if more convenient, but expect them to grow less vigorously. If summer is hot, plant them against a north wall. In most areas, plant in the open, but be sure soil moisture is constant. Set the plants a little deeper than they grew in the nursery.

Feeding and mulching

The plants are heavy feeders and require a regular program of feeding with nitrogen. The leaves will begin to yellow if soil nitrogen level is low. Mulch will help keep weeds down and maintain constant moisture.

Soil

Almost any soil will do, but a rich, well-drained loam is best.

Pruning

No pruning is necessary if you want only light crops on plants that are mainly ornamental. The plants bear the best fruit on the base of stems of the previous season, and on spurs along two-year-old stems. To prune, remove stems that are more than three years old during the dormant season. You can leave 9 to 15 stems, depending upon the age of the plants.

Plants produce for up to 20 years in ideal climates, less in warmer, southerly climates.

Pale American gooseberry reddens up when ripe.

Choose 'White Imperial,' 'White Grape,' among white currants.

Pests and disease

Currants are attacked by the usual aphids, mites, and so on, requiring occasional sprays (or hosing with water for mites). The most serious disease does not affect the currants themselves. Spores of white pine blister rust from miles away spend part of their lives on the currants, then transfer to pines growing within about 300 feet. Currants are banned where there is a white pine timber crop, but check your own and neighbors' gardens for pines with bundles of five needles, and if you find them, don't plant currants.

The variety list

Currants are listed first, then gooseberries. Gooseberry stems are thorny.

Currants

'Perfection.' An old variety with red fruit of medium size in loose clusters. The plant is upright with good foliage, vigorous, and productive. Recommended in Washington and Oregon. Available: wide distribution.

'Red Lake.' Minnesota, 1920. Recommended everywhere that currants will grow. The medium-to-large berries are light red in long, easy-to-pick clusters. The plants are slightly spreading. Highest yield in Canadian trials. Produce well in California. Available: wide distribution.

'Stephens No. 9.' Ontario, 1938. Good Great Lakes variety with fairly large berries of medium red in medium clusters. Plants are spreading and productive. Locally available.

'White Grape.' A white variety that is widely sold, but perhaps surpassed in quality by 'White Imperial' if you can find it. Available: (28), (32).

'Wilder.' Very old variety from Indiana that is still available in the Midwest. The dark red berries are firm but tender, very tart. Plants are large, hardy, and long-lived.

Gooseberries

'Clark.' Ontario. The fruit is large, red when ripe, on plants that are usually free of mildew. Good Canadian variety. Available: (32).

'Fredonia.' New York. The large fruit is dark red when ripe. Plants are productive and vigorous, open growth. Available: (32).

'Oregon Champion.' Oregon. Good variety for all West Coast growing areas. The medium-sized fruit is green. Available: (3), (7), (10), (15).

'Pixwell.' North Dakota, 1932. Very hardy variety for Central and Plains States. The berries hang away from the plant, are easy to pick. The canes have few thorns. Available: wide distribution.

'Poorman.' An American type with red fruit, recommended in the Pacific Northwest and the Central States. The plants are spiny and spreading. Available: (32).

Red currants add extraordinary beauty to the garden.

Easy to grow, red currants make the finest jelly.

Small fruits

Pests and diseases

The more energy your plants expend recovering from the effects of these spoilers the less fruit they will bear. Here are some tips on giving them a helping hand which will be amply rewarded at harvest time.

Fruit pests

The pests listed here are among the most common, although you may meet others.

Birds

Birds are at their worst with cherries, blueberries, and other smallish fruit that they can remove entirely. For these plants, when fruit begins to ripen cover the entire tree with plastic net available from nurseries and hardware dealers. Throw the net directly over the tree, or build a simple frame of lumber for dwarfs and bushes. For larger fruits you may find that cotton twine is discouraging enough. Throw the ball over the tree repeatedly from different sides. The strands annoy the birds when they try to land. The twine will rot away over winter.

Cherry fruit fly

Cherry (pear) slug

Small, wet-looking green worms are larvae of a wasp. They skeletonize leaves, leaving a lacy patch. Spray when you notice them (probably June and again in August) with malathion or a contact spray registered for control of the pest. Follow label direction. Once is usually enough.

Cherry (pear) slug

Codling moth

Birds

Cherry fruit fly

A pest in the Pacific Northwest. The fly larvae are white, burrow through the cherries leaving a hole. Spray with Diazinon or other product registered for control of cherry fruit fly at 7-day intervals as soon as you notice flies or maggot damage.

Codling moth

The major apple and pear pest. The moths lay eggs in the blossoms and the larvae tunnel in the fruit, leaving holes and droppings (frass). Spray after petals fall and continuing at 7 to 10-day intervals as directed with Diazinon.

Flatheaded borer

A Western pest that burrows into bark that has been damaged. Often found in sunburned trees. To avoid the pest, avoid the damage. Paint or wrap trunks and don't run into them with tools or machinery. When you find tunnels and droppings, cut away bark and wood and dig out the borer. Be sure you have them all, then paint the wound with tree seal or asphalt emulsion. For apples, cherries and pears, use a lindane product registered for control of this pest.

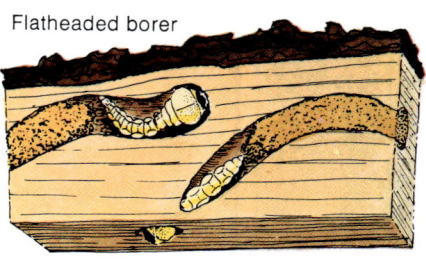
Flatheaded borer

Leaf roller

This moth larva hides in rolled leaves and feeds on both foliage and fruit. Once rolled in, they are protected from spray, must be unrolled by hand. Spray when pests first appear and at intervals recommended on the label of the Diazinon product you use.

Leaf roller

Mites

Spraying for insects may bring on a mite attack, since it removes their enemies. You'll see silvery webbing on the bottoms of leaves, perhaps curling or bronzing. Mites love dust, so wash off foliage with a jet of water in dusty seasons. Kill overwintering

Mites

mites with dormant oil spray. During growing season, use Diazinon or malathion products labeled for mite control on fruit trees.

Peach tree borer

There are two kinds. One bores into twigs (peach twig borer) and one into

Peach tree borer

the trunk at the soil line. The second is very common. Dig soil away from the trunk and check for tunnels and droppings. Kill the worm by pushing a bit of wire down its tunnel. (Check cherry and plum trees for the same pest). Spray trees with Diazinon, carbaryl, or lindane product according to directions.

Pear psylla

The youngest stages collect on leaves like aphids and suck juices. The honeydew they drop may cause a fungus growth that coats the leaves and interrupts photosynthesis weakens the tree. Dormant oil spray helps, and youngest stages can be controlled with carbaryl sprays, but do not use carbaryl during bloom. Malathion also can be used to control psyllids, but do not use within one day of harvest.

Pear psylla

Plum curculio

Serious on many stone fruits east of the Rockies. The pest belongs to the beetle family and the larvae attack the fruit right after blossom time. Spray with carbaryl or another product labeled for control of this pest. Follow all directions on the product you choose.

Plum curculio

Rodents

Mice, moles, and rabbits all like the bark of young trees, especially when it is covered with mulch or snow in winter and better food is lacking. If enough bark is removed, the tree will die at the first growth surge of spring. Protect the lower trunk in winter or all

Rodents

year with a cylinder of hardware cloth. Be sure it doesn't become tight as the tree grows. Check during the season and loosen or replace it.

Rosy apple aphid (and other aphids)

Aphids are another leaf-rolling creature that can damage immature fruit and prevent its proper development. A dormant oil spray kills overwintering eggs, and a contact spray of malathion, carbaryl, or Diazinon helps con-

Rosy apple aphids

trol them during the growing season if you notice them on a tree. Other aphids may roll leaves or collect on young growth. A dormant oil, followed by contact spray when you see them, usually keeps them controlled.

San Jose scale

Becoming serious in the West again. You'll see red spots on fruit, or simply masses of the scale insects when attacks become serious. They can kill a plant in a season or two. Use a delayed dormant oil spray, (garden type—not fuel oil) to control mature scales before crawlers hatch or are born. Crawlers can be controlled with malathion or Diazinon products labeled for this use. Follow all directions.

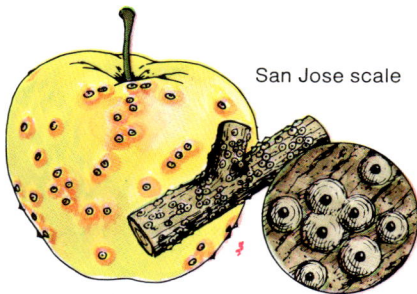
San Jose scale

Diseases of fruit trees

The following are a few of the many diseases that may appear, but these are the most common. Some are easily controlled with proper sprays (the right season is very important); others are best fought by choosing resistant plants; and some require removal and burning of infected parts.

Any disease is easier to deal with if you keep the orchard or garden fruit trees well pruned, and the ground around them clean of fallen fruit and leaves. Pick shriveled fruit that hangs on and burn it or seal it in a bag to discard.

Be sure to prepare soil properly, plant high, and keep the tree watered and fed. A healthy plant is much more resistant.

Apple scab

The disease lives over on fallen leaves, so adequate garden cleanup is important. Two kinds of spores are

Pests and diseases 75

produced by the old fungus, one in spring, another in summer. Both attack foliage and fruit, growing whenever rains fall. The disease is no problem in dry-summer climates. Both apples and crabapples are affected and need sprays. Choose resistant plants when possible.

To control scab, apply a fungicide labeled for scab control on apples at regular intervals as directed on the product. The spray schedule on the product label is for optimum results from that product.

Apple scab

Bacterial leaf spot
Primarily on cherries and plums. The disease lives over in old leaves, then produces spores in spring. The spores begin infections in rainy periods, causing colored spots on leaves that turn brown, become holes and widen. The fruit spurs may be attacked, causing fruit drop.

To control, spray with a fungicide labeled for control of bacterial leaf spot at petal fall, covering the leaves thoroughly. Spray as directed on the product label.

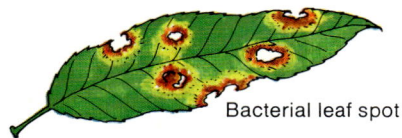
Bacterial leaf spot

Bacterial gummosis
Gumming along stone fruit branches is fairly common and may occur because of mechanical damage, insect damage, or because of a number of diseases. Several serious bacterial diseases with this symptom almost rule out the planting of certain fruit varieties in some areas. There is no spray treatment. Following are some of the diseases that affect variety choice.

Bacterial canker of cherries. In wet climates avoid 'Bing,' 'Lambert,' 'Napoleon,' 'Van.' Resistant are 'Corum' and 'Sam.' The disease causes long, narrow, damp-looking patches on trunk or branches with gum at the edges. Branches die as they are girdled. The disease can affect apricots, blueberries, peaches and prunes. Choose resistant peaches from our variety list.

Coryneum blight of peaches. This is a fungus disease, primarily of peaches, but also of cherries, apricots and prunes. Spotty leaves and fruit are followed by darkened bark that ruptures and exudes gum. This is a controllable disease. Use fixed copper

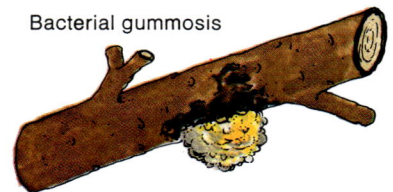
Bacterial gummosis

in October, then use wettable sulfur as a spray 1 week after petal fall and again after rainy periods.

Brown rot
Serious on all stone fruits, but especially on nectarines. In some areas these are nearly impossible to grow to the edible stage. A characteristic of brown rot is that the fruit shrivels and dries on the tree, forming mummies that must be removed by hand to prevent reinfection.

The first attack of the disease causes blossoms to brown and turn wet-looking, then drop. The amount of blossom blight determines the amount of fruit that may be spoiled.

To control the blossom-blight phase, spray as the first pink shows, using a fungicide such as Benlate, captan, Cyprex, ferbam, ziram, or lime sulfur. Spray as directed on the product label.

To control attack on fruit, spray as the fruit begins to ripen and repeat

Brown rot

if there is a period of wet weather. Green fruit is rarely attacked.

On peaches and nectarines, the disease may attack twigs and live over within them. Pruning out any dead twigs helps control the disease in the following year.

Cedar apple rust
The disease appears only where the alternate host, red cedar, grows near apples. The leaves first show orange spots and odd, cup-shaped structures, then yellow and fall. Remove red cedars or avoid planting them. If you have ornamental cedars, remove the galls in summer. They are brownish and globe-shaped, looking like part of the tree. Spray the apples

Cedar apple rust

with a product registered for control of cedar apple rust (ferbam or zineb products).

Crown gall
The disease is of bacterial origin, and occurs in some soils. It attacks young trees, producing soft galls or swellings on the crown and roots. The galls grow until they girdle and kill the tree. There is no chemical control.

Avoid buying young trees that show galls, and plant young trees carefully

Crown gall

to avoid injury that allows bacteria to enter the plant. Older trees with galls can only be removed and destroyed. Recently some experimental work has suggested that young plants can be innoculated against the disease, and so it may become inconsequential in the future.

Crown rot
A serious and common disease of almost any plant that is planted so that the trunk is constantly wet at the soil line during spring and fall. The disease is caused by a fungus and appears late in the growing season when a branch reddens and its foliage yellows or discolors. Look at the bark below the soil line to see whether it is dead, and if so, scrape it away and pull back soil so air can reach the infection.

Avoid crown rot by planting high and watering well out from the trunk except immediately after planting. The soil should never be wet at the crown. The high planting will help to keep it dry even where rainfall is heavy.

Fire blight

The disease is spread by insects during the bloom period and shows later in spring as new growth wilts, turns dark, and finally blackens as if burned. The infection spreads rather quickly

Fire blight

down branches, eventually killing infected pears and damaging or killing apples.

No treatment has proved very effective for the home gardener other than severe pruning of infected wood. It must be burned afterward. Choose resistant pears and where the disease is severe in apples, plant such resistant varieties as 'Cortland,' or 'Delicious.' Mild winters will increase the severity of the disease the following spring.

To control infection on resistant plants, cut any blighted branches several inches below the infection as soon as you notice an attack. There is some question about sterilizing pruning tools, but the classic method is to carry a strong solution of household bleach with you and dip the shears after each cut. Burn all prunings immediately.

Peach leaf curl

A disease that is easy to control but sure to attack peaches in many regions. Uncontrolled it will weaken the tree, killing it after a number of seasons. It interferes with blossom and fruit production.

To control curl, you must spray during leaf fall and again during dor-

Peach leaf curl

mancy with a fixed copper spray or lime sulfur, and you must wet every twig and branch completely. If rain falls immediately after treatment, repeat it.

The disease shows as a reddening of leaves. They then curl into blisters that may have a powdery look. Finally they fall and a second crop of leaves grows which is not affected. No spraying is effective once the disease has appeared, but the copper spray or lime sulfur will remove it completely if you spray every year.

Powdery mildew

Powdery mildew is a fungus disease that causes a grayish, powdery coating to form over young shoots, leaves, and flower buds. It can deform or kill them.

Powdery mildew thrives where air circulation is poor and grows best in shade. Be sure fruit plants grow where air moves freely and receives sunlight most of the day.

Rinse dust and mildew spores from the foliage occasionally during the spring and summer.

Where an infection begins, clip off severely mildewed twigs and spray

Powdery mildew

with Actidione PM, karathane, or wettable sulfur. Sulfur should not be used during the hottest part of the day.

The basics of fruit pest control

Complete control of insects and diseases on fruit crops requires a thorough and comprehensive spray program. Proper timing, good coverage of foliage, and correct chemicals are essential.

Here, we present a simplified spray program that should meet your essential needs. But keep in mind that some pests are difficult to control, so you might find some blemished fruit even after following these recommendations. And your neighbor's spray program is important, too. If he is negligent, then you may find his problems become your problems.

Apples and pears

Winter: Before leaves are out, apply a dormant oil spray to control scale, mites, and other pests. This can be the most important spray of the year. Follow directions explicitly for best results.

Spring: The next important spray is when fruit buds show pink at the tips. Spray with an insecticide such as Diazinon to control aphids, leaf rollers, and many other pests, and with a fungicide such as captan to control apple scab, fruit spot, and bitter rot. When three-fourths of petals have fallen, spray an insecticide again to stop codling moth which appears at this time. Where apple scab is a problem, consistent use of a fungicide such as captan is required for control.

Summer: The first summer spray is 10 to 14 days after petal fall. Use an insecticide, fungicide, or both as your trees need. For perfect fruit, continue to spray through summer with insecticide and fungicide as needed.

Fall: Spray as necessary, but pay strict attention to label instructions regarding time intervals between sprays and harvest.

Peaches, apricots, cherries, and plums

Winter: Same as above. Where peach leaf curl is a problem, timing is very important. Lime sulfur sprays such as 26% calcium polysulfides should be applied in October or November after leaf drop but before heavy rains begin. Apply another full-coverage spray in January or February before buds begin to swell. Note: if buds have begun to swell or open, it is too late to obtain satisfactory control, as infection has already occurred. For best results, we recommend both sprays be applied.

Spring: When blossom buds show color — pink for peaches, red for apricots, popcorn stage for cherries, and green tip stage for plums — spray an insecticide such as Diazinon to control insect pests. A fungicide such as captan is often needed for brown rot control. Spray an insecticide and fungicide again when three-fourths of petals have fallen.

Summer: Same as above.
Fall: Same as above.

Space-saver training

If you have a small garden, forget all the old advice about distances between trees. Fruit can be grown successfully as hedges, garden dividers, boundary plantings, and espaliers. In this chapter, we show you how to crowd a lot of plants in small spaces.

With dwarfing rootstocks and a little training you can confine fruit trees within tiny spaces. The French, for example, grow apples as a foot-high border around beds of vegetables. That technique will work only for cool-climate gardeners, but there are close planting and training methods for mild-climate gardeners as well.

Home gardeners are not the only ones concerned with limited-space-planting these days. Commercial growers are experimenting with training methods that let them grow fruit in hedgerows and harvest their crop without hauling ladders and climbing 30 feet up a standard tree. The methods we outline here combine commercial experience with the training methods that French gardeners call espalier and cordon training. You can be as formal as you like in shaping the plants, but the modern tendency is toward less formal shapes that are easier to achieve and maintain.

Growing fruit in tight spaces is really no harder than maintaining a healthy rosebush, but keep the following points in mind to avoid frustration:

✓ Be especially careful about planting and general maintenance. Prepare your soil well and use low raised beds where drainage is a problem. Feed and water on a regular schedule. Spray before damage occurs (some pests and diseases do their work before you can really see the results). Don't let new growth escape from you and spoil the pattern. Look your plants over often.

✓ In limited-space planting, training continues at all seasons for the life of the plant. Since the plant is right beside you in the living-space garden, inspecting it is really no chore, but be ready to pinch or snip at any time. Major pruning is still a winter task, but in summer you head or cut away wild growth and suckers, and you may need to loosen or renew ties or add new ones.

◊

Formally espaliered trees like these serve four purposes; they define property boundaries; break up expanses of garden or lawn; enhance the landscape with their aesthetic, spreading branches; and provide generous fruit harvest in a limited space.

How does your tree grow?

Be sure you understand the normal growth pattern of the plant you intend to train. For example, a dwarfed apple or pear tree grows slowly and bears its fruit in the same places for years. The little fruiting twigs, called spurs, may need to be renewed over the years, but you can confine the trees to very formal shapes and keep them there. A peach or nectarine fruits on branches that grew the previous year. Old branches won't bear, so you cut them away like berry canes and replace them with new growth from the base of the tree. This heavy pruning means that rigid patterns are impossible. A peach can be fanned out over a wall or grown as a hedge, but cannot be held to a strict cordon or candelabra shape.

This informally espaliered cherry tree effectively complements the stark vertical lines of the supporting picket fence.

Photographs of variety test plot in Mid-Columbia Experiment Station at Hood River, Oregon. Apples on M.9 root stock were planted 2 feet apart and trained at a 45° angle to induce early fruiting. Bent in this fashion the central leader operates like a lateral branch of a regular orchard tree. The bending increases the number of fruiting spurs. Additional spur development is encouraged by both dormant and summer pruning.

Rootstocks

In the section on dwarfing (pages 12–15) you will see the effects of various dwarfing rootstocks on apple trees. Unfortunately, these stocks are not labelled separately in most retail nurseries, and the salesmen may not be able to tell you what you are buying.

As a general rule, apple varieties sold as dwarf trees will be budded on the rootstocks called Malling 7 and Malling 26, which can produce trees of rather large size if the fruiting variety is vigorous. The smallest trees on these roots will be spur varieties which are already partially dwarfed since they produce shorter branch segments between each fruiting twig, or spur.

Very vigorous fruiting varieties will have to be controlled by more frequent summer pruning. If you find that one tree in a hedge or row regularly overgrows and escapes the pattern you have chosen, you would do well to remove it and plant a less vigorous tree.

How deep to plant

Dwarfing rootstocks cause dwarfing because they are not themselves very vigorous or deep rooted. Trees on the smallest stocks may blow out of the ground unless they have support. Many nurserymen now are placing the bud of the fruiting variety rather high on the rootstock, up to 6 or 8 inches above ground. On the tree you buy, this bud union shows as a bulge with a healed scar on one side. Plant the tree with the union about 2 inches above the soil. This is deeper than it grew in the nursery and accomplishes two things: first, the deep planting makes the tree a little more stable; second, the rootstock is less likely to send up suckers from underground.

Deep planting can be dangerous in poorly drained soil where rot is a problem. If your soil is wet and heavy, use a raised bed or mound to bring the soil *up* to the bud union instead of planting deep.

Be very careful never to bury the bud union in soil or mulch at any time during the life of the tree. If moist

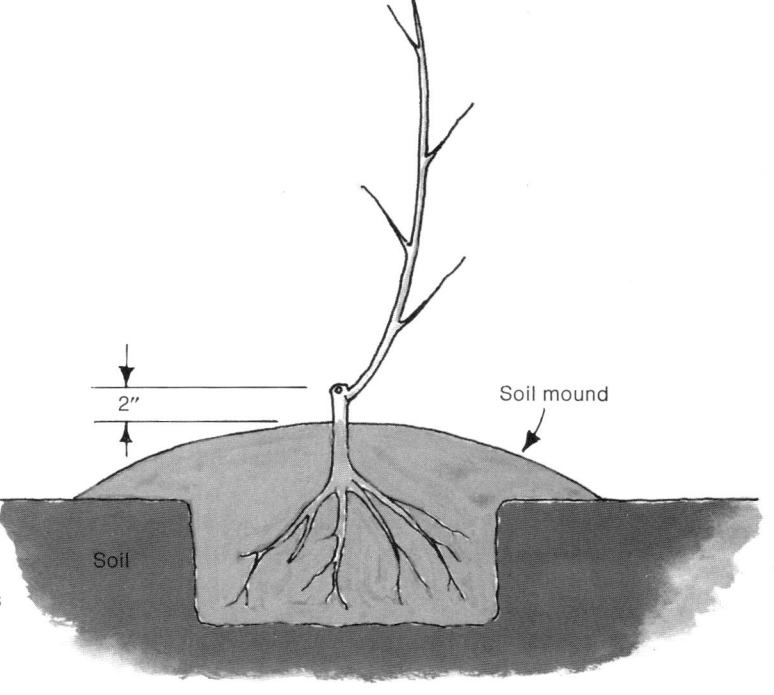

material touches the union, the upper fruiting part will root and its vigorous root system will produce a full-sized tree instead of the dwarf you bought. Check the bud union frequently for signs of rooting and keep mulches a few inches away from it.

Summer pruning

Summer pruning weakens a plant by removing the leaves that manufacture nourishment. On trees in limited space this pruning is the main means of confining them, since winter pruning has the opposite effect and causes a vigorous burst of spring growth. On the other hand, too much summer pruning can damage a tree. You will learn the proper amount by doing the work, but here are general guidelines.

First, and most important, don't be too timid. You are unlikely to kill your plant, but if the worst should happen, a dwarf replacement tree (trained informally) will grow into place and begin to fruit in a season or two.

In early summer, remove only excessively vigorous sprouts that threaten to take over the tree. These may suddenly shoot out much farther than any other growth. Cut them off at the base. Also, remove any suckers from below the bud union, cutting to the base. Paint large wounds with pruning compound.

When the *new* growth matures and slows its pace, begin snipping it back. The season will vary, depending on weather, your feeding, and watering, but by July you can begin with some branches, finishing up by early September. Cut off all but about four leaves of the current season's growth on each new branch. Then give your trees a last feeding of nitrogen to produce new fruiting wood. Don't thin out branches. You can do that during winter pruning if necessary.

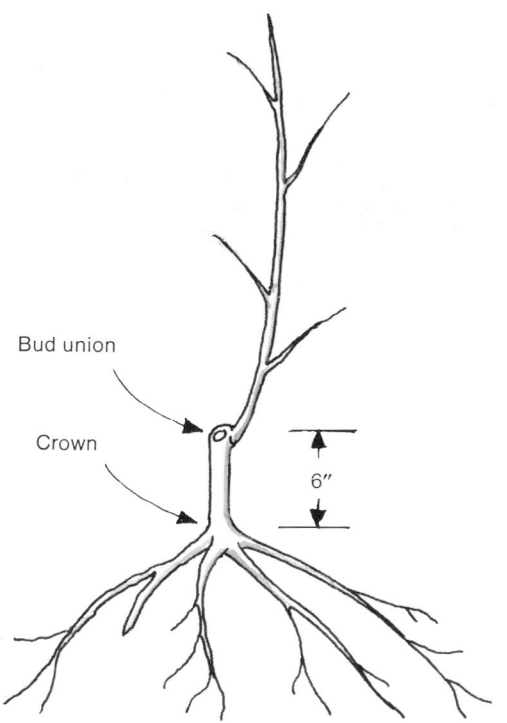

Training to fit your space

You have a broad choice of possibilities in training fruit trees to limited space. Dwarf apples and pears can be trained to formal patterns and still produce fruit, since the flowers and fruit are produced on spurs along old branches. Apricots and European-type plums also produce much fruit on old wood, but since they grow more vigorously they require more of your time to hold a shape. They will not grow or fruit well in rigid patterns. Peaches and nectarines fruit on branches that grew the previous year. You can train them in simple fans or hedges and replace branches that produce fruit with new growth in the fall.

In warm climates you may wish to try training a fig or citrus. The fig fruits twice where the season is long, first on new growth of the previous season then on new growth of the current season. You will lose most of the first crop with severe pruning, but can hope for the second. You can train some citrus (lemons, Rangpur lime) along wires for a fence, or espalier them on walls.

Grapes make good subjects for fences or walls, and a variety that requires a little more heat than your region can offer may produce good fruit when grown on a south or west wall.

You can train cane berries flat against fences or walls, and treat them something like peaches, since you must replace all canes that have fruited with canes of the current season.

The poorest subjects for limited-space training are the quince and cherry. The quince fruits at the tips of new twigs, and the cherry is normally too large to confine and will not fruit at all without a pollinizer close by. Both of these plants can be trained, but your effort is better spent with something more rewarding.

Natural training

Apples and Pears. Both dwarf apples and pears grow and fruit well when trained as hedges against horizontal wires. Use wooden rails in very cold climates. Set posts about 8 feet apart. Stretch a bottom wire between them at 24 inches above ground. If your nurseryman can guarantee Malling 9 rootstocks, place the upper wire at 4 or 5 feet. For Malling 7 or 26 roots, the more common in nurseries, place a third wire at 6 or 7 feet.

Plant the young bareroot trees about 3 feet apart, beginning next to an end post. The last tree will go in about 2 to 3 feet short of the final post. If you buy unbranched trees, bend the trunk, called a whip, at a 45-degree angle and tie it to the wire. If there are any branches with wide crotches, cut them so only two leaf buds remain. Clip off those with narrow crotches at the trunk. Do not feed.

During the first season, train the trunk and any new branches at about 45 degrees, tying loosely where they touch the wires. Pinch off at the tip any branches that seem badly spaced, or that point at right angles to the fence but wait until winter to do this.

The first winter, remove badly placed branches at the trunk. Remove the tips from well-placed branches, cutting to a healthy bud on the top of each branch. Feed lightly as growth begins.

The second summer, continue training shoots at the ends of branches upward at 45 degrees. Cut side growth to four buds beginning in July. Feed again lightly.

Each winter thereafter, remove tangled or damaged growth and cut remaining long shoots to four leaf buds. Feed as growth begins. Each summer, cut out suckers and excessively vigorous sprouts as they appear. Shorten new growth to four leaves from July on, and feed the trees in early August to encourage fruiting wood.

This training method allows side branches to grow outward, away from the fence. Your hedge will eventually become three to four feet wide. You can hold it at that width by pulling some of the outward growth back toward the fence with string, but check ties frequently or they will cut the branches. If parts of your hedge begin to escape and grow too far outward, trim those branches back to healthy side branches in May. To maintain the proper height of five to eight feet, cut top growth back to a healthy side shoot near the top wire in May.

Peaches and nectarines. Since a peach hedge must have its fruiting wood renewed annually, you will need long replacement branches each year. For a hedge, plant as described under apples, using three wires at two, four, and six feet. Cut the whips to about 24 inches long and shorten those side branches that point along the fence to two buds each. Cut off other branches at the trunk. Train all new growth at 45 degrees in both directions. Remove any suckers from below the bud union, cutting to the trunk.

The first winter, cut out about half the new growth at the base, choosing the weakest branches for removal. Cut off the tips of branches you retain if they have grown beyond the hedge limits. Feed lightly as growth begins.

Apple or pear

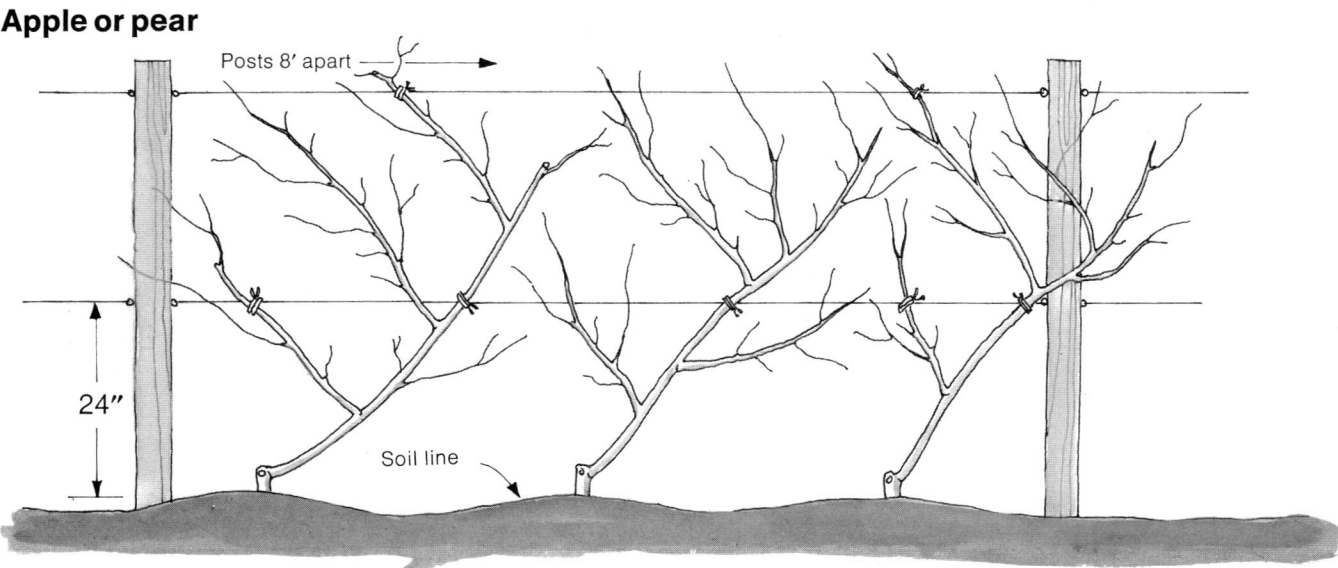

Peach

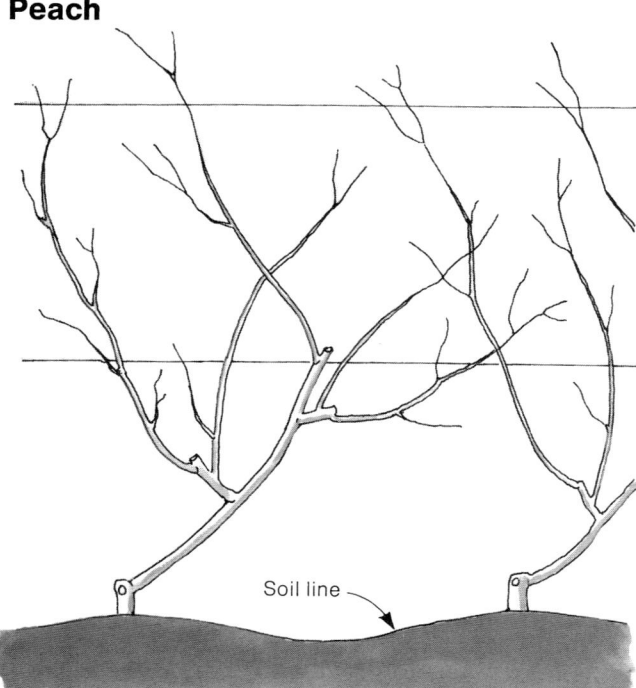

Fruit will form on the branches that grew the previous summer. The original trunk and the lowest branch will form an approximate V-shape at or below the lowest wire. During the second summer, choose the healthiest shoots from the lower portions of these main branches, and pinch back all other growth, especially growth above the second wire, after it produces six to eight leaves. The lower shoots will replace the entire upper structure and should be tied back loosely to the fence. Continue to remove suckers below the bud union, and feed lightly twice during early and midsummer.

When leaves drop in fall, cut out all branches that have fruited, and head back the V-shaped main structure to the middle wire. Paint all wounds with pruning compound and train the new growth to the fence. Feed as growth begins. During the summer, again encourage the lower shoots and pinch back the upper growth, feeding twice. Always be sure that new growth is *above* the bud union.

A note on peaches: in parts of the country, the disease known as peach leaf curl attacks both peaches and nectarines each year. If you have this disease in your region, you must spray with a copper fungicide when trees are *dormant,* drenching every branch and twig on all sides. In wet winter climates, spray in fall while the last leaves are still clinging, then again in early winter during a dry spell of at least two days duration.

In drier climates you can wait to apply the first spray until the beginning of winter, and apply the second in midwinter or early spring before the buds swell.

The training method outlined here for a hedge will work well against a wall in cool regions where the wall will supply a little extra heat to ripen fruit. Form a wall-trained tree into a fan shape with the outer branches nearly horizontal, the central branches nearly vertical.

Apricots and plums. Use approximately the same technique described for peaches, but instead of replacing all growth each year, replace about a third and head back new growth on the remaining branches to four to six leaves during the summer.

Fig

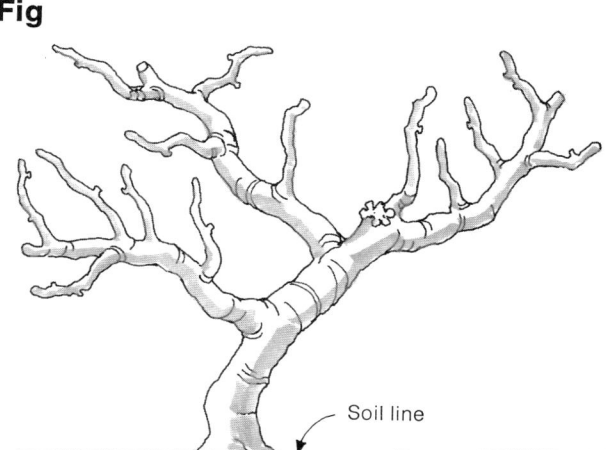

Figs. In warm regions where figs grow well, train the young tree to form an irregular, permanent scaffold of trunk plus two to five short branches. These should be headed at two or three feet long, with the trunk at 45 degrees and branches from 45 degrees to horizontal. New growth from these scaffolds should be cut to about 15 inches long in winter and thinned so that the summer hedge is contained at the size you wish. These branches may produce a little fruit in June or July. In summer, trim very lightly to hold the shape. The new summer growth will fruit in fall. Figs are likely to sucker badly and will need attention several times during the growing season.

Where figs can be grown in most years, but freeze back occasionally, grow them as shrubs rather than training them.

Grapes. See grape training methods under Pruning on page 95. A double cordon can be used for fences or against a south or west wall.

Cane Berries. Canes of the previous season can be trained to a fan or column shape against a wall or used as a fence on a two-wire trellis. See cane berries under Pruning, page 97. New canes should be gathered into loosely tied bundles and placed lengthwise along the wall or fence until old canes fruit. After fruiting, cut out old canes and put the new ones in place. Where disease is a problem, as in many areas of the South, cut and destroy all canes immediately after fruiting and use late summer growth for the following year's crop.

Cane berry

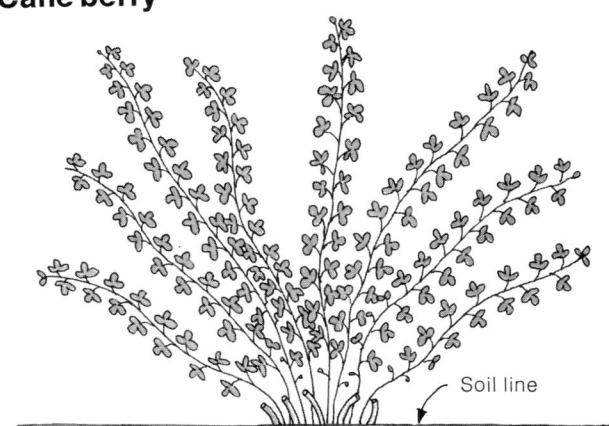

Formal shapes

Only apples and pears can be trained in formal shapes, and pears may be a disappointment in regions where such diseases as fire blight are a problem. Some formal plants, already trained, are available from nurseries and you can plant these and maintain them with no initial effort, but they will be expensive.

The principle of formal training is simple. You encourage buds to grow at fixed places on a young tree, tie them in position as they lengthen, then hold them in place by light pruning through the year. Malling 7 or Malling 26 rootstocks are fine for formal shapes. Pears will grow on quince rootstock.

A warning on any form of training: ties must be checked frequently, since a tight tie left in place will cut the branch and kill it.

How to encourage bud growth

On any tree, the leaf buds farthest from the ground will grow best. On a horizontal branch, the buds on top will grow best, and those near the trunk will leaf out sooner than those near the tip. In addition, branches grow most vigorously when vertical, and growth slows as a branch is bent toward horizontal.

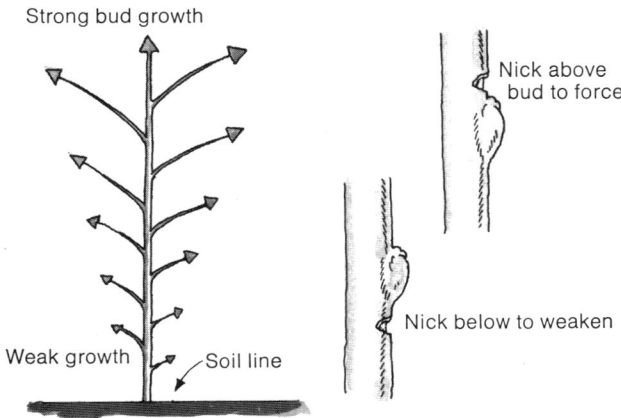

Cutting a branch forces bud growth below the cut. You can produce a similar effect by cutting a small notch in the bark just above a leaf bud. The bud below the notch will tend to sprout. You can weaken a bud by nicking bark just below it.

Three basic shapes

The three basic shapes that underlie all formal training are: the straight vertical, the 45-degree angle, and the straight horizontal. A single tree is trained in only one shape, but it can be repeated with several branches so that the tree has several vertical, angled, or horizontal members as shown in the sketches. The single members of a formal tree are called *cordons*. A tree trained flat with horizontal cordons is called an *espalier* (used loosely to mean any flattened shape), and a tree trained with angled cordons is called a *palmette*. Vertical training may be adapted to freestanding, three-dimensional shapes.

Training vertical trees

Single cordon. Plant the young tree with the bud union about 2 inches above the soil surface. Cut any side shoots to two buds. The tree may be trained against a wall, pillar, post, or wire trellis, but it must be on the south or west side.

Allow the tree to grow through the first summer with no further pruning. The first winter after planting, cut the central leader back by a third to a half, cutting the minimum amount if side growth is vigorous, more if it has grown weakly. More cutting will force more growth the following summer. New branches should be cut to three buds. New growth on older branches is cut to one bud.

The following summer, beginning in July, cut new branches to three buds, new growth on previously trimmed branches to one bud. Do not cut the top vertical branch until it reaches the height you desire. An exception occurs if the tree fails to produce much side growth. You may then cut new growth on the main stem by a quarter to a third in winter.

When the tree reaches the height you desire, clip the leader about two buds below that height in May. Thereafter, trim all new branches to three buds, and all new growth on old branches to one bud during the summer. In winter, trim any branches you missed earlier. Feed and water carefully to prevent excessive growth.

Forming several vertical cordons

To form a number of vertical cordons on the same tree, you must encourage two or more buds on opposite sides of the trunk, then cut away the trunk above them. To be sure that the right buds grow, you make use of bark notches.

Begin by finding two buds low on the trunk but above the bud union. They should be close together and pointing in opposite directions. Place a horizontal support (wire, wooden rail) an inch or two above the buds. If the support is fixed to a wall, the wall should face south or west.

Just above the lower bud, cut a small notch in the bark. Above the upper bud, nick the bark to the wood. Remove the next two buds entirely, then cut a deep nick in the

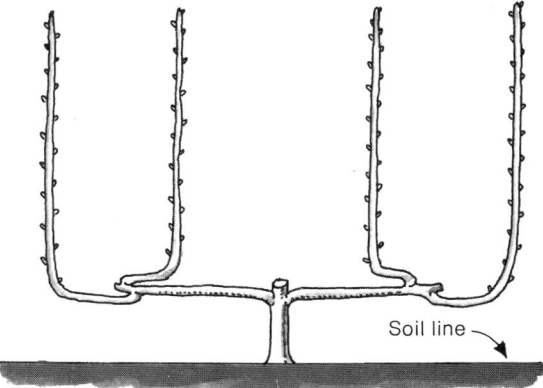

bark just *below* the next higher bud. Snip off the trunk above this bud.

The effect will be as follows: the notch and nick above the lowest buds will force them into growth, since nutrients will stop at the cuts. The topmost bud will grow too, but weakly, since you have cut the bark below it. This last bud helps the tree to draw nutrients past the two buds you wish to keep.

In late summer, tie the new shoots from the lower buds to the horizontal support. If one is weaker, let it remain somewhat vertical. In winter, cut the trunk just above the pair of new branches. For a U-shaped double cordon, let the new branches grow vertically again after they form the bottom of the U. After the first season, treat them as you would a single vertical cordon. You can also train the new shoots at 45 degrees or horizontally. Pruning for these shapes is the same as for a vertical cordon.

To form a double U-shape, train the first two shoots into a broad U, becoming vertical when the branches are two feet apart. Let the verticals grow at least two feet up from the bottom support (may require a second season). Repeat the notching and trimming as before on each vertical, training the buds into twin U's one foot across.

Espaliers and palmettes

To form an espalier or palmette with a central trunk and a number of opposing branches you will use a slightly different method. For the first pair of horizontal or angled branches, notch and nick two opposite buds below the

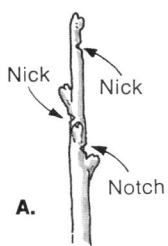

A.

Plant the young tree and set the frame on stakes about 18 inches above the ground. The frame is temporary and may be removed when the training is complete.

Encourage three or four buds about 6 inches below the frame. For three, notch above the first, nick above the second, leave the third alone, then remove the next two and nick below the next. Cut away the trunk above it. Train the shoots horizontally with even spacing

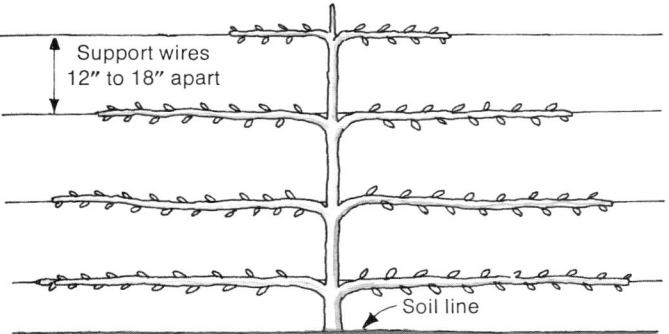

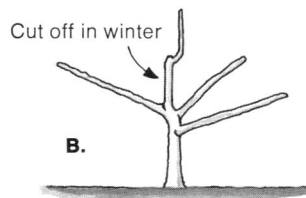

B.

In winter, cut away the vertical central stem, leaving the horizontals.

support as before, and remove the next two buds. Do *not* nick the bark below the next bud. You want it to grow strongly to form the central trunk. Cut off the trunk above it. In fall, tie the two lower shoots for an espalier or angled palmette and begin normal summer and winter pruning. Choose two more buds on the central stem for

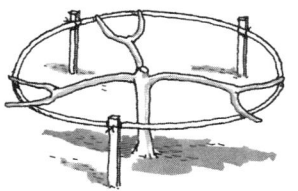

C. Choose buds to form "Y"

On each horizontal, search for two buds about 5 inches away from the center and growing on the sides of the branches, not the top or bottom. Nick the bark beyond the first and cut the branch beyond the second. Remove any buds on the top of the branch nearer the center or they will take over.

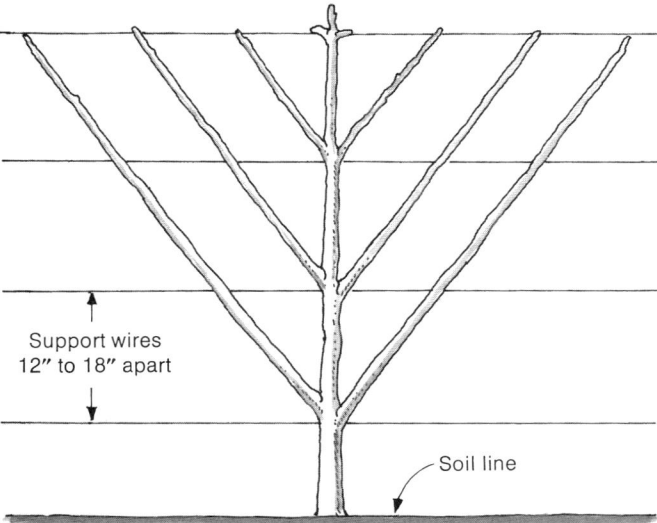

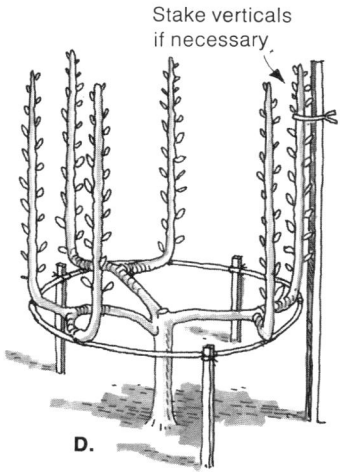

D.

When the three pairs grow beyond the hoop, begin training them upward and treat them as ordinary vertical cordons. Trim away any growth on the horizontal portions as soon as you notice it. For four buds the technique is the same, except that you notch the two lower buds, nick the next, and leave the next.

When vertical members reach the height you wish, clip the leader about two buds below that height in May and thereafter trim as described under Training Vertical Trees, page 84.

encouragement, remove the next two, and cut off the trunk above the third. Continue for each pair of horizontals.

Three dimensions

For a three-dimensional shape the technique is the same, but you will encourage three or four closely spaced buds placed evenly around the trunk. Three buds will be divided again for six upright cordons; four buds will produce eight uprights. After shoot growth has begun, you will have to use a hoop or a square frame to train the horizontal portion of your tree. Use a hoop about two feet across for the simple vase shape illustrated. A pointed cone shape will require a hoop three feet across or, for eight verticals, a square frame three feet on a side.

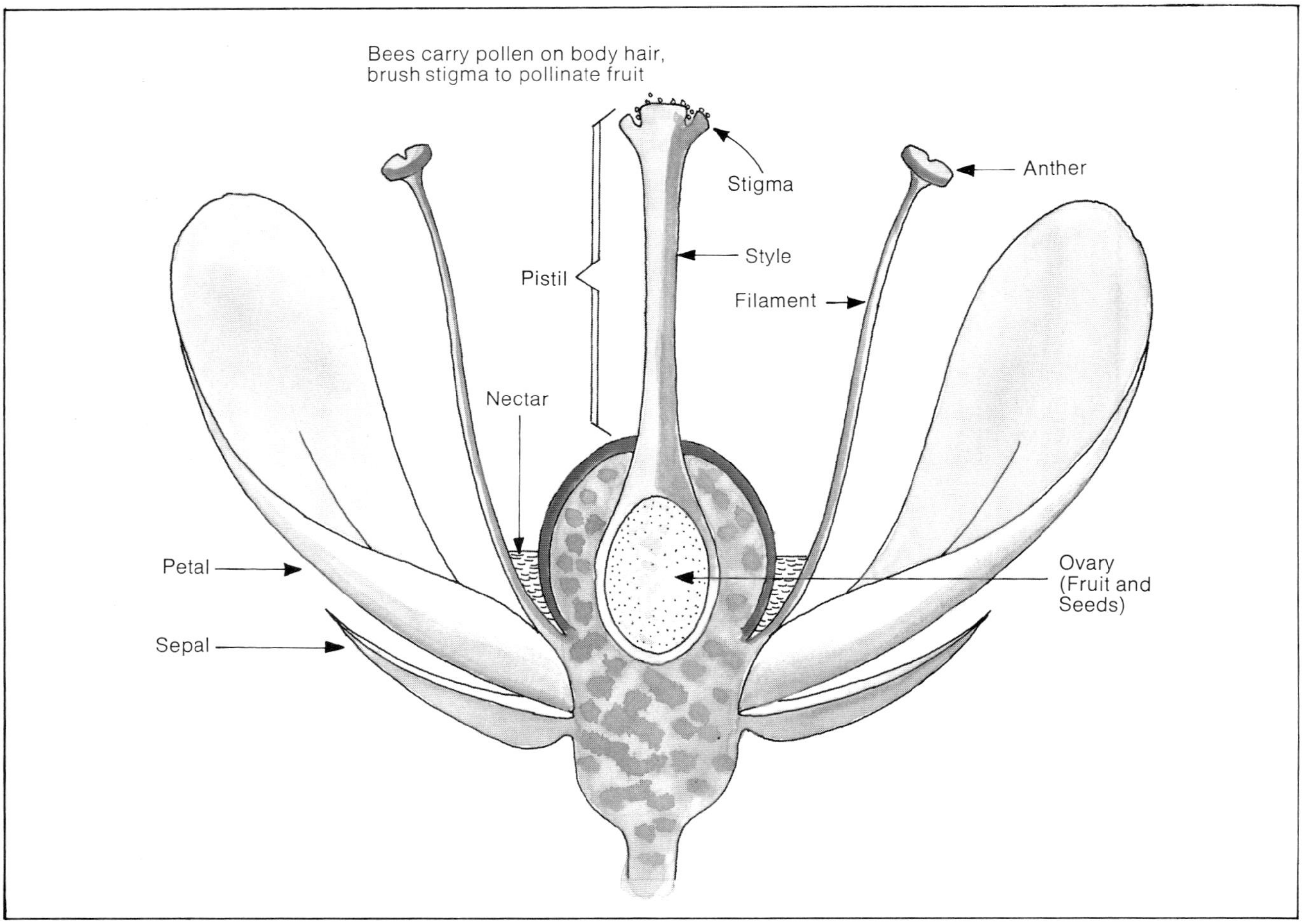

Bees carry pollen on body hair, brush stigma to pollinate fruit

- Stigma
- Anther
- Pistil
- Style
- Filament
- Nectar
- Petal
- Sepal
- Ovary (Fruit and Seeds)

How to achieve proper pollination

Plant close to a pollinating variety

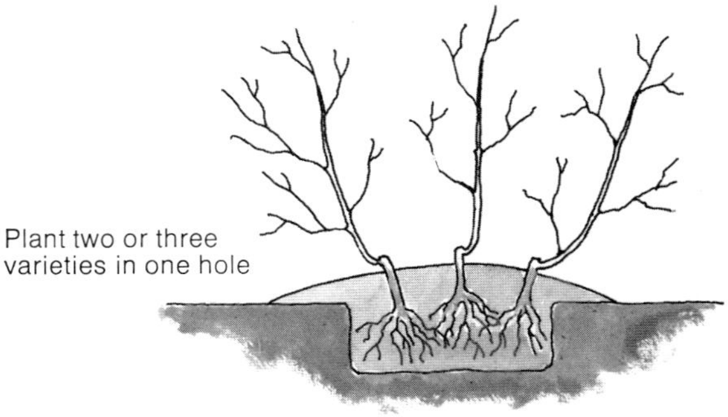

Plant two or three varieties in one hole

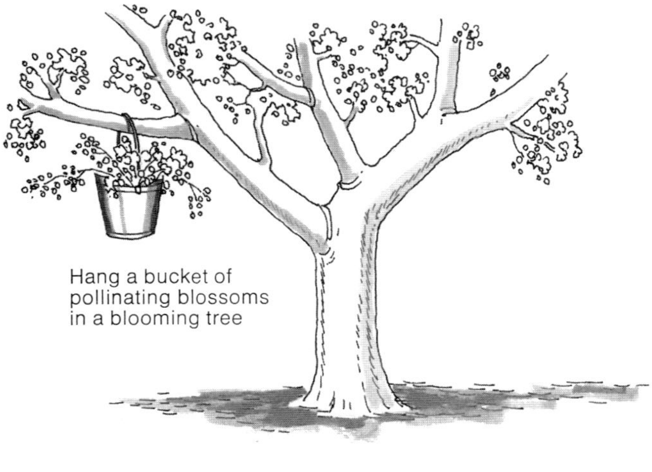

Hang a bucket of pollinating blossoms in a blooming tree

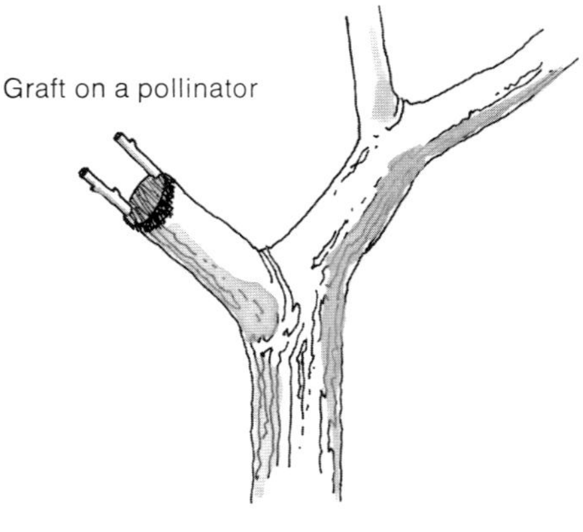

Graft on a pollinator

Pollination, pruning, and grafting

Pollination, Pruning, and Grafting

**Make the most of your fruit garden by understanding its nature.
How does spring bloom mature into a summer crop?
How can you best train a young plant for strength and abundant fruit?
How can you ripen many varieties on a single tree? Your answers follow.**

Plant breeding may seem like a subject that only a bush or a botanist could love, but every time you bite into an apple or a peach you're tasting the results of breeding. As a general rule, the fruit is only there because the seed has been fertilized.

What should you know?

You may feel that once you plant a tree you've done your part, and the rest is up to it. That idea can lead to fruitless fruit trees. Before you ever lift a shovel, you'll need to understand a little of how fruit is produced.

With a few exceptions (certain figs, for example), fruit will not form unless pollen from the male parts of a flower is transferred to the receptor of the female part. Most of the transferring for the fruits discussed in this book is done by bees. Even when you see bees at work, though, you may not get a crop. The pollen they carry must be of the right sort. Apple pollen, for example, will never pollinize a pear blossom, but more important, apple pollen won't always pollinize an apple blossom.

The right combinations

Some plants are called *self-fruitful*. This means that their blossoms can be fertilized by pollen from another flower on the same tree, or from another tree of the same kind. Self-fruitful plants will produce fruit if they are planted far from any other plant of their kind.

Even self-fruitful plants sometimes give more fruit if another plant of a different variety grows close by. Among the self-fruitful plants are many apples, most peaches and apricots, and the citrus group. Sour cherries are also self-fruitful.

Other plants set fruit only when they receive pollen from a plant of some other variety. Their own pollen is often entirely sterile. Many apples, cherries, and plums fall into this group. The Napoleon (Royal Ann) sweet cherry needs another cherry tree with fertile pollen within at least 100 feet of it, or it bears no fruit. The individual entries for each fruit in this book will tell you the right combination of plants for a crop.

Never assume that because you have a bearing fruit tree you can be sure of a crop on a new tree of a different variety. Check the entry on that variety for good pollinizers. Plants must bloom at about the same time for cross-pollination to be successful, so a very early apple with sterile pollen needs another early apple as a pollinizer. A late-bloomer may not work well even if its pollen is fertile.

Some plants bear male and female flowers on separate trees. Figs and persimmons are among these. Fortunately, most figs and persimmons available to the home gardener will produce fruit without pollination. If, by some chance, you have a Calimyrna fig tree or an American persimmon in the garden, you will get no fruit unless the tree is female and has been pollinized.

Planting for pollination

A fruit plant that needs a pollinizer needs it close by. The maximum recommended distance is 100 feet between plants, but the closer the better. This is because the bees that do the pollen carrying must fly back and forth between the plants, and they won't if the distance is too great. If your neighbor has a pollinizing variety across the back fence you're in good shape. If not, do one of the following: 1. Plant two trees fairly close together; 2. Plant two to four trees of the same kind in a single planting hole; 3. Graft a branch of a variety with fertile pollen onto a tree that needs pollination.

Sometimes, even though a good pollinizer is close to the tree that needs it and blooms at the same time the bees are uncooperative and your crop is poor. If this happens, trick the bees by gathering a bouquet of flowers with fertile pollen and placing them in a vase of water in the branches of the second tree. Do it early in the morning when the bees are working hard and the temperatures are fairly low.

Common sense pruning

Don't expect to take this book out to your garden, stand in front of your unpruned fruit tree, and know exactly what cuts to make.

You have probably read several publications on pruning and have found that no sketch or photograph of a tree looks exactly like yours.

There is only one way to free yourself from pruning fear or frustration. Just do it!

You need only keep two objectives in mind:
  Cut to create a strong scaffold.
  Cut to admit light to leaves and fruit.

The leaves of the tree produce the sugars which are stored in the fruit. Leaves grow where they receive light.

A properly pruned tree will produce fruit throughout the tree—on low and interior branches. An unpruned tree produces fruit on the light-exposed branch tips.

Use the gentle approach. First cut off poorly placed or weak branches leaving the best ones to grow. If you make a mistake, it's normally self-correcting. The plant will send out new growth to replace what you remove.

So, if the tree needs shaping or reshaping, make the necessary cuts—without fear.

But you need guidelines to select a shape to aim for. We hope to give you the necessary guidelines in these pages. But, be flexible, there are many ways to reach the final objective—fruit.

Pruning and growth

Pruning has a direct effect on the growth of a plant. If you cut part of a bare branch in winter or early spring, the remaining piece will grow more vigorously, producing several shoots for every one you cut. On the other hand, if you cut leafy branches in late summer or fall, you weaken the plant (the missing leaves can't produce food for growth). New growth will follow, but it is less vigorous. In general then, winter pruning stimulates new growth, summer pruning controls a plant.

The illustrations below will help you to recognize the various parts of a plant so that you know what to look for when you go out with clippers and saw.

Buds
Look at a dormant plant in winter and you will see rows of buds on the branches, more numerous on small twigs than on old wood. Since the last bud on a branch tends to grow best, you can direct growth by finding a bud that points toward the area where you want a branch and cutting just above it.

Terminal Bud.
The fat bud at a branch tip will always grow first and fastest if you leave it. Cut it, and several buds will grow behind it.

Leaf Bud.
Flat triangle on the side of a branch. To make one grow, cut just above it. Choose buds pointing outward from the trunk so the growing branch will have space and light.

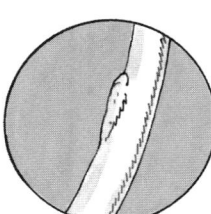

Spurs.
Twiglets on apples, pears, plums, apricots. They grow on older branches, produce fat flower buds, then fruit. Don't remove them.

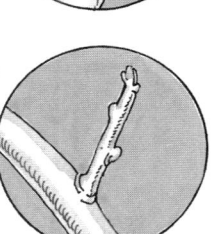

Flower Bud.
Plump compared to leaf buds and first to swell in spring. On stone fruits they grow alone or beside leaf buds. On apples and pears they grow *with* a few leaves.

Node
On a leafy branch, the point where stems are attached. Pull off a leaf with its stem, and just above the scar you can see a young bud hidden in the *axil*. Growth enzymes are concentrated there.

Leaf growing from a node.
In the angle of its stem is the axil. Cut above this node and a bud will sprout from the axil.

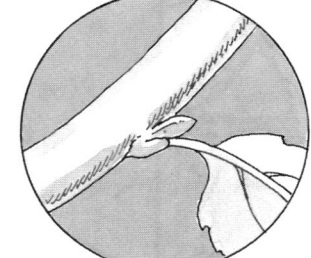

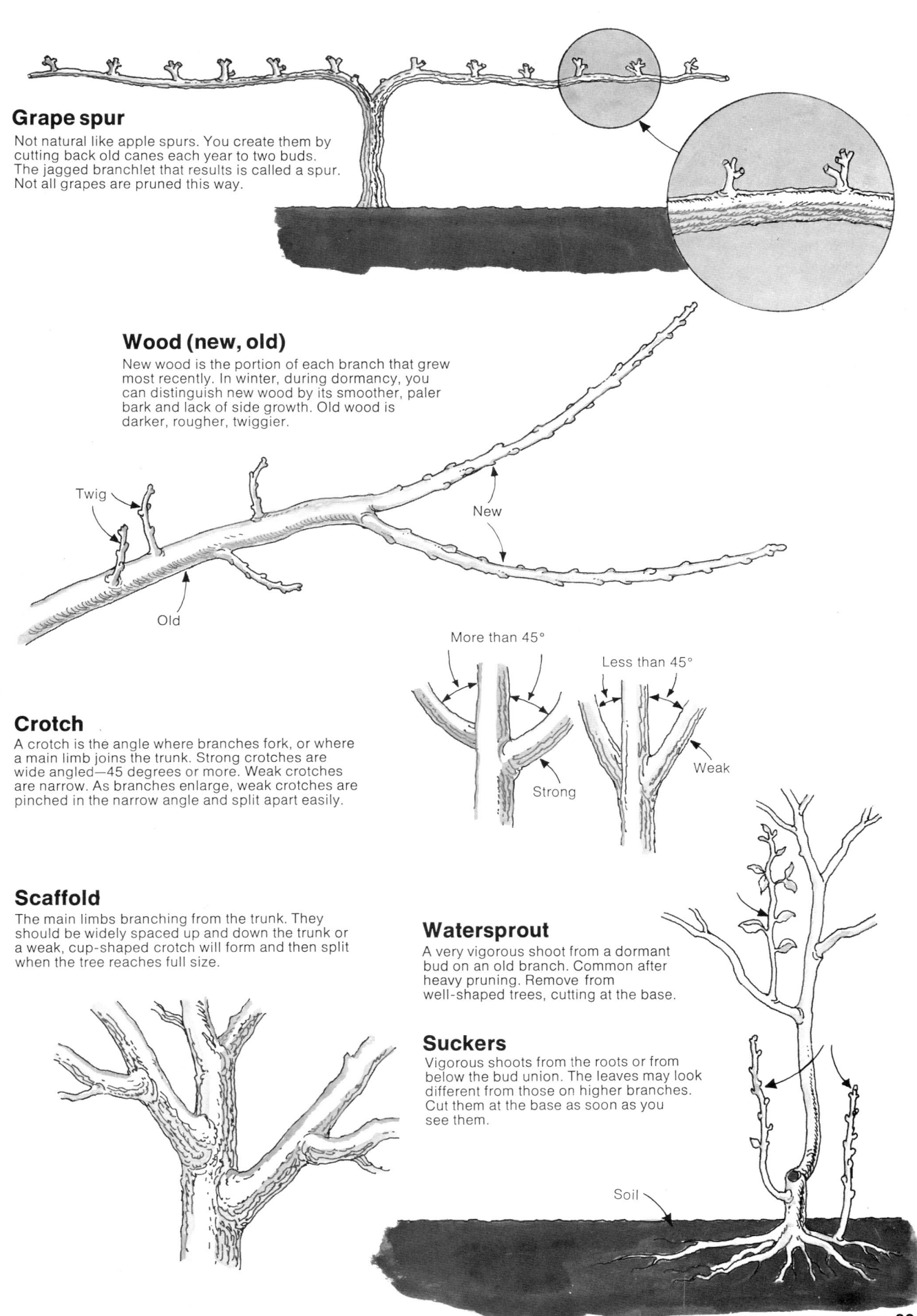

Grape spur
Not natural like apple spurs. You create them by cutting back old canes each year to two buds. The jagged branchlet that results is called a spur. Not all grapes are pruned this way.

Wood (new, old)
New wood is the portion of each branch that grew most recently. In winter, during dormancy, you can distinguish new wood by its smoother, paler bark and lack of side growth. Old wood is darker, rougher, twiggier.

Crotch
A crotch is the angle where branches fork, or where a main limb joins the trunk. Strong crotches are wide angled—45 degrees or more. Weak crotches are narrow. As branches enlarge, weak crotches are pinched in the narrow angle and split apart easily.

Scaffold
The main limbs branching from the trunk. They should be widely spaced up and down the trunk or a weak, cup-shaped crotch will form and then split when the tree reaches full size.

Watersprout
A very vigorous shoot from a dormant bud on an old branch. Common after heavy pruning. Remove from well-shaped trees, cutting at the base.

Suckers
Vigorous shoots from the roots or from below the bud union. The leaves may look different from those on higher branches. Cut them at the base as soon as you see them.

Pollination, pruning, and grafting

Making a cut

When you cut away parts of a plant, you leave a wound where pests or disease organisms can enter. To avoid trouble, try to make wounds as small as possible, and protect them until they heal if they are over a half inch in diameter.

The smallest possible wound is made when you remove a bud or twig. If a new sprout grows in toward the trunk, or threatens to tangle with another branch when it's longer, pinch it off right away and save pruning later. If you see the bud of a sucker down near the soil, rub it off with your thumb.

Make your cuts close to a node. The branches grow only at these nodes, and if you cut between them, the stub will die and rot. Cut at a slight angle so no straight shoulder is left to attract disease or burrowing pests.

Do major pruning in early spring, just as the buds swell. New growth will begin to heal the cuts immediately.

Angle your cut

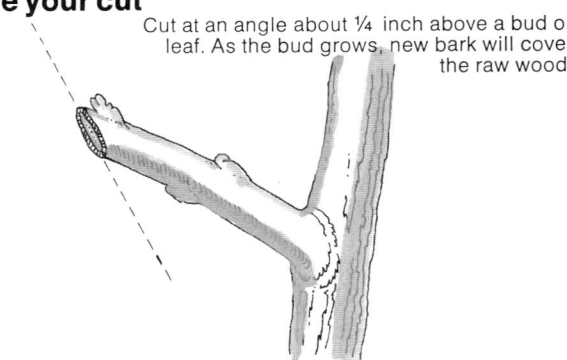

Cut at an angle about ¼ inch above a bud or leaf. As the bud grows, new bark will cover the raw wood.

Removing a stub

Never leave a projecting stub. It will rot and can damage the branch it is attached to. Cut stubs close to the trunk at a point where the wound will be about the same diameter as the branch you cut. Cutting *very* close leaves a larger wound.

Cutting a big limb

When you remove a big branch, first undercut at a short distance from the trunk (A). Then saw off the branch beyond the undercut (B). Finally, cut the stub close to the trunk (C). This technique will prevent a falling branch from tearing the bark. Paint the wound with a pruning compound.

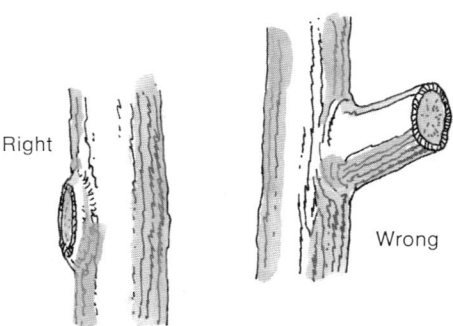

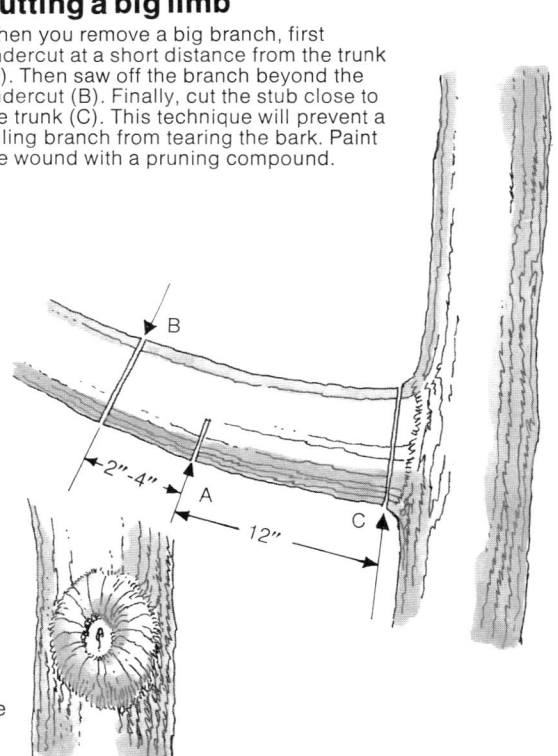

Well-healed cut

New tissue grows from the edge of a wound toward the center. If your cut was smooth, the scar will close evenly with a dimple in the very center.

Tools

Illustrated here are the main pruning tools: You should buy 1) quality shears, 2) a lopper for larger branches, 3) a saw for very large cuts. (Saws may be folding, straight, or with replaceable blades.), 4) a large rasp, 5) pole saw and pole pruner. Have shears and loppers sharpened every year, and never force them through too large a branch. You will also need pruning compound and pruning paint to protect fresh cuts.

You may find a large rasp handy for evening up rough edges and smoothing off shoulders. You can rent or buy pole saw and pole pruner for cutting high branches without climbing.

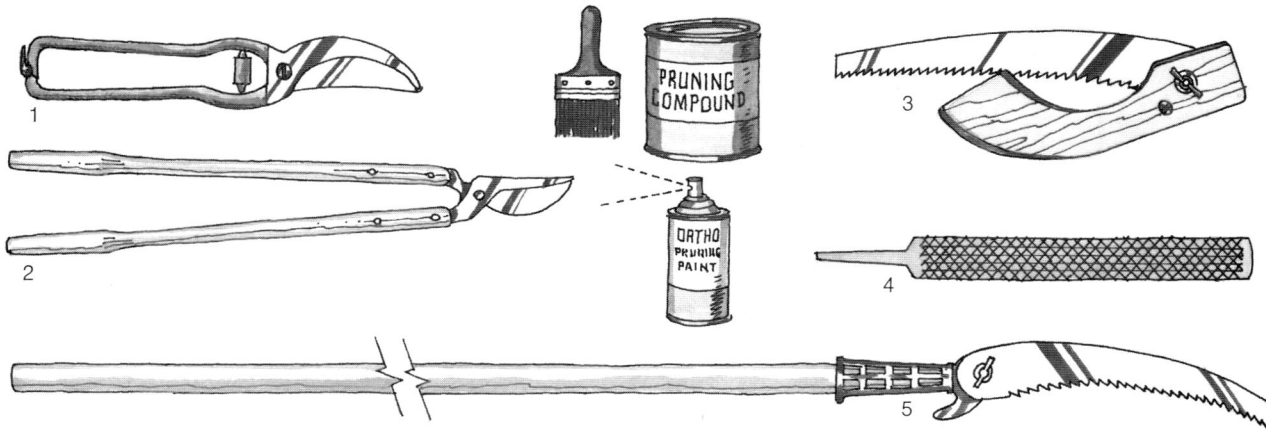

Starting right

When you first plant a young bareroot tree it will consist of a thin vertical shoot, called a whip, and possibly some twiggy side branches. You must cut it back immediately to balance the loss of root system cut away when the tree was uprooted—remaining roots cannot maintain the whole top. Then too, cutting forces more vigorous growth and you will have a better choice of branches the following winter when you choose your scaffold. Partial exceptions to the rule are certain espaliers (See page 85).

A young tree's calendar goes like this: First dormant season means the first winter after planting, about a year after you bought the tree. Second dormant season is the next winter, two years from purchase. In these first two dormant periods you will prune fairly heavily to establish a sturdy framework. It is best to prune as lightly as possible after that. The tree will grow faster and bear younger if you leave all but a few tangled twigs intact. Apples and pears will require the least pruning up to maturity, apricots and plums a little more, and peaches the most. When a tree reaches bearing age, pruning consists of maintaining the form you have already established.

Shaping young trees

From the first dormant season, you are aiming toward a mature tree of a certain shape. With fruit trees there are two possibilities, the vase shape and the central-leader shape. There are advantages to each, but the modern tendency is to vase pruning.

Vase Pruning. The mature tree will have a short trunk and then spread outward with three or four main limbs. These in turn will branch outward with five to seven secondary limbs. The center of the tree is open so that light penetrates and encourages fruit on the lower branches. This shape is always used with apricots, plums, and peaches, often used with pears and apples.

Central Leader. As the name implies, the mature tree will have a central trunk with a number of major limbs branching outward at various levels. The center of the tree is shaded and produces little or no fruit, and the tree will be tall and hard to prune. On the other hand, it tends to be very strong, holding the weight of a crop well and standing up to weather.

Central-leader pruning is still used for the smallest dwarf apples in a variation called the spindle bush. Since the tree is tiny, shade and pruning are not a problem. Another technique, called delayed-open-center, combines some of the strength of a central trunk with the sunny center of a vase shape. The trunk is allowed to grow vertically until it reaches 6 to 10 feet, then clipped to a side branch.

We recommend the vase shape and describe it below, but also include a description of spindle-bush training (page 92) for dwarf apples on Malling 9 rootstock.

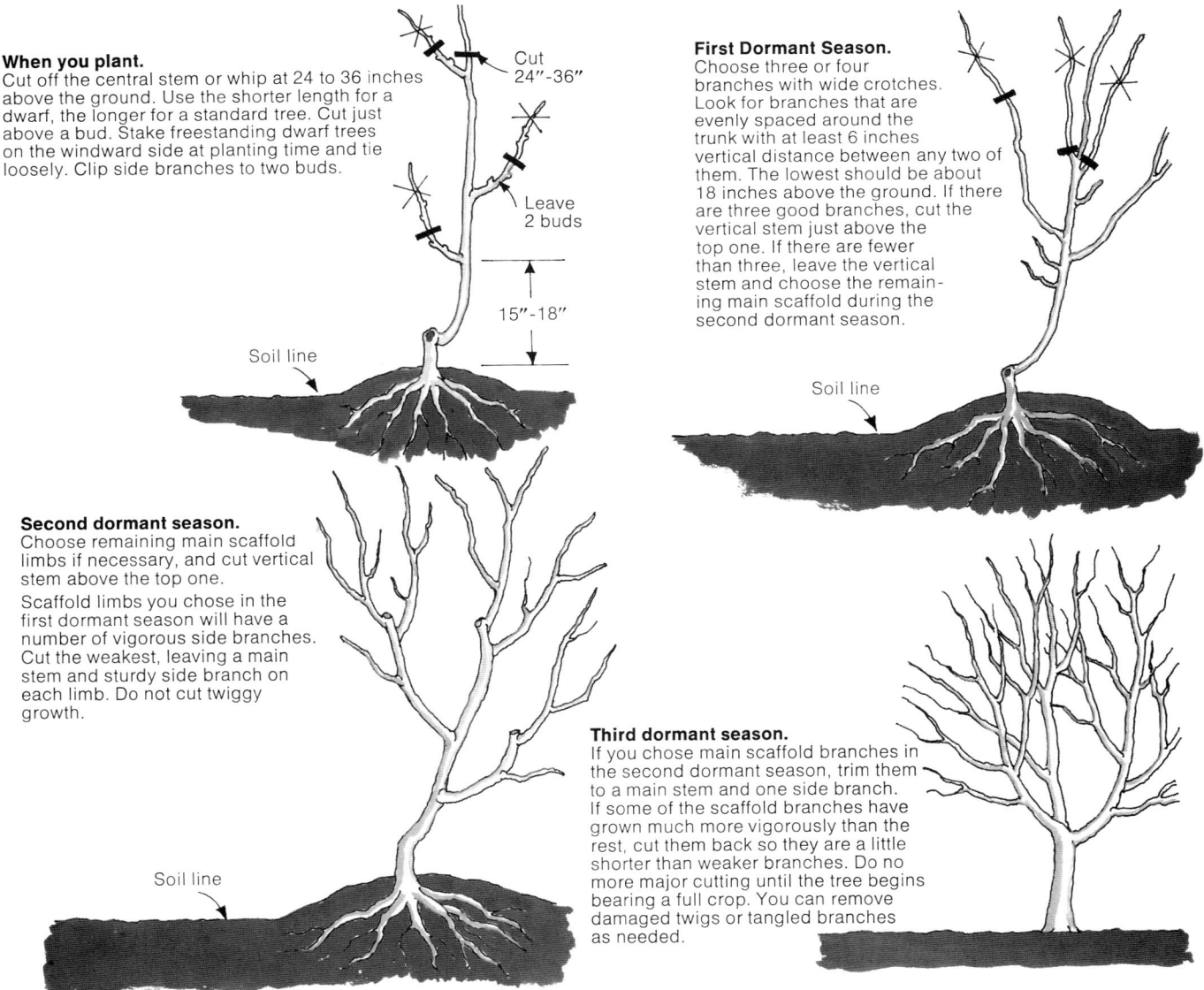

When you plant.
Cut off the central stem or whip at 24 to 36 inches above the ground. Use the shorter length for a dwarf, the longer for a standard tree. Cut just above a bud. Stake freestanding dwarf trees on the windward side at planting time and tie loosely. Clip side branches to two buds.

First Dormant Season.
Choose three or four branches with wide crotches. Look for branches that are evenly spaced around the trunk with at least 6 inches vertical distance between any two of them. The lowest should be about 18 inches above the ground. If there are three good branches, cut the vertical stem just above the top one. If there are fewer than three, leave the vertical stem and choose the remaining main scaffold during the second dormant season.

Second dormant season.
Choose remaining main scaffold limbs if necessary, and cut vertical stem above the top one.
Scaffold limbs you chose in the first dormant season will have a number of vigorous side branches. Cut the weakest, leaving a main stem and sturdy side branch on each limb. Do not cut twiggy growth.

Third dormant season.
If you chose main scaffold branches in the second dormant season, trim them to a main stem and one side branch. If some of the scaffold branches have grown much more vigorously than the rest, cut them back so they are a little shorter than weaker branches. Do no more major cutting until the tree begins bearing a full crop. You can remove damaged twigs or tangled branches as needed.

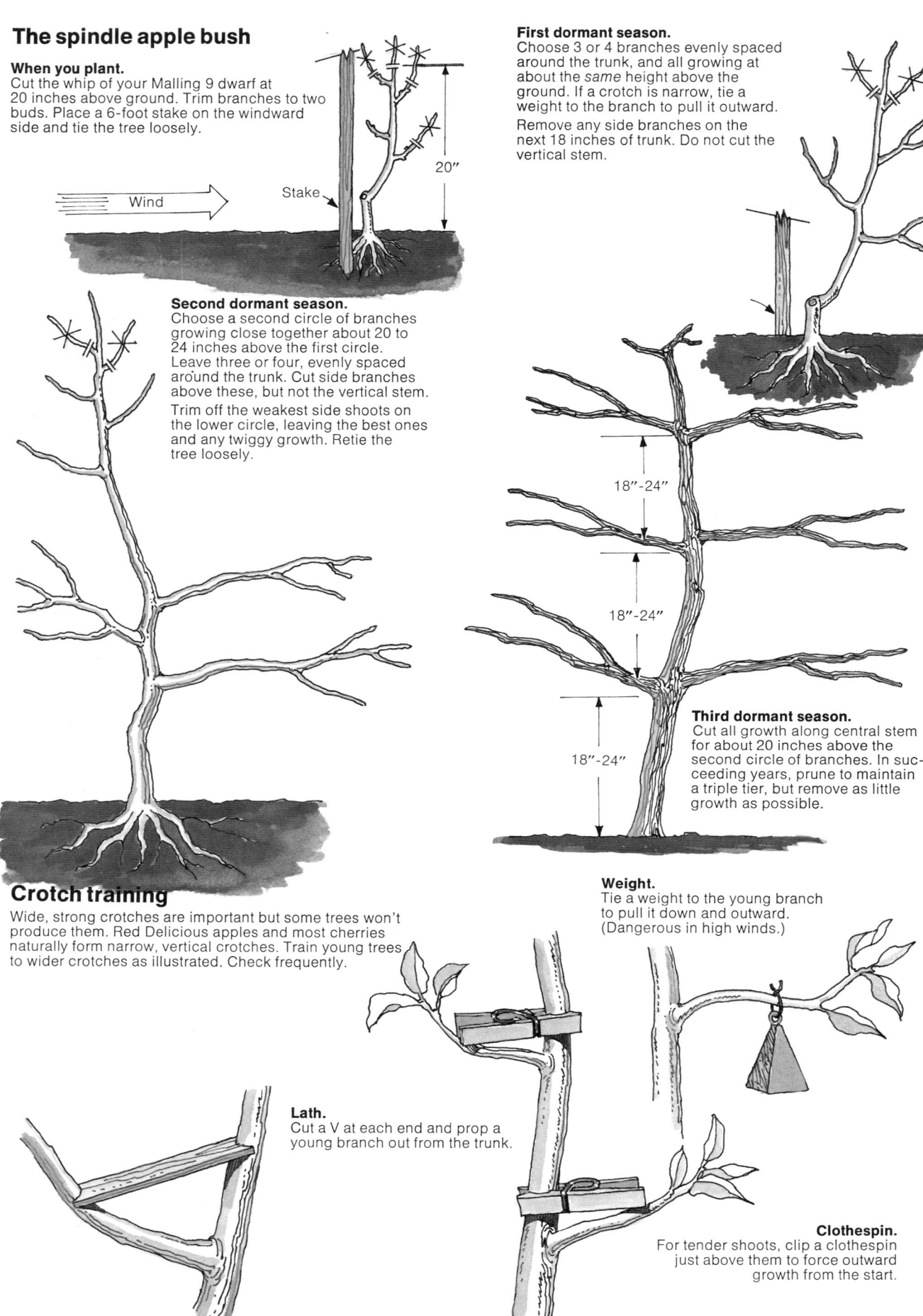

The spindle apple bush

When you plant.
Cut the whip of your Malling 9 dwarf at 20 inches above ground. Trim branches to two buds. Place a 6-foot stake on the windward side and tie the tree loosely.

First dormant season.
Choose 3 or 4 branches evenly spaced around the trunk, and all growing at about the *same* height above the ground. If a crotch is narrow, tie a weight to the branch to pull it outward.
Remove any side branches on the next 18 inches of trunk. Do not cut the vertical stem.

Second dormant season.
Choose a second circle of branches growing close together about 20 to 24 inches above the first circle. Leave three or four, evenly spaced around the trunk. Cut side branches above these, but not the vertical stem.
Trim off the weakest side shoots on the lower circle, leaving the best ones and any twiggy growth. Retie the tree loosely.

Third dormant season.
Cut all growth along central stem for about 20 inches above the second circle of branches. In succeeding years, prune to maintain a triple tier, but remove as little growth as possible.

Crotch training

Wide, strong crotches are important but some trees won't produce them. Red Delicious apples and most cherries naturally form narrow, vertical crotches. Train young trees to wider crotches as illustrated. Check frequently.

Weight.
Tie a weight to the young branch to pull it down and outward. (Dangerous in high winds.)

Lath.
Cut a V at each end and prop a young branch out from the trunk.

Clothespin.
For tender shoots, clip a clothespin just above them to force outward growth from the start.

Each fruit is different

Although early training of fruit trees is similar, the growth habit of each kind is different. Apples and pears grow relatively slowly and produce fruit on short spurs along the old branches. The spurs produce for as long as 10 years. Spur-type apples and pears sprout more productive spurs per foot of branch and grow more slowly than ordinary trees.

Cherries produce fruit on spurs, but their main branches may shoot up into long poles. These can be headed back in the first years to encourage branching. Otherwise, cherries need less pruning than other fruit.

Apricots, plums, and prune-type plums grow spurs, but also send out vigorous new shoots at branch tips and need heading and thinning.

Peaches and nectarines produce fruit on new wood of the previous season. They need severe pruning to force new wood.

Remember that . . .

Any heavily pruned tree sends out lots of new growth in spring. If a tree bears on older wood, you will cut back fruit production by heavy pruning. If it bears on new wood, you will stimulate production in the season after the *following winter*.

Pruning always removes *some* fruiting wood. An unpruned tree may bear too heavily, producing small fruit and next to no new growth. Pruning evens the crops over many seasons.

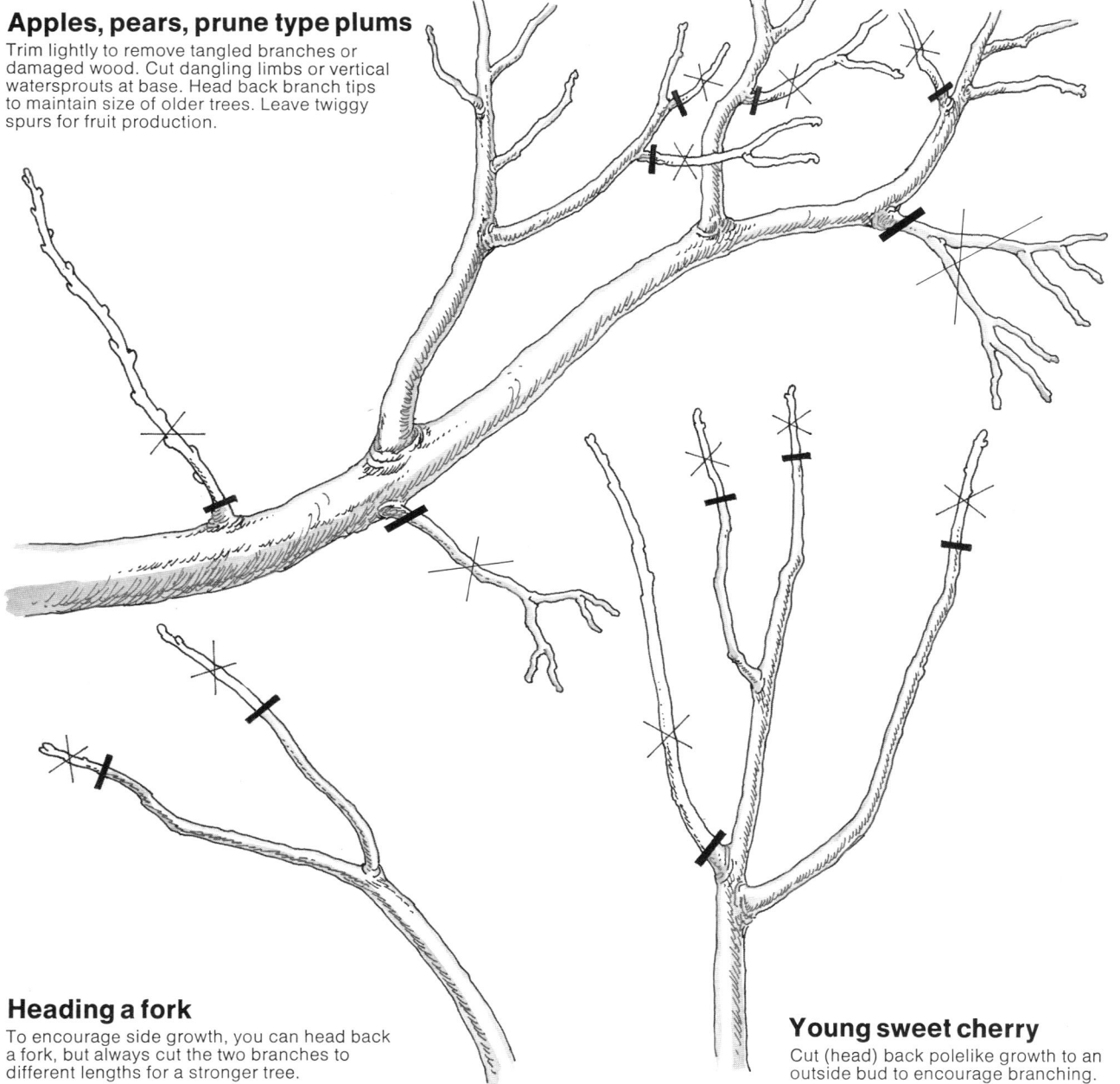

Apples, pears, prune type plums
Trim lightly to remove tangled branches or damaged wood. Cut dangling limbs or vertical watersprouts at base. Head back branch tips to maintain size of older trees. Leave twiggy spurs for fruit production.

Heading a fork
To encourage side growth, you can head back a fork, but always cut the two branches to different lengths for a stronger tree.

Young sweet cherry
Cut (head) back polelike growth to an outside bud to encourage branching.

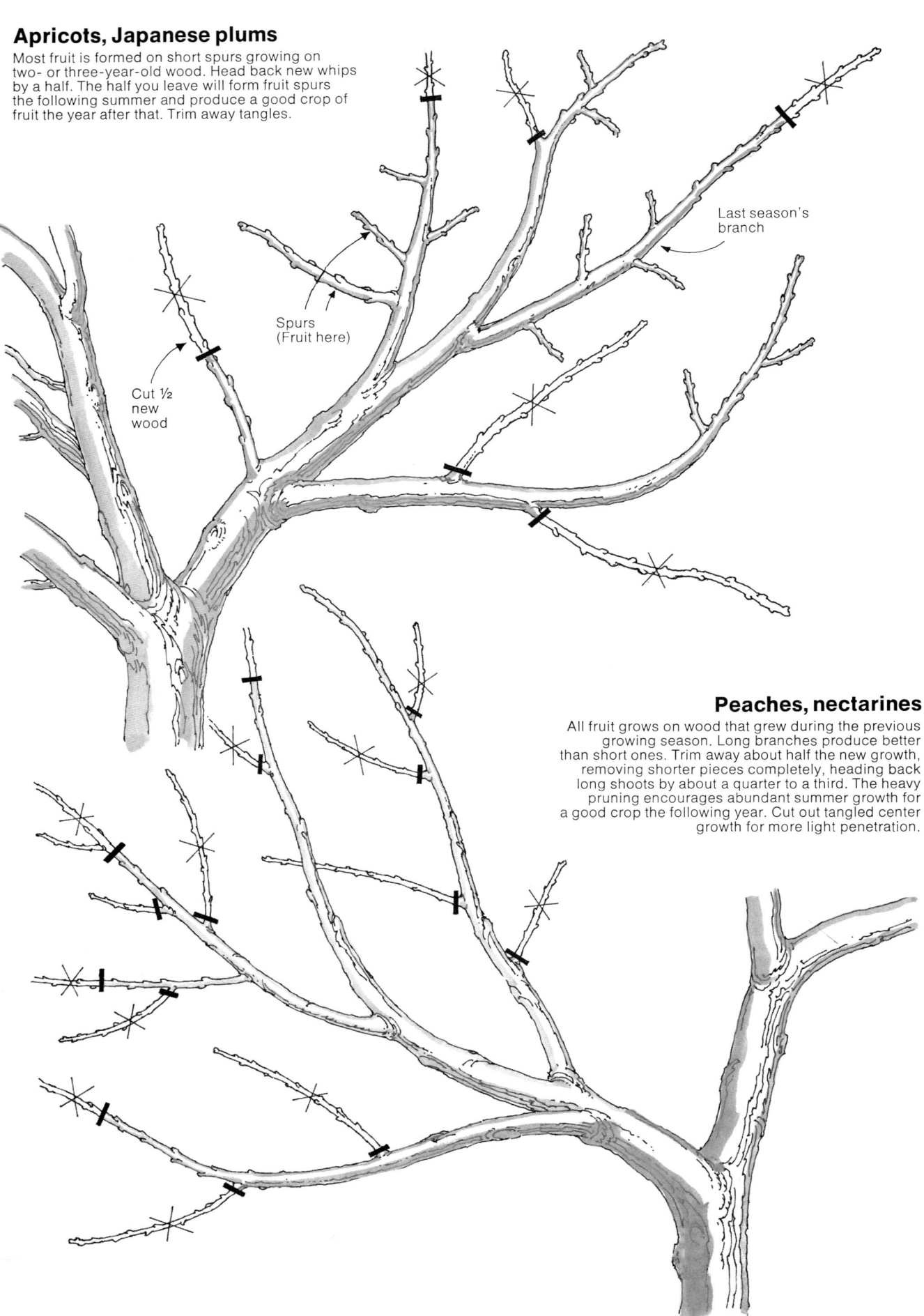

Apricots, Japanese plums
Most fruit is formed on short spurs growing on two- or three-year-old wood. Head back new whips by a half. The half you leave will form fruit spurs the following summer and produce a good crop of fruit the year after that. Trim away tangles.

Last season's branch

Spurs (Fruit here)

Cut ½ new wood

Peaches, nectarines
All fruit grows on wood that grew during the previous growing season. Long branches produce better than short ones. Trim away about half the new growth, removing shorter pieces completely, heading back long shoots by about a quarter to a third. The heavy pruning encourages abundant summer growth for a good crop the following year. Cut out tangled center growth for more light penetration.

Grapes—what kind do you have?

All grapes require heavy pruning to produce fruit, but different kinds need different pruning. Wine grapes and muscadines will usually need spur pruning in which all side branches of a mature plant are cut to two buds in fall or winter. Two new shoots grow on the spur you leave, and each produces a cluster or bunch of fruit.

Some grapes do not produce fruit on shoots that grow too near the main scaffold. Thompson Seedless and many American grapes such as Concord are among these. For these grapes you must cane-prune. Instead of cutting to a short spur in winter, leave two whole canes from the previous growing season. When fruit forms from side growth along this cane, clip the cane off beyond the next set of leaves. At the same time, you encourage two new canes that will bear fruit the following year.

Both spurs and canes grow from a permanent trunk or trunk plus arms that you train on a trellis or arbor.

The variety list from page 68 on indicates whether you should practice spur or cane pruning on a listed variety. In general, all muscadines need spur pruning. Americans of the Concord or "foxy" group take cane pruning. Grapes of the wine-producing sort usually will take spur pruning. For any grape not listed, inquire at your Cooperative Extension Office, or experiment by cane-pruning a portion of a mature vine, spur-pruning another portion.

When you plant.
Plant a rooted cutting with two or three buds above the soil, then bury those in light mulch. Grapes root deep, need good soil.

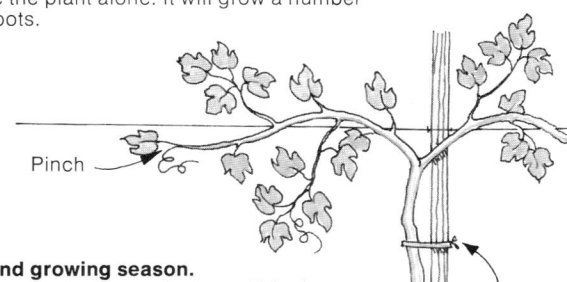

First growing season.
Leave the plant alone. It will grow a number of shoots.

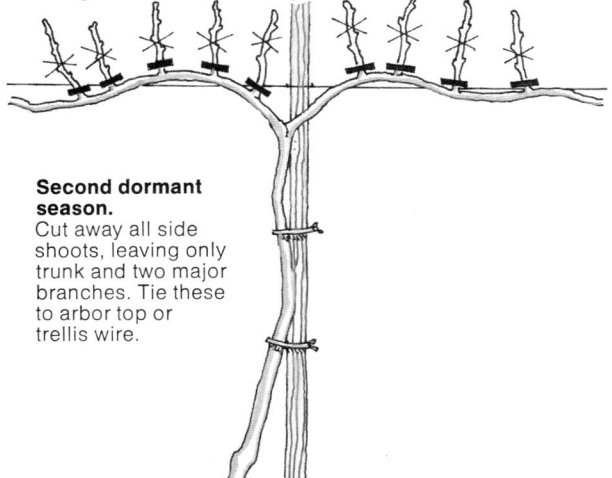

First dormant season.
Choose the best shoot and cut others to the base. Head remaining shoot to 3 or 4 strong buds.

Second dormant season.
Cut away all side shoots, leaving only trunk and two major branches. Tie these to arbor top or trellis wire.

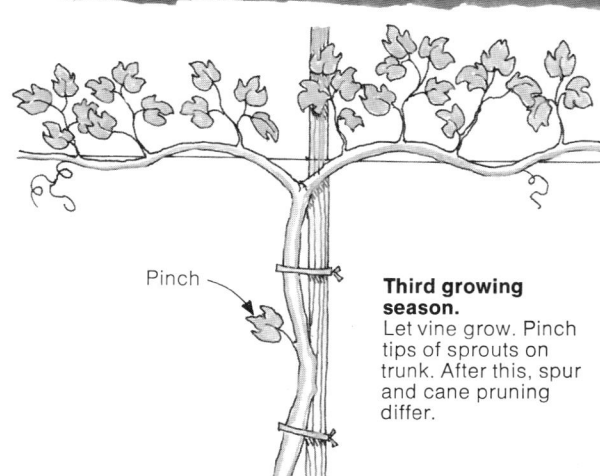

Second growing season.
When new shoots reach about 12 inches long, select the most vigorous and pinch off others at the trunk. Tie remaining shoot to a support (arbor post, trellis post). When the shoot reaches branching point at arbor top or trellis wire, pinch it to force branching. Let two strong branches grow, pinch any others at 8 to 10 inches long.

Third growing season.
Let vine grow. Pinch tips of sprouts on trunk. After this, spur and cane pruning differ.

Pollination, pruning, and grafting

Shapes for vines

You have a choice of arbor training, cordon training, head training, or trellised canes. An arbor is an overhead frame on posts at least seven feet tall.

The overhead portion should be at least eight to ten feet on a side. Train a vine up each vertical post with two branches crossing the top horizontally. It may take more than two seasons to reach the top and begin training the horizontals.

A cordon is a horizontal permanent branch on a wall or trellis. Train each vine to either two or four cordons. For four, allow three shoots to grow during the second growing season. Train two of the shoots horizontally, tie the other vertically until it reaches the upper support then pinch and select two horizontals.

A head-trained vine is free-standing but may not give you much fruit. This method is attractive and you can use it for spur or cane grapes. Stake the young trunk and allow up to four shoots to grow, beginning about 24 inches above the ground or higher. To spur-prune, cut each shoot to two buds in winter each year. To cane-prune, gather the fruiting canes upward and tie them together toward the tip. Let growth from renewal buds trail.

Trellised canes are grown on wire like a four-arm cordon, but the permanent wood is confined to short stubs near the trunk and the fruiting canes are tied to the wire.

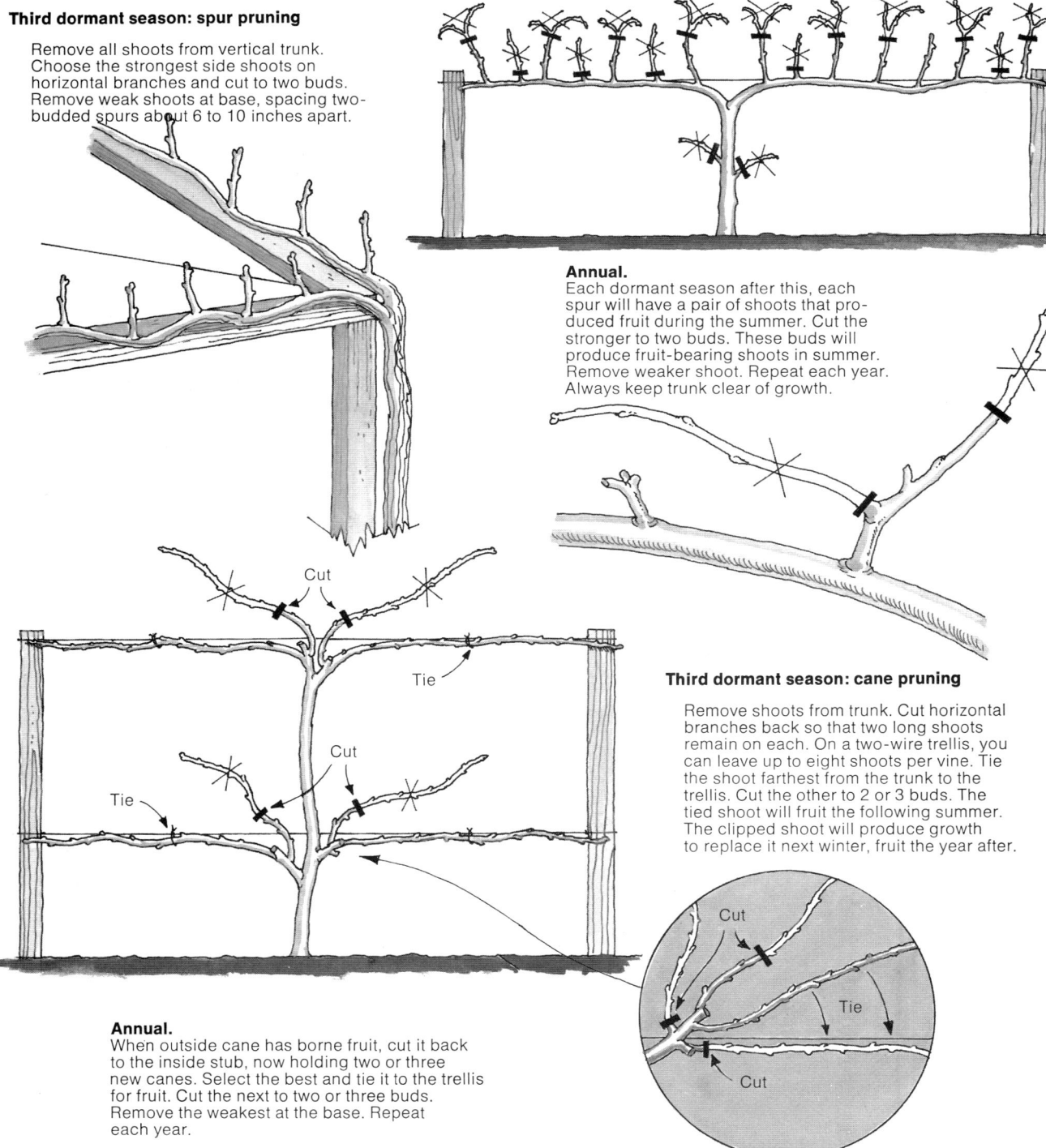

Third dormant season: spur pruning

Remove all shoots from vertical trunk. Choose the strongest side shoots on horizontal branches and cut to two buds. Remove weak shoots at base, spacing two-budded spurs about 6 to 10 inches apart.

Annual.
Each dormant season after this, each spur will have a pair of shoots that produced fruit during the summer. Cut the stronger to two buds. These buds will produce fruit-bearing shoots in summer. Remove weaker shoot. Repeat each year. Always keep trunk clear of growth.

Third dormant season: cane pruning

Remove shoots from trunk. Cut horizontal branches back so that two long shoots remain on each. On a two-wire trellis, you can leave up to eight shoots per vine. Tie the shoot farthest from the trunk to the trellis. Cut the other to 2 or 3 buds. The tied shoot will fruit the following summer. The clipped shoot will produce growth to replace it next winter, fruit the year after.

Annual.
When outside cane has borne fruit, cut it back to the inside stub, now holding two or three new canes. Select the best and tie it to the trellis for fruit. Cut the next to two or three buds. Remove the weakest at the base. Repeat each year.

Cane berries and bush berries

All cane berries fall into two groups: those with rigid canes that grow upright, and those with trailing canes that tend to creep. Both types produce fruit on canes that sprouted the previous year. Cut these canes to the ground as soon as you have harvested the crop. Leave about eight of the best new canes, cutting the rest. Everbearing raspberries differ slightly in that a light crop forms at the top of new canes in fall. Cut only the portion that fruits. The lower portion will bear the following year.

Rigid-caned berries. (Blackberry, blackcap raspberry, purple raspberry.) Cut old canes after fruit harvest. Pinch young blackberry canes when they reach 36 inches; pinch blackcaps and purple raspberries at 24 to 30 inches. Pinched canes will send out lateral growth. In winter, cut blackberry laterals to 15 to 18 inches, raspberries to 10 to 12 inches. Paint the bases white to distinguish them from summer growth. If you wish, tie the erect canes to a single wire, stretched at 18 inches above ground.

Trailing Raspberries. For single-crop berries, cut canes as soon as harvest is over. Train new canes to a post, vertical wire, or to horizontal supports. In summer, as new canes grow, gather them in bunches, tie very loosely, and lay them along the ground until time for training.

For everbearing raspberries, cut canes that fruit early in the season and train young canes. These will fruit at the top in fall. Cut the fruiting portion after harvest but leave the rest.

Trailing blackberries (dewberries). You can treat blackberries like raspberries, although canes are longer and more vigorous. Or try this method: stretch a wire 36 inches above the row of berry plants. After harvest, remove old canes and cut new ones off at 48 inches. Canes that sprawl left are then pulled back to the right side of the wire. Canes that grow right are pulled to the left side. Tie if necessary. Extremely long laterals will grow outward, knitting together. Train them as needed along the wire.

Shrubby fruit plants

The shrubby fruit plants such as currants, gooseberries, and blueberries tend to bear very heavily if left completely unpruned. You can clean them up by removing the oldest shoots, those three and four years old, in winter, and thinning out the worst tangles among the twigs. You need not be too conscientious. If berries are very small one year, thin the following winter. If they are large, skip the thinning.

If you grow elderberries, mahonia, or other berry plants, the same rules apply. Thin tangles if they're bad, and remove the oldest growth if the plant needs thinning.

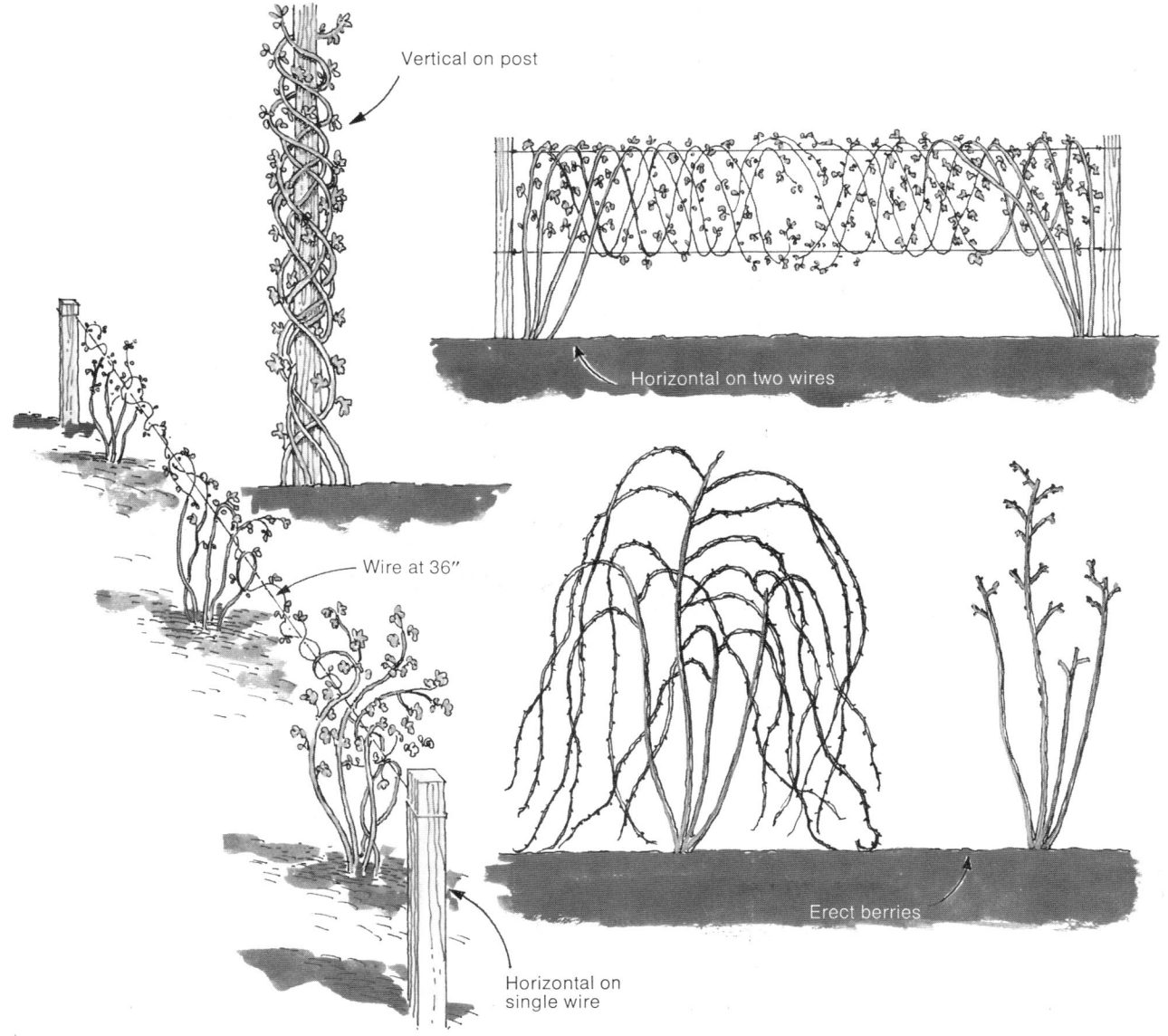

Vertical on post

Horizontal on two wires

Wire at 36″

Erect berries

Horizontal on single wire

Pollination, pruning, and grafting

Grafting is easy

Grafting lets you take full advantage of limited garden space. A grafted tree can bear up to four or five varieties of fruit, and pollination is much improved when a pollinizing branch grows on the same tree with a variety that needs its pollen.

You can, of course, plant up to four young trees in the same hole with the same space-saving advantages of a grafted plant, but if you inherit a full-grown tree this technique won't do, while grafting is still possible.

Nurseries occasionally sell trees that already bear a number of varieties, but they are likely to be very expensive, and the mixture may not be what you would choose for yourself. Fortunately, grafting is not much more difficult than rooting a cutting, and some methods do next to no damage to the tree even if you fail the first time.

Grafting terms

Understanding terms is important to any skill, and especially important to grafting. The four basic terms involved are *cambium, scion* (SIGH-un), *stock,* and *callus.*

Cambium. This is the growing layer of most garden plants, lying between the bark and the woody portion of a trunk or stem. When you graft a new branch to an old plant the cambium layers of the two pieces must touch.

Scion. This is the new shoot or branchlet that you will attach to an existing plant.

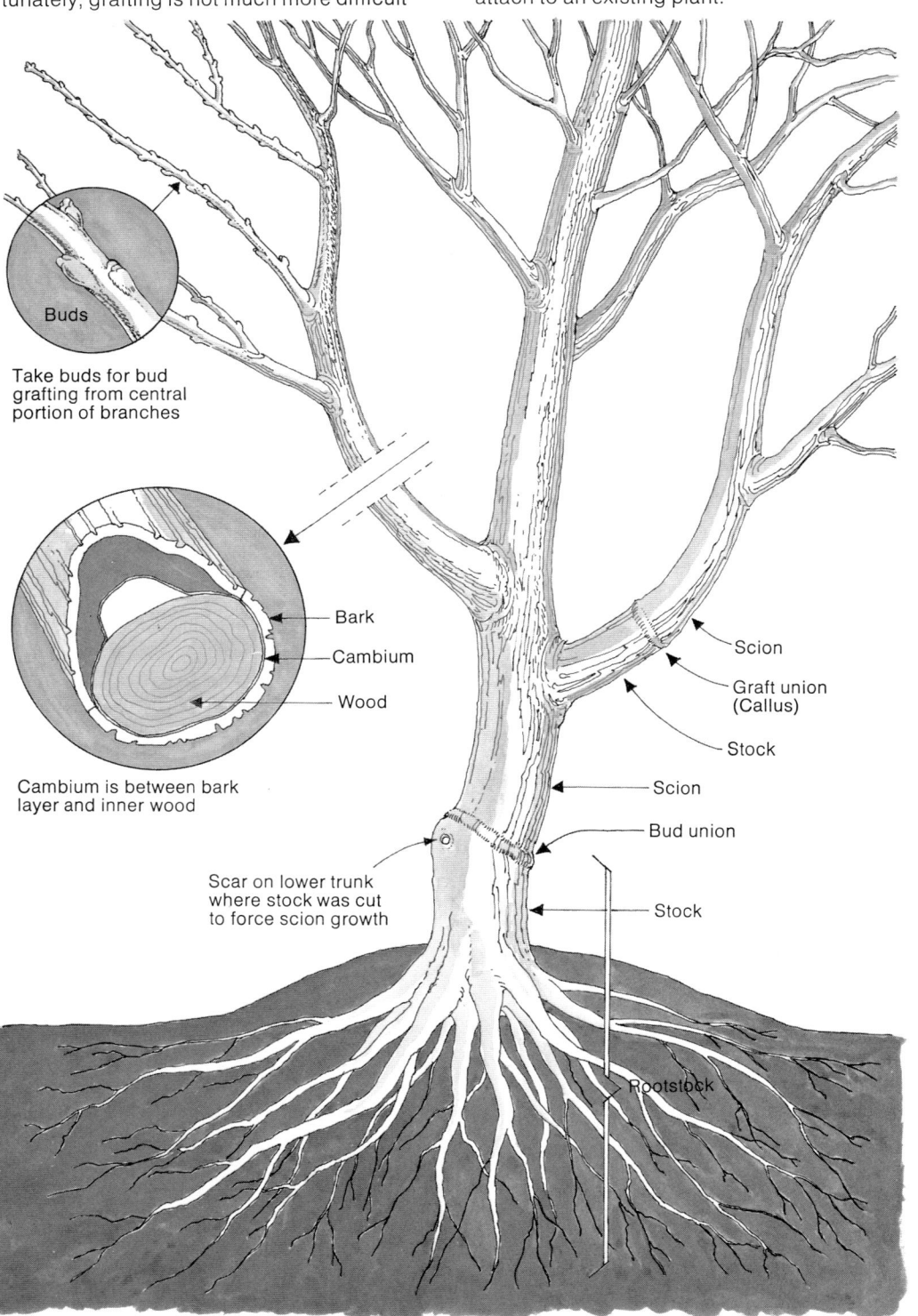

Take buds for bud grafting from central portion of branches

Cambium is between bark layer and inner wood

Scar on lower trunk where stock was cut to force scion growth

Bark
Cambium
Wood

Scion
Graft union (Callus)
Stock
Scion
Bud union
Stock
Rootstock

Pollination, pruning, and grafting

Stock. The stock, or rootstock, is the existing plant to which you attach a scion. Scion and stock must usually be closely related, for example pear on pear or apple on apple, but this is not invariably true. (See "Grafts you can Try" following.)

Callus. Both scion and stock grow a mass of special cells as they join together. It is these new cells, called *callus,* that form the actual joint. Callus cells grow best at temperatures above 55 degrees Fahrenheit, and when the plants are active, so grafting is usually done when spring growth is beginning. A special form of grafting called *budding* is possible in summer or fall.

Why graft?

Tree fruits do not, as a general rule, reproduce themselves from seed. Seedlings bear fruit that is different and usually inferior. The only way to grow a new Golden Delicious or Winesap is to graft a piece of the tree to an apple rootstock. Young nursery trees show the graft as a kind of lump on the lower trunk called the bud union.

Grafting can increase the number of varieties you grow at home. If you have space for only one apple tree, you can graft new varieties onto some of its branches. If you do this kind of grafting, match the growth habits of stock and scion. A very vigorous apple branch grafted to a slow-growing spur-type tree may take over and shade out the other branches.

You can also use grafting to correct mistakes. Perhaps you inherit a fruit tree that does poorly in your area for some reason. Instead of replanting, graft on a better fruit. You'll have a crop much sooner than by starting over. Or perhaps your garden tree won't bear because it needs a pollinizer. Graft in a branch of the proper variety and you'll have a good crop and two kinds of fruit.

Nurserymen use grafting to produce trees of smaller-than-normal size. Special roots that slow growth are grafted to desirable varieties of apples, pears, and other fruit, and the resulting trees stay small. You may want to try your hand at this form of grafting in order to save space. The easiest way is to buy a dwarf or semidwarf tree and add varieties of similar growth habit, but you can also propagate new rootstocks from suckers. We discuss dwarfing rootstocks below.

What equipment do you need?

There is much special grafting equipment available, but a home gardener can make do with a sharp pocket knife, a good pair of pruning shears, a roll of plastic electrician's tape (the kind that stretches), and a can of water-base asphalt tree sealer. You may want to add a small cleaver, a hammer and nails, and a pruning saw for grafting larger limbs.

Grafts you can try

Usually you are safe in grafting any apple variety onto an apple stock, or any other fruit onto a tree that bears the same kind of fruit. There are odd exceptions. Peach scions, for example, often join better on almond stock than onto peach stock, and any stone fruit like the peach, plum, or apricot is a bit trickier than the pome fruits such as apples and pears. For any graft, be sure the scion is pointed in the *right direction.* Notice the position of the buds when you cut your scions, and position the graft so that they point the same way, away from the trunk.

Graft combinations above right are listed by stocks with scions following. Those with an asterisk (*) make a weak union that may break or die after a time (possibly several years).

ALMOND: any almond; peach; nectarine

APPLE: any apple (but not vigorous and slow varieties together).

APRICOT: any apricot; peach*; plum; nectarine*

CHERRY, sour; any cherry, sweet or sour

CHERRY, sweet; any cherry

ORANGE: any orange; grapefruit; lemon

PEACH: any peach or nectarine; almond; apricot; plum

PEAR: any pear

PLUM, European: any European plum; almond; apricot; peach*; nectarine; Japanese plum

PLUM, Japanese: any Japanese plum; European plum*; apricot; peach*; nectarine

QUINCE: any quince (*Cydonia*); pear (not Bartlett)

Dwarfing rootstocks

Fruit varieties grafted onto certain rootstocks are dwarfed to a certain extent. Apples are usually dwarfed on the Malling and Malling-Merton series of rootstocks, each of which gives a mature tree of a different size. See the illustration on page 13 for comparative sizes of mature apple trees on these numbered roots.

Apricots are dwarfed to some extent when grafted onto the Western sand cherry, *Prunus besseyi.*

Sweet cherries are slightly dwarfed on roots of 'Stockton Morello' sour cherry.

Many citrus varieties are dwarfed on roots of the trifoliate orange.

Peaches are somewhat dwarfed on Nanking cherry roots.

Pears are dwarfed on quince roots, but since some varieties of pear will not form a union with quince, a double graft is often necessary, with quince at the root, a trunk section or interstock of Old Home or Hardy pear, and a top of the desired fruiting variety. Quince is an unsatisfactory rootstock in cold climates.

Plums are somewhat dwarfed on Western sand cherry roots.

Quince and sour cherry are not normally dwarfed by grafting.

Where to look for scionwood

An obvious source of scions for grafting is a neighbor's or friend's tree, but any nursery in bareroot season will have a large supply of scions, since the young trees must be cut back for planting. To obtain scions of old varieties, refer to sources in the "Old Apples" section beginning on page 28. Hold any scionwood in moist, cold surroundings until grafting season. A crisper in the refrigerator is a good place for scions. In cold climates, scions may be cut before the ground freezes and then bundled and buried below freezing level. The hole must be well drained and each variety should have a label so you won't confuse them.

Most scions should be cut in late fall or winter, but budsticks are also cut in spring and summer. See the pages on grafting methods for more detail.

T-budding

Use the budding method on stock branches from pencil size to 1 inch across. You have a choice of seasons: a. in spring at the first signs of stock growth (use dormant scions from storage); b. in May or early June when the new growth has mature leaves; c. in summer, from July through September, if bark is still loose on stock branches.

You can bud only when the bark of stock plants "slips," that is, when it detaches easily from the wood beneath. This happens during periods of active growth. Check the bark before beginning by making the T-shaped cut described below. If the bark sticks or breaks in spring, wait a while. If bark sticks in later summer, water thoroughly and wait a week.

Cut budsticks for early spring budding in winter and store them in a moist, cold place. Cut budsticks for May and June, or for summer just before you need them. Since they will have mature leaves you must cut these off, but leave the stems attached. They can serve as handles when you slice off individual buds. (The buds on new wood are just above the leaf stems.)

Use leaf buds and not flower buds in budding.

Normally, leaf buds are small, flat, and pointed, while flower buds are more rounded and protruding. If you are not sure, compare all the branches from which you intend cutting budsticks, and choose the smallest, flattest buds. If you find that you have made a mistake in early spring, you can try again in May or in summer.

Buds inserted in the spring months will grow during the same season. Check them three weeks after budding, and if they look healthy or show signs of expanding, cut the stock branch off above the next leaf or shoot. Cut this short piece when bud is well grown. Again, if you're not sure, wait a week or two. Buds inserted in summer will not grow until the following spring. Do not cut the stock away until growing season begins. You can be fairly sure that the bud will grow if the bit of stem you leave drops away, leaving a healthy-looking bud. If the stem shrivels without dropping and the bud turns black you have failed. Try again if the bark is still slipping.

Step 1
With a sharp knife, make a cut about 1½ inches long down the middle of a smooth stock branch. Cut through bark to wood. Cut across to form a T; pry up a corner. If bark is not loose, water and wait, or try again the following spring.

Step 2
Cut a pencil-sized branch or budstick. Snip leaves, if present, leaving stems. Cut off immature wood at branch tips. Avoid large, rounded buds. They may be flower buds.

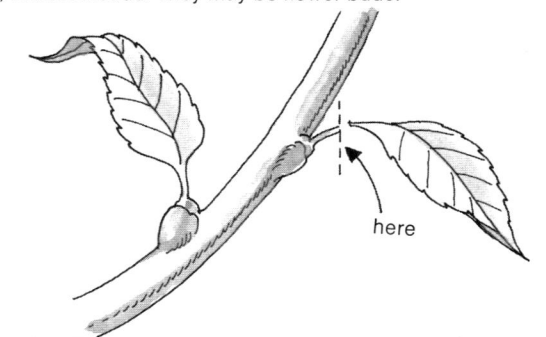

Step 3
With very sharp knife, slice upward from ¾ inch below bud to 1 inch above. Take a sliver of wood with the bud. Back of bud should be flat.

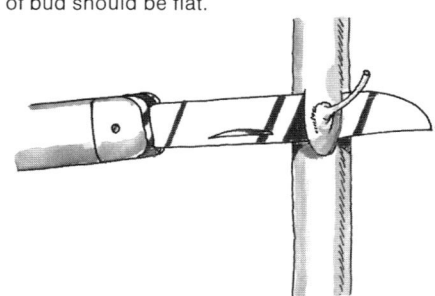

Step 4
Cut across the top of bud sliver (shield) about ¾ inch above the bud. Lift it off without touching raw cut. Use knife blade or stem segment to handle.

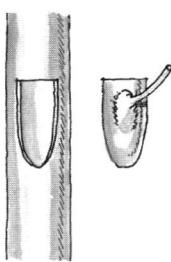

Step 5
Slide bud shield into T-cut, using point of knife below bud to push it down. Straight top of shield should match top of T-cut on stock. Wrap with a length of flat rubber band, winding end into first loop. Finish tie by inserting end in last turn.

Step 6
If bud joins to stock, remove rubber and cut stock in 6 to 8 weeks for early-season budding, or wait until following spring for summer budding.

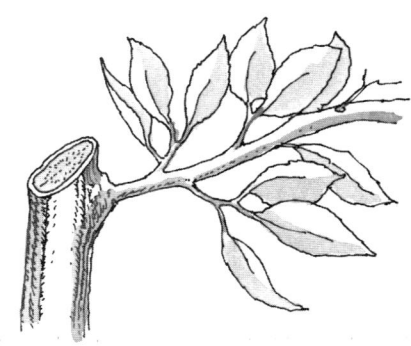

Whip graft

The whip graft is easy for a beginner, and can be used either to graft a desired variety to a young rootstock or to add varieties to upper branches of a young tree. Use it to join branches from ¼ to ½ inch in diameter.

Whip grafts should be made in very early spring, either at the earliest signs of stock growth, or just before growth begins. The bark need not slip. Scion wood can be cut in late fall and winter and stored, or cut when you graft.

The technique described below is the standard method, used for grafting branches, or for grafting a section of root to a scion for a new plant. There are variations that also work well if you are careful.

For topworking new varieties into a young tree, you can make only the sloping cut omitting the reverse cut in drawing 3 below.

For grafting a small scion to a larger stock, you can match the cambium on one side of the stock only, leaving part of the cut on the stock uncovered.

Do not graft a large scion to a smaller stock. It is likely to dry out and die and, if it grows, the callus tissue will be excessive, forming a large knot at the joint.

Scions should be 2 or 3 buds long for whip grafting, but if a longer piece is easier to handle, clip it once the graft is tied, then wax the end cut.

You will know that the graft is successful if the scion grows.

Plastic stretch tape may be left in place through the first growing season. Ties that will not stretch must be carefully cut once growth is well started. It is a good idea to apply a tree seal or pruning paint to the graft area after tape is removed. This gives protection from the sun and other elements.

Step 1
Compare scion and stock. Scion should be of same diameter as stock or somewhat smaller. Find a section of each that is free of buds.

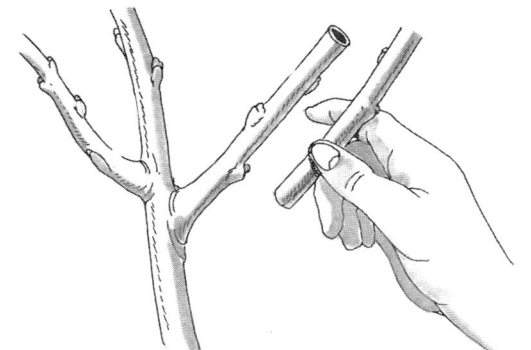

Step 2
With a very sharp knife, make a smooth, sloping cut on stock and scion from 1 to 2½ inches long. A wavy cut will join poorly or fail to join.

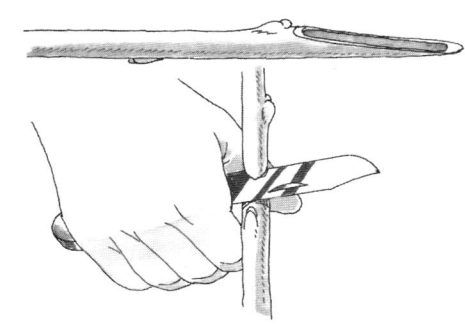

Step 3
Make reverse cuts on both scion and stock, beginning about a third of the way from tip. (It is possible to skip this step if you join cambium carefully.)

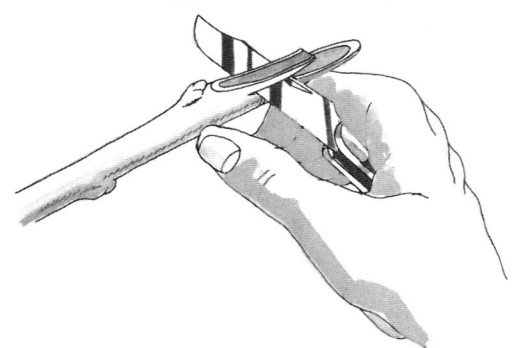

Step 4
Slide scion and stock together so that cambium is carefully matched on at least one side of stock. Stock can be slightly wider than scion.

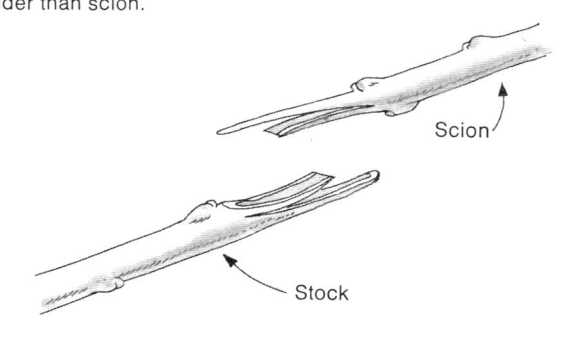

Step 5
Bind with plastic stretch tape or with budding rubbers or raffia. Cover entire length of cut and wax. Snip all but 3 buds.

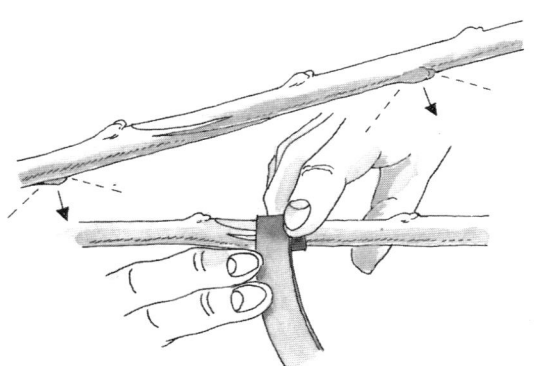

Step 6
When growth begins, cut nonstretch ties such as raffia. Stretch tape may be left until following season.

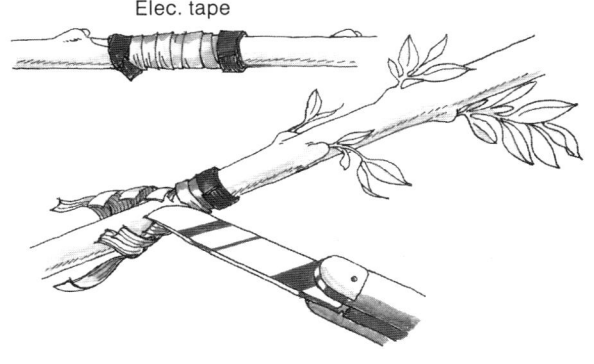

Pollination, pruning, and grafting

Cleft graft

Cleft grafts can be made on stocks from 1 to 4 inches in diameter. The scions used are much smaller, approximately pencil-sized. The season for cleft grafting is very early spring when buds first begin to swell, although it is possible to graft during winter if it is more convenient. The bark should not yet be slipping or it may come loose when the stock is split.

The season for cleft grafting will vary, depending on the kind of tree to be grafted. Almonds or apricots begin growth and bloom earlier than apples or pears, so the proper season may extend from January to March or later in cold climates.

Scions can be cut and stored, or cut when you graft. Since the scions will be much smaller than the stock, be especially careful to match the cambium layer. If bark is thick on the stock, then the scions when properly matched will sit well in from the stock surface.

Two or three scion buds should protrude from the stock, but you can work with a longer scion, then snip and wax it once grafts are in place.

In cleft grafting, waxing is especially important. Wax thickly after matching scions and stock, then check every few days and rewax any splits. Use grafting wax or water-base asphalt tree seal applied with a flat stick. Never use sprays to coat grafting wounds as they are not thick enough. If you think that sunny weather may follow your grafting, paint stock and scion with an interior latex paint to prevent sunburn.

Don't worry if wax covers the scion buds. They easily push through when they begin to grow.

For very small branches where the cleft does not hold the scions firmly, wrap the stock with plastic tape for more security.

Step 1
Find a branch 1 to 4 inches in diameter with a very straight smooth portion. Saw the branch straight across, leaving this smooth area for splitting. Use a heavy knife, cleaver, or special tool for splitting, placing it across the center of the cut and tapping with a mallet. Split 2 to 3 inches down.

Step 2
Push a large screwdriver or chisel into the center of the split to hold it open for the scions.

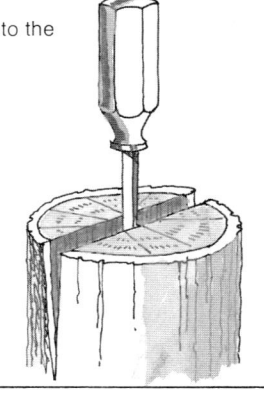

Step 3
Use two scions. Cut into a wedge shape with the angle of the cut made to match the opening in the stock. Insert scions with cambium touching cambium of stock along length of wedge cut. Remove screwdriver to pinch scions in cleft.

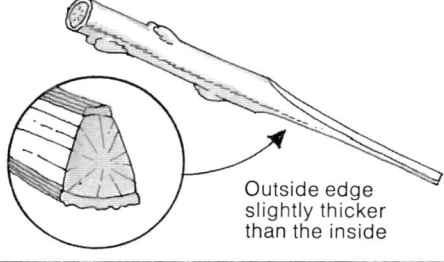

Outside edge slightly thicker than the inside

Step 4
End view of scion in stock should look like this. Side view of scion should look like this.

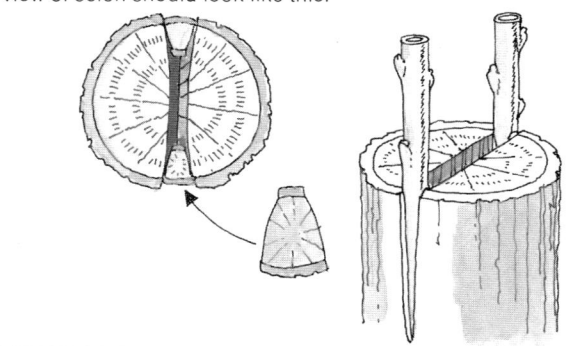

Step 5
Wax stock, filling cleft, and coat scions heavily along sices. Clip to 3 buds if necessary and wax end cut. Paint with white interior latex in sunny weather.

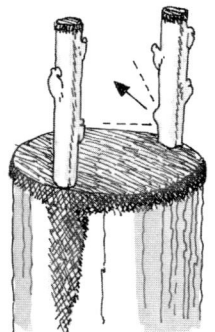

Step 6
If only one scion grows, cut stock at an angle and paint with pruning compound. If both grow, head back the weaker, but leave it to help heal stock.

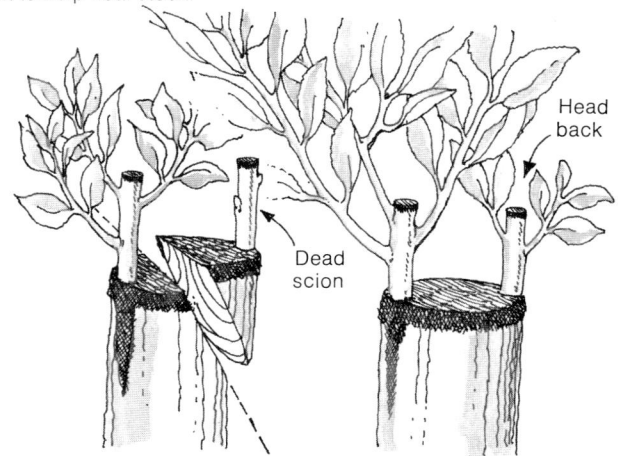

Head back

Dead scion

Bark grafting

Bark grafts can be performed on stock branches from 1 inch to 12 or more inches in diameter, but very large stocks are less satisfactory since the cut heals slowly or not at all. Optimum size of stock is from two to five inches in diameter.

The season for bark grafting is later than for either the whip or cleft method, since the bark must "slip" or detach easily. Check for slipping on a small branch before making a major cut.

Scions must be cut early and held in a cold place, since otherwise they will not be fully dormant at the season when bark is slipping. Insert several scions of the same kind around the stock, and allow the strongest to grow. Head the others back, but keep them for several seasons to improve healing of the stock.

The method described here is one of several, each differing in the way the stock bark is cut and the scion trimmed. This method offers double cambium contact of scion and stock and the simple trimming of the scion is easy for a beginner. Cooperative Extension pamphlets are available describing other methods. Again, thorough waxing is most important. Check frequently for splits and rewax if necessary.

You can use bark grafting to replace an entire tree if it is not too large. Cut off the top, leaving one foot of smooth-barked trunk, then graft on your scions. This method will only work on deciduous material. To replace the top of an evergreen, you must leave a "nurse" branch of the original tree until the scions are well grown.

Step 1
First choose 3 or 4 scions of about pencil size and snip them to about 6 inches long. Then find a smooth, straight section on the stock and saw it straight across. See pruning section for proper three-step cut to prevent torn bark.

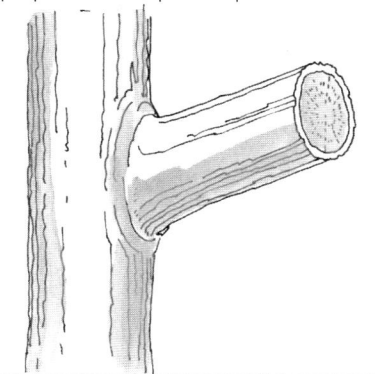

Step 2
Hold a single scion against the bark of the stock and nick the stock on each side of it. Then cut downward through the bark of the stock 1 or 2 inches and peel back the flap.

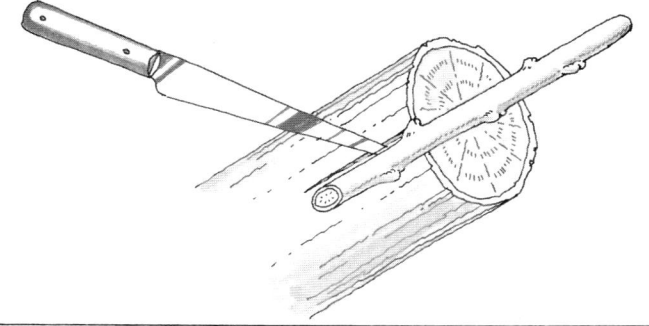

Step 3
Slice the base of the scion at an angle to form a sloping cut as long as the flap of bark on the stock. On the other side of the scion, make another sloping cut about ⅓ as long.

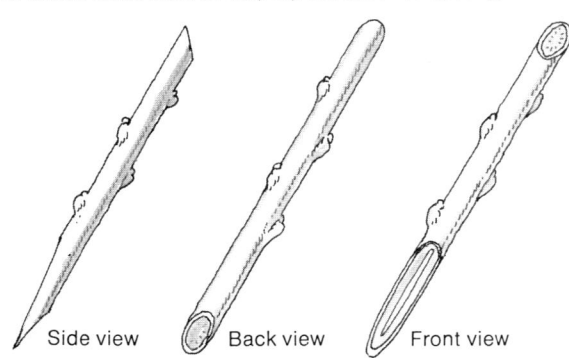

Side view   Back view   Front view

Step 4
Place the long cut flat against the wood of the stock. Nail it with a small nail near the top of the stock. Press the bark flap against the scion and nail it below the first nail. You can cut any section of flap beyond the short cut on the scion. Repeat steps 2, 3, and 4 for each scion up to 4.

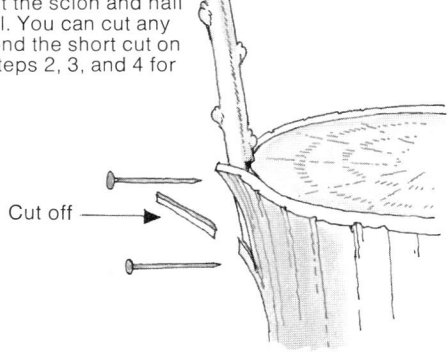

Cut off

Step 5
When all scions are tacked in place, wax heavily to cover all joints. Snip scions to 2 or 3 buds and wax end cut.

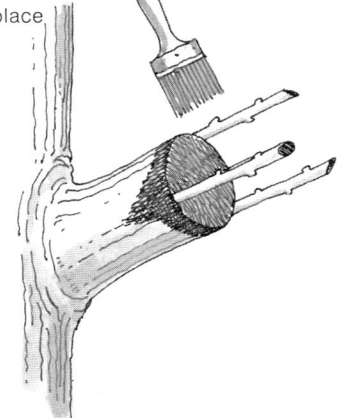

Step 6
When scions are well grown, head back all but the strongest. Keep weak scions until stock has healed. If only 1 scion grows, cut the stock on an angle and coat with pruning compound.

Pollination, pruning, and grafting

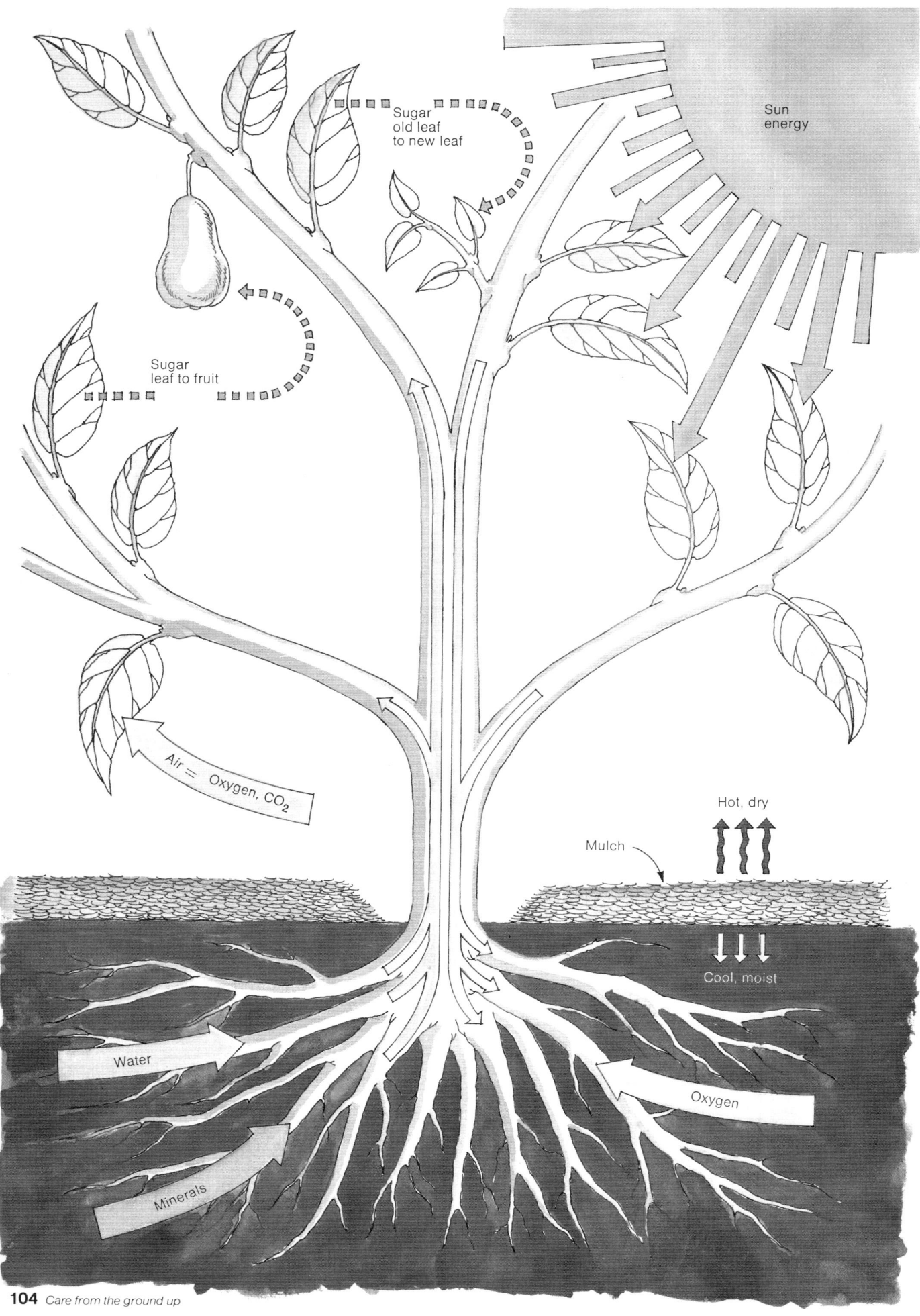

Care from the ground up

When the roots are happy, the plant is healthy. Here's how to plant, feed, water, and mulch to keep things growing smoothly under the garden floor.

The fruiting plants discussed in this book have been selected over the centuries because they produce much finer crops than their wild relatives. The extra crop, though, means that there's more stress on the plant . . . it has, so to speak, more mouths to feed. You have to help by providing an ideal environment.

The illustration on the opposite page will give you an idea of the day-to-day work of a fruit plant.

Sweetness and light

All plants need a lot of sugar. They make it themselves in their leaves, using carbon dioxide, water, and the energy of sunlight. You help out by planting in a sunny spot, pruning and training for good leaf exposure, keeping water in the soil, and keeping leaves free of dust, pests, and disease so that they can do their work. Each growing piece of fruit needs some 30 leaves working for it, not to speak of leaves supplying nourishment to the roots and branches.

Here's what you buy

The first step in producing fruit is buying a plant. Most deciduous fruit plants are sold bareroot. The leafless plant is pulled out of the ground in late fall or winter and shipped to the nursery where it is held in moist sand or wood shavings. Sometimes each root is enclosed in a plastic bag full of moist shavings. A bareroot plant is fragile and must be kept cool and moist. Plant it as soon as possible after you get it, instructions follow on page 108.

Evergreen plants are sold with their roots wrapped in soil and burlap, or they are growing in metal or pulp containers. The burlapped form is sold at the same season as bareroot plants and should go into the ground quickly. The container form may be sold at any time and you can wait a while to plant if you don't cut the container.

Bareroot plants are sometimes put into containers at the nursery. If you buy them in winter, or while they're still dormant, you can bare the roots again to plant them. If they have leafed out, grow them in their containers until May or June, so the root system has time to knit the container soil together.

Bare root

Burlap-wrapped

2-gal. can

papier-mâché pot

Deep-down goodness

While the leaves are busy topside, the roots spread out underground, searching for water and minerals. They won't spread very fast or far in dense, wet soil with no air spaces, since they need a good supply of oxygen. You help to supply it by adding organic material, such as compost, to densely packed clay soils.

Roots grow only where there's the right amount of moisture, and you help here too by watering deeply and regularly, and covering the surface with a mulch to keep things cool and damp.

Apart from moisture, the roots are looking primarily for minerals. The one that's always in short supply is a usable form of nitrogen. You have to add it several times from early spring into summer. Sometimes your soil will turn out to be short of some other mineral. Your Cooperative Extension Agent can tell you whether you should add such things as potassium, iron, or zinc, and how to do it. Don't worry about these things unless your tree starts to look strange. It may turn yellow or red, drop leaves out of season, or produce an odd-looking crop. Describe symptoms or show an odd branch and the Extension Office can take it from there.

The enemy

Since you like fruit, it's no surprise that many other creatures do too, from birds and mice, to insects, to fungi and bacteria. Part of the battle is keeping the plant clean and growing. Supply what it needs and hose it down if it's dusty. Sprays won't do their job if a plant is filthy and starving.

Common pests and diseases appear on pages 74 to 77. Most of them have done their damage once you notice them, so you spray ahead of time. For example, codling moths lay eggs in flowers. You spray when petals have fallen. It's no good spraying when you see wormholes and misshapen fruit.

Your soil—what's it like?

Here's what plants need down where the roots grow:
1. Air in the soil
2. Constant moisture (but not standing water)
3. A supply of mineral nutrients

You'll supply these needs best if you examine your soil. Is it rock-hard when dry, and gummy when wet? Then you probably have the very fine soil called clay or adobe. It holds moisture so well that there's often no room for air. Fluff it up with organic material like compost or peat moss. Spread four or five inches of organic matter over the soil and stir it in, mixing evenly. Ideally, you should add the material wherever the plant's roots might spread when it's mature, and they'll spread more widely than the branches.

Does water sink right in without spreading much? Does the soil dry up just a few days after watering? Sandy

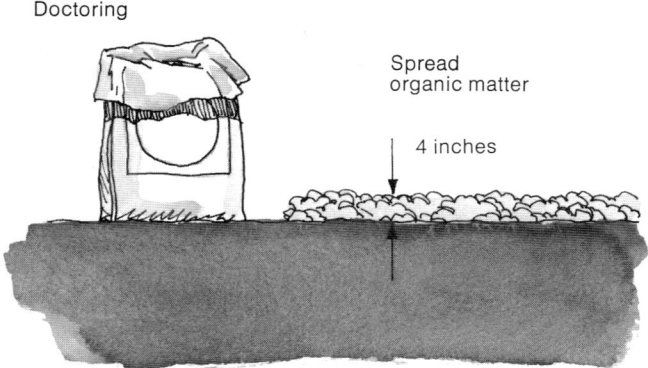

Doctoring — Spread organic matter 4 inches

Dig it in to 10 inches

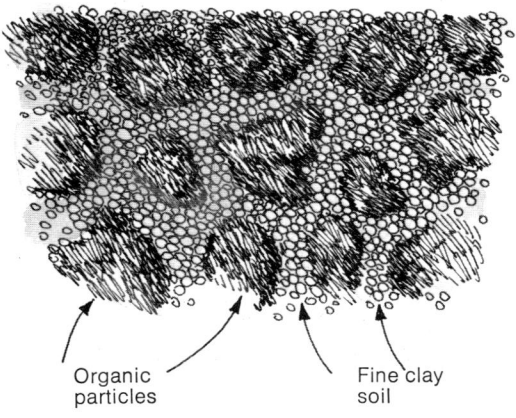

Clay is fluffier — Organic particles, Fine clay soil

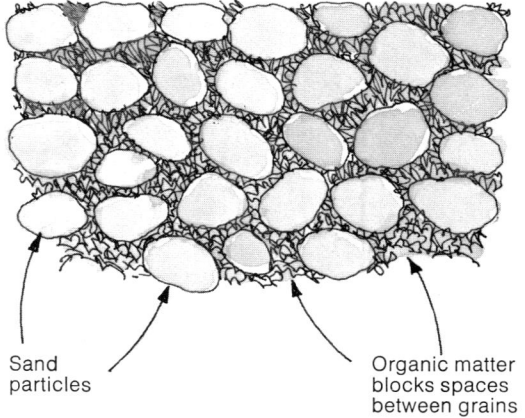

Sand holds water — Sand particles, Organic matter blocks spaces between grains

soils are like this. They have lots of air, but moisture and nutrients disappear fast. Organic matter helps here too, by filling in spaces between the coarse soil particles and holding onto the water you deliver. Peat moss, compost, and manures are especially good materials for sandy soil. Sawdust and ground bark are less good at water holding and poor at hanging on to nutrients.

If you have soil that feels moist for days after watering, but still crumbles easily when you pick up a handful and squeeze it, then its just right.

Keeping soil healthy

Once a planting area is in good shape and your plant is in the ground, keep it growing by protecting the soil. Sun and wind will cause bare soil to crust over at the surface. Then, air and water can't penetrate evenly and roots near the crust die out. Cover the soil surface as suggested under Mulch on page 110.

Foot traffic beats down the soil until air is driven out and water won't penetrate. A mulch helps here too, since it makes a cushion of resilient material over the root area.

Plants aren't all the same

Some plants tolerate dense, airless, soggy soil better than others. This list may help you decide what to plant, but keep in mind that in gardens with extremely dense soil you can still plant air-lovers in a raised bed one to three feet deep and wide enough to accommodate a good root system, perhaps six feet by six feet for a standard tree.

Tolerate dense or wet soil: pear, quince, cranberry

Tolerate short airless periods: apple, crabapple

Need fair drainage: apricot, cherry, fig, nectarine, peach, plum, grape, currant

Need good drainage: strawberry, cane berries, citrus

Need perfect drainage: blueberry

In a container

Think of a container as any limited area of good soil, and you'll see that it can be more than just a pot. If you dig a large hole in extremely poor clay soil and add a lot of organic material, the plant you put in the hole may never send roots beyond its borders. You have planted in a container within the soil. If you lift a plant above the soil in a raised bed, you create a kind of container. And of course if you plant in a pot or box on your deck or paving, you are planting in a container.

Container soil must be especially good, since the roots of the plant within it can't grow outward in search of a better life. It should drain very quickly, but hold moisture and nutrients. Normally a fruit plant will need a large volume of container soil, and it is cheaper to mix it yourself than to buy ready-mixed kinds.

Synthetic soils

The mixes, such as Jiffy-Mix and Redi-Earth, are referred to as "soilless mixes" or "synthetic soils." However you should not translate the word synthetic as *artificial*. The ingredients are as natural as Mother Nature could make them.

Jiffy-Mix, the most widely available synthetic soil, is made up of 50% peat moss and 50% vermiculite. When mined, vermiculite (Terralite) resembles mica. Under heat treatment the mineral flakes expand with air spaces to 20 times their original thickness.

Jiffy-Mix contains just enough nutrients to sustain initial plant growth. Use it to germinate seeds and for growing flower and vegetable transplants.

It provides what a plant needs for optimum growth:

1) Fast drainage of water through the "soil."

2) Good aeration—a high percentage of air in the "soil" after drainage.

3) A reservoir of water in the soil after drainage.

Air and water retention. The airspace after drainage and the water retention properties of various mixes and the materials that go into them has been measured. The figures shown in the chart below indicate percent by volume. Physical properties of clay loam are included in the list for comparison.

Material	Total Porosity	Water Retention	Air Space After Drainage
Clay loam	59.6	54.9	4.7
Sphagnum peat moss	84.2	58.8	25.4
Fine sand	44.6	38.7	5.9
Redwood sawdust	77.2	49.3	27.9
Perlite, 1/16-3/16"	77.1	47.3	29.8
Vermiculite, 0-3/16"	80.5	53.0	27.5
Fir bark, 0-1/8"	69.5	38.0	31.5
1:1, fine sand: fir bark	54.6	37.4	15.2
1:1, fine sand: peat moss	56.7	47.3	9.4
1:1, perlite, peat moss	74.9	51.3	23.6

The synthetic mix is free of disease organisms, insects and weed seeds. It eliminates disease problems often present in regular soil.

It is light weight—half the weight of soil when both are wet. The light weight is an advantage when growing plants in containers on roofs or balconies.

You can use the mix just as it comes from the bag. But thorough wetting before use is absolutely necessary. And "thorough wetting" is not easy with dry peat moss. We wet it by putting the amount we want to use in a plastic bag, adding *warm* water, and then squeezing and mixing the bag by hand.

One 4-cubic foot bag will fill a planter box 24 by 36 inches, by 8 inches deep.

Many gardeners add top soil to the mix when planting shrubs and trees in containers. This gives them a soil of good physical properties, but all the advantages of sterilization are lost.

We make our own mix when planting a number of trees and shrubs, or when filling a raised bed. The properties for a mix to be used in landscape plantings might be:

9 cubic feet of fine sand
18 cubic feet of ground bark or
nitrogen-stabilized sawdust
or
9 cubic feet of fine sand
9 cubic feet of peat moss
9 cubic feet of ground bark
add to either of the above:
5 pounds of 5-10-10 fertilizer
7 pounds of ground limestone
1 pound of iron sulphate

Planting

The illustrations here will give you an idea how to plant a tree from the nursery. Here are some special points to remember:

✓ Never plant if the soil is very wet. Working wet soil packs it and traps roots. In very rainy climates, you can dig holes for bareroot and burlap-wrapped plants in fall and protect the soil removed from the hole with a weighted plastic sheet. It will be workable any time.

✓ Never let bareroot or burlap-wrapped plants lie around unprotected. If you must bring bareroot plants home before youn can plant, dig a shallow trench, lay the plants on their sides with roots in the trench, and cover roots with moist soil. Wrap burlapped plants in a sheet of plastic so the soil ball stays moist.

✓ Plant high. Notice in the illustrations that the planting soil is mounded above the normal soil line. The most fragile part of a woody plant is the crown, that section where soil touches the trunk and the roots branch. It must be dry most of the time and especially in spring and fall. Raised planting minimizes crown rot (which could be fatal to the plant) by making it impossible for water to puddle near the trunk. If you plant at soil level, you're inviting disaster because the soil in the planting hole will settle and your plants will sink downward.

Fertilizing

When you feed a fruit tree, you are supplementing the mineral elements in the soil. Nitrogen is the element most commonly in short supply so it becomes the key nutrient in a fertilizer program. Most fruit tree fertilizers will contain higher amounts of nitrogen than other nutrients, for example, 12-6-6 or 12-6-10. Straight nitrogen forms are ammonium nitrate, calcium nitrate, urea, and ammonium sulfate. The choice of nutrients to use depends upon several factors.

Since fruit trees are grown in so many different types of soils, it is virtually impossible to pin down the specific fertilizer needs. Also, there are many selections and

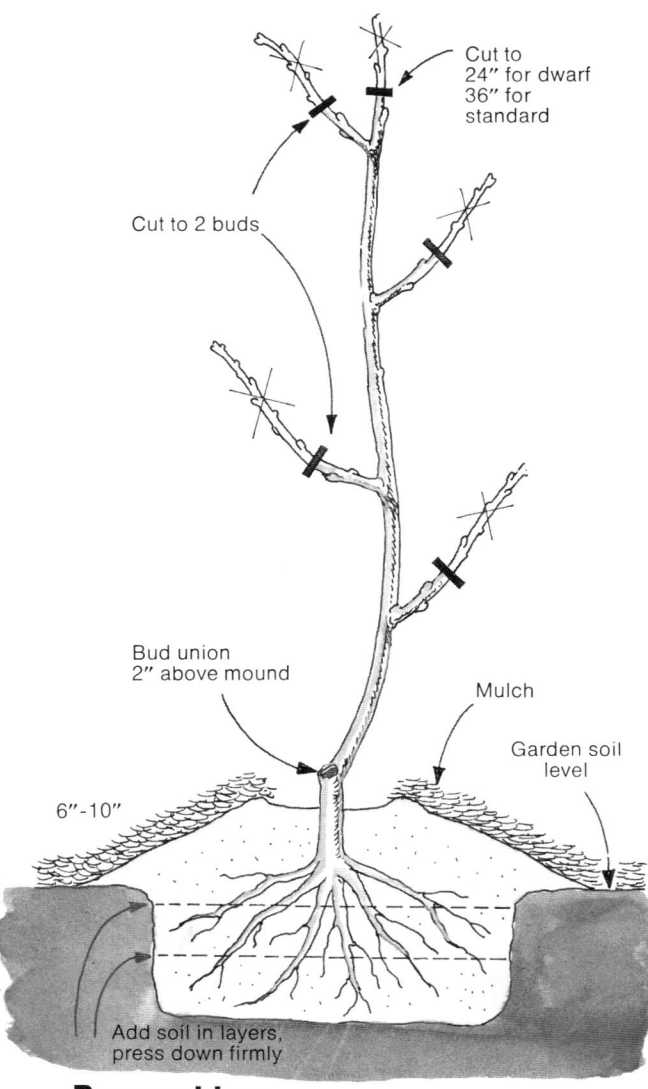

Bareroot tree

Clip off broken roots, leaving clean cut. Rub off fine root hairs. Hole must be wide enough for roots to spread. Soak soil after hole is refilled, make volcano-shaped mound, soak again from top, running water slowly so it sinks in. Mound higher in dense soil, lower in good soil.

Burlap wrap

Do not jar the root ball or you may damage plant. After first layer of fill is pressed down, lay back the burlap and fill again. Soak, make mound, soak. Protect from winds or strong sun.

varieties that respond differently. The trees themselves can often serve as indicators of needs. If growth is vigorous and healthy and leaves appear normal, then nutrient requirements are being met. But, if growth is limited and the leaves are small or pale green or chlorotic, fertilizer is needed.

It's not a good practice to let your trees demonstrate these needs; preventing these deficiency signals is a much better practice.

When to feed . . . how much

We suggest applying one-half of the fertilizer in the spring, and the other half after harvest for early-bearing trees or about mid-June for later-bearing varieties. Keep the fertilizer at least a foot away from the trunk and apply evenly under the tree canopy.

A general rule of thumb is to use about ¾ lb. of nitrogen for each mature tree (not dwarf varieties) per year. This means that for fertilizer having 12% nitrogen you will need to apply 6 pounds. Young trees will need correspondingly lesser amounts and newly planted trees should not be fertilized with nitrogen until the root system becomes well established. Follow label directions on the fertilizer package.

Potassium and other nutrients. Potassium is commonly deficient in fruit trees, particularly in high rainfall areas and where trees are grown on sandy or gravelly soils. Be sure to include potassium in the fertilizer program where these conditions exist. Manures contain potash so this nutrient is added when manures are used.

Phosphorous fertilizers should be added to the planting hole and mixed with the soil since phosphorus is very important when the root system is limited. If after following the usual fertilizer program, growth is still weak and leaves show abnormal appearances, then zinc, magnesium, iron, manganese, and boron could be deficient. A foliar spray during the growing season may be the best way of applying these elements.

Feeding with animal manure. Animal manures are suitable as fertilizers but use them with caution since they often contain harmful amounts of salts and obnoxious weed seeds. Also remember that bird and rabbit manures contain from 3-6 times more ntirogen than cattle or horse manure, so use lesser amounts. About 30-60 pounds of bird or rabbit manure and 100-200 pounds of cattle manure per tree will supply the nutrient needs of full size mature trees. Spread it under the branches in the fall or early spring. For young trees use about ⅓ pound of bird or rabbit manure, or one pound of cattle manure per tree each year. Double the amount each year to maturity.

Judging the results. Using the appearance of the tree as a fertilization guide is a good practice if you don't let them get overly deficient. Use sufficient fertilizer each year to keep the trees growing well — excess growth means to cut back — deficient growth means to use more. Follow the label directions of reputable fertilizer companies and the advice of your informed nurseryman.

Dwarf and container plantings

Since these never grow very big, they require lesser amounts of fertilizers. Start out with ¼ cup of a 12-6-6 grade fertilizer (or similar analysis) after the tree is well established. Repeat this application annually, supplementing it with small additions (⅛ cup increments) every two to three months during the growing season until the tree seems to be doing well. Adjust if growth is too slow or too vigorous.

Watering

A standard fruit tree needs deep watering. Dwarf trees on shallow-rooted stocks may not need as much but any tree must have a constant moisture supply. Here's how to provide it.

At planting time. Water each layer of soil in the planting hole. If the garden soil is dry, soak the hole itself before you put in the plant. Finish by soaking from the top of the planting mound, creating a volcano-like depression to hold the water. Let the hose trickle so water won't run over the side.

After planting, and before growth begins, don't water again unless the soil seems unusually dry. The roots are not in active growth, and soggy soil will rot them.

When growth begins, give the plants a soaking when the top inch or so of soil dries. Dig down to be sure water is needed. Water with a trickling hose at the top of the planting mound. This is especially important with burlap-wrapped plants, since the soil in the ball may not take up water unless you trickle it straight into the ball.

When first-season growth is abundant. In midsummer, when plants are growing well, stop watering from the top of the mound. Create a shallow ditch right at the base of the planting mound and soak the soil in this circular ditch about every two to three weeks, or when the top inch or two dries.

Watering after the first season. Make a shallow ditch about 6 to 12 inches wide around the plant and just outside the tips of the branches. Move the ditch outward as the plant grows. Soak thoroughly about once every three to four weeks. This is a rough guide. Your tree may need water every two weeks in very sandy soil, or not for six weeks in heavy soil. Dig down to check the moisture in the upper few inches before watering. Conserve the water you provide by spreading a 2-inch layer of mulch over the roots from the mound area to the outside of the watering ditch.

How long to water. You want to soak the soil long enough to force water down to the deep roots. On dwarf trees the deepest roots may stop 30 to 36 inches below the surface. On big trees, the roots may extend many feet. Then too, water sinks quickly through sandy soil, but very slowly through clay. A day after keeping your watering ditch full for two or three hours, check penetration by pushing a 4- or 5-foot length of stiff wire into the wet soil. It will penetrate only wet soil, so when it refuses to go down any farther, pull it out and check the depth of penetration. Soil should be moist down to at least 2½ feet for dwarfs, 3½ to 4 for big trees.

Trees in a lawn area should have a deep soak about twice a summer, in addition to lawn watering.

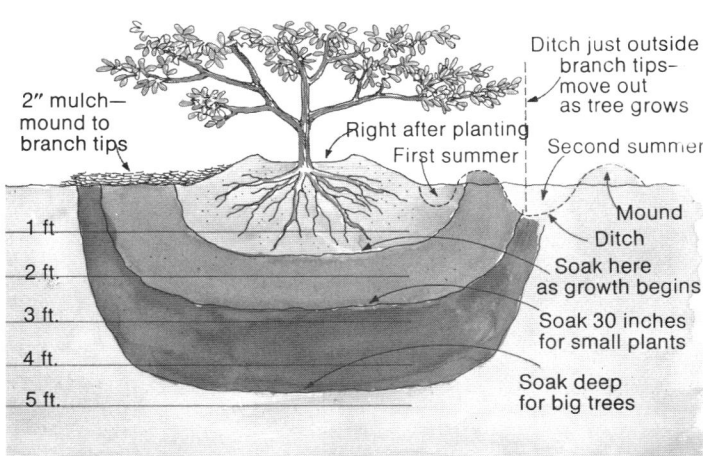

Mulch the root zone

Mulch is just a cover over the soil. It might be gravel, plastic, ground fir bark, manure—or even grass clippings, leaves, or brown paper bags. It is important for many reasons.

✔ Mulch keeps wind and sun from baking and crusting soil.
✔ Mulch smothers weed seeds.
✔ Mulch protects soil from foot traffic.
✔ Mulch holds in water even at the surface.
✔ Mulch keeps surface soil cool.
✔ Mulch keeps soil from freezing and thawing, which causes heaving of plants.
✔ Organic mulches rot, improve soil texture.

When and where to mulch

Cover the soil with a mulch from the planting mound to the branch tips if you can. Use at least two inches of a porous material like manure. Slash waterproof mulches like thick paper or plastic so water can pass through. Beautify a plastic mulch with gravel, pebbles, or bark chips spread over the surface about an inch deep. To hide paper mulches cover them with a thin layer of ground bark.

In warm, dry climates, spread mulch in spring and then turn it into the top two inches of soil in late fall. In cold climates where ground may freeze, add more mulch in late fall, up to six inches. You may even want to cover this deep mulch with evergreen boughs for added protection from freezing, and to keep the mulch in place when strong winds blow. Snow adds to the usefulness of any mulch.

Never pile any mulch against the tree trunk or plant stem. Keep it at least six inches away. Wet mulch there can cause rot, and dwarf trees mulched to the bud union will take root and grow to full size. An exception: in very cold climates, mulch deeply over the bud union when real cold begins, remove the mulch when severe cold is over.

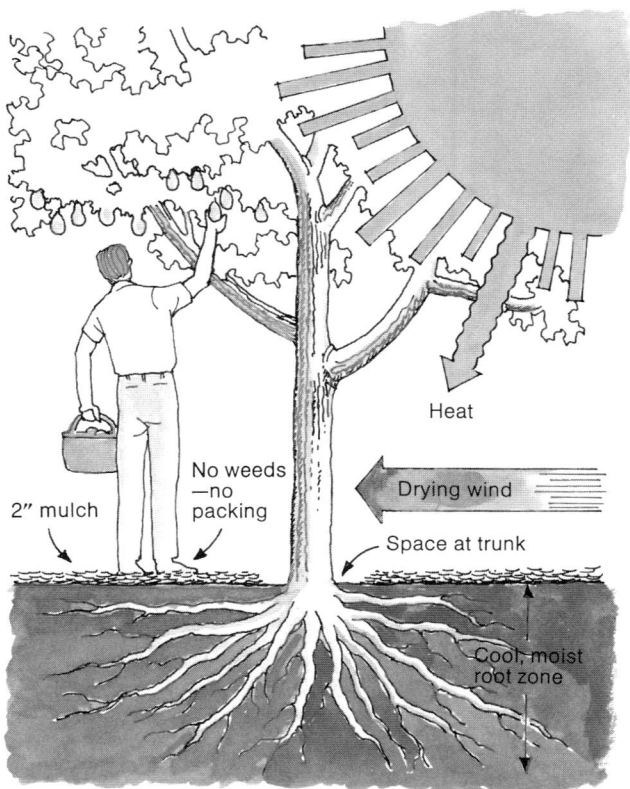

Mulching materials

Material	Remarks
Rotted manure	May contain weed seeds.
Sawdust Wood chips Wood shavings	Low in plant nutrients, decomposes slowly, tends to pack down. Well-rotted material preferred. Can be fresh if nitrate of ammonia or nitrate of soda is added at the rate of 1 pound per 100 sq. ft. Keep away from building foundations; may cause termites.
Peat moss	Attractive, available, but expensive for large areas. Should be kept moist at all times.
Ground corn cobs	Excellent for improving soil structure.
Pine needles	Will not mat down. Fairly durable.
Peanut hulls Cotton screenings Tobacco stems (shredded)	Supply plant nutrients and improve soil structure. Fairly durable.
Tree leaves (whole) Tree leaves (shredded)	Excellent source of humus. Rot rapidly, high in nutrients. Oak leaves especially valuable for azaleas, camellias, and rhododendrons.
Hay Grass clippings	Unattractive, but repeated use builds up reserve of available nutrients which lasts for years.
Straw	Same as above, but lower in nutrients although furnishes considerable potassium.
Buckwheat hulls	Very attractive but tend to scatter in windy locations.
Pecan hulls	Extremely durable, availability limited.
Gravel or stone chips	Limited use, but particularly good for rock garden plantings. Extremely durable, holds down weeds, but does not supply plant nutrients or humus.
Bark	Ground and packaged commercially. Especially attractive in this form. Sometimes available in rough form from pulpwood-loading sites.

List of catalog sources

Throughout the book, we give a list of source numbers after each variety name. You will notice an "s" or "D" after some numbers. This means that semi-dwarf or dwarf plants are available.

The numbers in the varieties lists are the same as those shown below. They show which firms to write to for catalogs.

In our listing of available catalogs we have given a brief description of each source. By reading those descriptions you can determine the companies that are specialists in fruits and those that cover the entire spectrum of garden material.

Many of these catalogs are the equivalents of garden books containing good reference material. They reward the careful reader.

Our catalog search was made with 1976 information. You can expect changes in the catalogs of later dates. What is scarce today may be widely available in future years, but our search will uncover the most likely sources of hard-to-find varieties.

Look at the source listings to see if they are wholesale or retail dealers. Wholesale cannot sell directly to you, but you can refer your nurseryman to them.

1. Adams County Nursery & Fruit Farms
   Aspers, PA 17304
   Fruit specialists. 22-page catalog. Wholesale and retail

2. Bountiful Ridge Nurseries, Inc.
   Box 250
   Princess Anne, MD 21853
   Specialists in fruits and nuts. 50-page catalog and planting guide. Wholesale and retail.

3. Bowers Berry Nursery
   94959 Hwy 99 E
   Junction City, OR 97448
   12-page catalog of berries and grapes. Wholesale and retail.

4. Bunting's Berries
   Selbyville, DE 19975
   40-page catalog. 24 pages strawberries. Fruit trees, berries, and nursery stock.

5. Burgess Seed and Plant Co.
   P.O. Box 82
   Galesburg, MI 49053
   Two catalogs are offered:
   1. 44-page general seed catalog. Flowers, vegetables, and nursery stock. 4 pages on fruit.
   2. Especially for the limited space gardener. Full color, 32-page catalog with one page on fruits to grow indoors.

6. W. Atlee Burpee Co.
   Warminster, PA 18974
   Clinton, IA 52732
   Riverside, CA 92502
   180-page general seed catalog. Flowers, vegetables, garden aids, and nursery stock. 10 pages on fruit.

7. C & O Nursery
   P.O. Box 116
   1700 N. Wenatchee Ave.
   Wenatchee, WA 98801
   Fruit specialists, Exclusive patented varieties. 40-page catalog with 7 pages of ornamentals and shade trees. Wholesale and retail.

8. The Clyde Nursery
   On Highway U.S. 20
   Clyde, OH 43410
   10-page catalog of fruits and berries.

9. Columbia Basin Nursery
   Box 458
   Quincy, WA 98848
   Colored brochure and price list. Seedling rootstock, dwarfing apple rootstock, dwarf and standard budded fruit trees. Wholesale and retail.

10. L. E. Cooke Co.
    26333 Road 140
    Visalia, CA 93277
    Fruits, berries, grapes, vegetables, and nursery stock. Specializes in dwarf and semidwarf fruit trees and genetic dwarf peaches. Wholesale only. Inquiries answered with information on retail availability.

11. Cumberland Valley Nurseries, Inc.
    P.O. Box 430
    113 Lind Street
    McMinnville, TN 37110
    1-page catalog specializing in plums, peaches, and nectarines. Wholesale and retail.

12. Farmer Seed & Nursery Co.
    Faribault, MN 55021
    84-page general seed catalog. Flowers, vegetables, and nursery stock. 5 pages on fruit.

13. Henry Field Seed & Nursery Co.
    407 Sycamore Street
    Shenandoah, IA 51601
    116-page general seed and nursery catalog. Flowers, vegetables, gardening aids, and nursery stock. 16 pages on fruit.

14. Dean Foster Nurseries
    Hartford, MI 49257
    80-page general catalog. Specializing in strawberries. Flowers, vegetables, dwarf fruit, and berries. Wholesale and retail.

15. Fowler Nurseries, Inc.
    525 Fowler Road
    Newcastle, CA 95658
    4-page price list of over 200 varieties sent on request. Commercial price list also available. 32-page catalog $1.

16. Grootendorst Nurseries
    Lakeside, MI 49116
    Specialists in dwarf Malling and Merton rootstock.

17. Gurney Seed & Nursery Co.
    1448 Page St.
    Yankton, SD 57078
    76-page general seed catalog. Flowers, vegetables, and nursery stock. 10 pages on fruit.

18. Haley Nursery Co., Inc.
    Smithville, TN 37116
    6-page price list. Fruit trees. Specializing in peaches and nectarines. Wholesale only. Ask your dealer to order.

19. Heath's Nursery, Inc.
    P.O. Box 707
    Brewster, WA 98812
    12-page catalog of fruit trees, shade and ornamental trees.

20. Inter-State Nurseries
    Hamburg, IA 51644
    84-page catalog. Fruit, flowers, berries, roses, and ornamentals. 14 pages on fruit.

21. Ison's Nursery & Vineyard
    Brooks, GA 30205
    16-page catalog specializing in grapes. Wholesale and retail.

22. J. W. Jung Seed Co.
    Station 8
    Randolph, WI 53956
    60-page general seed catalog. Flowers, vegetables, and nursery stock, 4 pages on fruit.

23. Kelly Bros. Nurseries, Inc.
    Dansville, NY 14437
    80-page catalog of fruit, nuts, flowers, and ornamentals. 16 pages on fruit.

24. Lawson's Nursery
    Route 1, Box 61
    Ball Ground, GA 30107
    8-page fruit catalog. Specializing in old-fashioned and unusual fruit trees. Lists over 100 varieties of old apples.

25. Henry Leuthardt Nurseries, Inc.
    East Moriches, Long Island, NY 11940
    52-page fruit catalog and guidebook on dwarf and espalier-trained fruit trees.

26. Earl May Seed & Nursery Co.
    Shenandoah, IA 51603
    80-page general seed catalog. Flowers, vegetables, and nursery stock. 10 pages on fruit.

27. Miller's Nursery, Inc.
    Canandaigua, NY 14424
    Fruit specialists. 40-page catalog also includes garden aids and ornamentals.

28. New York State Fruit Testing Cooperative Association
    Geneva, NY 14456
    32-page fruit catalog. $4 membership fee, refunded on first order.

29. L. L. Olds Seed Co.
    2901 Packers Ave.
    Box 1069
    Madison, WI 53701
    80-page general seed catalog. Flowers, vegetables, and nursery stock. 3 pages on fruit.

30. Owen's Vineyard and Nursery
    Georgia Highway 85
    Gay, GA 30218
    12-page catalog specializing in muscadine grapes. Includes guidelines for growing and training. Southern rabbiteye blueberries available.

31. Rayner's Bros., Inc.
    Salisbury, MD 21801
    34-page fruit catalog specializing in strawberries. 3 pages on fruit trees.

32. Southmeadow Fruit Gardens
    2363 Tilbury Place
    Birmingham, MI 48009
    Probably the largest collection of fruit varieties, old, new, and rare, in the U.S. Their 112-page illustrated catalog is priced at $5 and worth it. A condensed 8-page catalog is free.

33. Stanek's Garden Center
    East 2929 - 27th Avenue
    Spokane, WA 99203
    34-page catalog of fruit, flowers, and ornamentals. 4 pages of fruit and berries.

34. Stark Bros. Nursery
    Louisiana, MO 73353
    40-page illustrated catalog and guide. 12 pages vegetables, ornamentals, and nuts.

35. Van Well Nursery
    P.O. Box 1339
    Wenatchee, WA 98801
    28-page fruit catalog. Fruits and berries. Wholesale and retail.

36. Waynesboro Nurseries
    P.O. Box 987
    Waynesboro, VA 22980
    48-page catalog on fruits, nuts and ornamental plant material. 21 pages on fruits and nuts.

37. Weeks Berry Nursery
    6494 Windsor Island Rd. No.
    Salem, OR 97303
    Specialists in small fruits. Wholesale and commercial plantings.

38. Dave Wilson Nursery
    4306 Santa Fe Avenue
    Hughson, CA 95326
    Fruits, berries, grapes. Specializing in Zaiger patented fruit trees. Wholesale only. Ask your dealer to order.

39. H. G. Hastings Co.
    Box 4655
    Atlanta, GA 30302
    64-page general seed catalog. Flowers, vegetables, and nursery stock. 5 pages on fruits and berries.

40. Archias Seed Store Corp.
    P.O. Box 109
    Sedalia, MO 65301
    42-page general seed catalog. Flowers, vegetables, and nursery stock. 4 pages on fruits and berries.

41. Whatley Nursery
    Route 1, Box 197
    Helena, GA 31037
    2-page price list. Specializing in muscadine grapes. Wholesale and retail.

42. Buckley Nursery Co.
    Rt. 2, Box 199
    Buckley, WA 98321
    44-page catalog. Fruit, shade, flowers, and ornamental trees. 13 pages devoted to fruit. Wholesale and retail.

43. C. D. Schwartze Nursery
    2302 Tacoma Rd.
    Puyallup, WA 98731
    5-page catalog specializing in apple trees and crab apple trees.

44. Hilltop Orchards & Nurseries, Inc.
    Rt. 2
    Hartford, MI 49057
    Widely recognized fruit tree specialists for commercial orchardists. Free, 38-page handbook and catalog.

45. Stribling Nurseries
    1620 W. 16th—P.O. Box 793
    Merced, CA 95340
    Fruit specialists. 44-page catalog of fruit, nut, and grape varieties. Includes tree-planting guides and ripening charts.

46. Armstrong Nurseries
    P.O. Box 473
    Ontario, CA 91761
    Specialists in fruit trees and roses. 40-page catalog lists genetic dwarf peaches and nectarines, as well as other exotic fruit trees. Vegetables and bulbs.

47. W. F. Allen Co.
    P.O. Box 1577
    Salisbury, MD 21801
    Strawberry specialists. 30-page catalog and planting guide lists over 30 varieties. Wholesale and retail.

48. Mayo Nurseries
    Route 14
    Lyons, NY 14489
    Fruit specialists. 8-page catalog includes many varieties of dwarf and semidwarf apples. Wholesale and retail.